MW00980399

COUNTER TERRORISM

Reassessing the Policy Response

Benoît Gomis

COUNTER TERRORISM

Reassessing the Policy Response

CRC Press is an imprint of the
Taylor & Francis Group, an **informa** business

CRC Press
Taylor & Francis Group
6000 Broken Sound Parkway NW, Suite 300
Boca Raton, FL 33487-2742

Printed on acid-free paper
Version Date: 20150603

International Standard Book Number-13: 978-1-4822-3715-3 (Hardback)

Visit the Taylor & Francis Web site at
http://www.taylorandfrancis.com

and the CRC Press Web site at
http://www.crcpress.com

CONTENTS

SECTION III How to Break the Cycle? Rethinking the Policy Response

FOREWORD

In politics, what begins in fear usually ends in folly.

Samuel Taylor Coleridge

Since the 2001 attacks, which became known as 9/11, terrorism has been a dominant theme in both the national security and international relations discourse. For many brought up in the paradigm of the Cold War military confrontation among states, the security world seemed to have been fundamentally transformed. Suddenly, a new threat was emerging from shadowy armed groups distinct from state militaries appeared, and governments, especially in the West, scrambled to reorganize their defenses.

In parallel with this surge of activity on the part of concerned governments and largely financed by them, an exponential growth in academic research and writing on terrorism occurred. Rarely has a security development been subject to such intense study, although the ultimate influence of this study on actual counterterrorism policies and practices is far from clear. As the Coleridge epigram suggests, governments and societies when acting out of fear frequently pursue policies that are excessive and can undermine the very values and interests they were meant to protect.

The need for objective, evidence-based policies and programs on counterterrorism is as real today as it was in the immediate aftermath of 9/11. The shock generated by the magnitude of the loss of civilian lives resulting from this unprecedented attack has dissipated over time. This, coupled with the gradual recognition that the toll from terrorism in the West stands at almost negligible levels in comparison with other dangers, should enable a more realistic assessment of the threat from terrorism, domestic or international. In the decade between 2002 and 2012, deaths due to terrorism amounted to 36 in the United States, 57 in the United Kingdom, 12 in France, and 1 in Canada. Even when considered globally, the fatality rate of homicide worldwide is 40 times higher than that as a result of terrorism. This level of violent fatalities is, in turn, dwarfed by the estimated 211,000 deaths attributed to illicit drug abuse in the single year 2011 or the 2.5 million and 6 million deaths originating with alcohol and tobacco usage, respectively. Have authorities been guilty of a massive overreaction to the terrorism threat? And if so, at what cost, both in terms of our security preparedness and democratic practices, not to mention the lost opportunities to redirect resources to other pressing national priorities?

It is this core question that Benoît Gomis explores in his insightful and comprehensive study of terrorism and its varied impact on contemporary public policies. After a concise history of terrorist action and a complementary exposition on the unresolved definitional questions surrounding the term, Gomis focuses on how the terrorism fixation has led to a series of distortions in a variety of major public policy files. From debunking the supposed narco-terrorist threat to deflating the hyped cyber terrorist threat, Gomis methodically examines the factual basis underlying many of these assertions and reveals them to be largely without foundation.

Counterterrorism has become a growth industry and a lucrative one at that. There will always be a temptation to inflate a national security threat on the part of those who will profit from the programs and procurement established to counter it. Getting a true picture of the scope and nature of counterterrorism policies is complicated by the tendency of governments to wrap the entire sector under a heavy cloak of secrecy. Gomis calls for greater transparency and accountability from governments in their management of counterterrorism and the avoidance of excessive infringements of civil liberties. Most importantly, he advocates maintaining a sense of proportion in assessing and responding to the threat posed by terrorism. It is through a realistic and measured response that those in authority can deal with the actual terrorist challenge while avoiding the pitfalls of an ill-informed and excessive reaction.

Gomis has written a fact-based and cogent account of terrorism as a contemporary security policy problem that will be of interest to students and practitioners alike. It is a revealing and refreshing contribution to the existing literature on the subject.

Paul Meyer*

---

* Paul Meyer is a former Canadian diplomat. During his 35-year career, he notably held the positions of Director General of the International Security Bureau (1998–2001) and Director General of the Security and Intelligence Bureau (2007–2010) at the Department of Foreign Affairs and International Trade. From 2003 to 2007, he served as ambassador and permanent representative to the United Nations and the Conference on Disarmament in Geneva. He is now a fellow and adjunct professor in international security at Simon Fraser University (Burnaby, Canada) and a senior fellow at the Simons Foundation.

ACKNOWLEDGMENTS

Many thanks to everyone who has helped me along my journey, in particular,

- My colleagues at Chatham House from whom I have learned so much. A special thank you to Paul Cornish for taking a chance on a young graduate—and a Frenchman at that!—and getting me into the terrorism and counterterrorism field.
- CRC Press for inviting me to write this book and assisting me along the way, and the Canadian Network for Research on Terrorism, Security and Society (TSAS) and the University of British Columbia (UBC) for hosting me during the writing process.
- Dave Clemente, Claudia Hofmann, Eelco Kessels, Jeronimo Mohar, Hugo Rosemont, and Heather Williams, who made time in their busy lives to review various sections of this book; Eugene Gibney, who provided thorough and brilliant edits and great encouragement throughout the process. While all of their comments, suggestions, questions, and corrections made a huge difference to the overall quality of this book, I am solely responsible for any factual errors this book may include.
- Gabriel Smetzer, my very talented graphic designer friend, for designing this cover. Check out his work at: www.gabrielsmetzer.com.
- Last but not least, my wife, Siobhán Gibney Gomis, for her love, motivational pep talks, and much-needed contagious cheerfulness after my long hours of trawling terrorism databases. Who would have thought I would luck out on such a wonderful life partner?

AUTHOR

Benoît Gomis is an international security analyst whose focus is on terrorism and organized crime. While writing this book, he was a visiting scholar at the Canadian Network for Research on Terrorism, Security and Society (TSAS), based at the University of British Columbia (UBC), Vancouver, British Columbia. He is also an associate fellow at Chatham House—with which he is currently working on a European Commission–funded project entitled "Countering Lone Actor Terrorism," he is an associate faculty at Royal Roads University—where he taught an MA course on international conflict, and a researcher at Simon Fraser University (SFU)—where he is conducting research on the illicit tobacco trade. In an independent capacity, he consults for a number of organizations including governments, think tanks, nongovernmental organizations (NGOs), companies, and universities.

He previously worked as a research analyst in the International Security Department of Chatham House in London, which the University of Pennsylvania ranks as the second most influential think tank in the world. There he led research projects on drugs and organized crime, counterterrorism, and Franco–British defense and security cooperation. He also worked at the French Ministry of Defense in Paris and the North Atlantic Treaty Organization (NATO) Parliamentary Assembly in Brussels; and was educated at Sciences Po in Aix-en-Provence, Loyola University (Chicago), and the London School of Economics and Political Science (LSE).

Gomis is the author of a number of reports and articles, including "Illicit Drugs and International Security: Towards UNGASS 2016" (2014) and "Franco–British Defence and Security Treaties: Entente While It Lasts?" (2011), which the United Kingdom's Chief of Defense Staff selected for his Recommended Reading List. He is a frequent contributor to international publications—including *European Geostrategy* (of which he is an associate editor), *IHS Jane's Intelligence Review*, and *World Politics Review*—and the media, including *Al Jazeera, ARD*, the *BBC*, *Christian Science Monitor*, the *Financial Times*, *France 24*, the *Global Post*, the *Los Angeles Times*, the *National (UAE)*, and the *Sunday Times*. He has spoken at numerous conferences and seminars, including at the British Parliament, the Conference Board of Canada, the Counter-Terror Expo, Georgetown University, King's College London, Public Safety Canada, and the United States Military Academy.

Counterterrorism: Reassessing the Policy Response is his first book.

INTRODUCTION

In 2008, Professor Andrew Silke estimated that between 2002 and 2007 one new book on terrorism was published in English *every 6 hours* (Silke 2008, p. 28). Then, you might ask, why another volume on the topic? Isn't the literature comprehensive enough?

The terrorism literature is substantial. Terrorism studies began in the 1960s and initially focused on the pro-independence, revolutionary, and anti-imperialist movements of the time. In the 1970s and 1980s, research centered on contemporary left-wing terrorist groups such as the Red Army Faction, the Red Brigades, and the Japanese Red Army. While the 1990s saw new research on national separatist groups (e.g., the Irish Republican Army—IRA, *Euskadi Ta Askatasuna* or Basque Fatherland and Liberty) and Islamist groups (e.g., Hezbollah, Hamas), the decade was also marked by a decrease in academic interest (Bakker 2014).

The 9/11 terrorist attacks led to a spike in academic research on terrorism. In the decade following the attacks, the amount of books ever published on the topic more than doubled (*Guardian* 2007). As Andrew Silke and others point out, despite recent progress, terrorism research has generally been of poor quality (Schmid and Jongman 1988, p. 177; Silke 2008, p. 30). In addition, a number of topics remain un- or underresearched in the field of terrorism studies, including measuring and evaluating counterterrorism policies, the terrorism–organized crime nexus, and citizen privacy, topics that will be explored in this book (Schmid 2011). More importantly, a number of books and other publications have reinforced the overall perception and political discourse that the terrorist threat to the Western world is very high, without always providing reliable evidence to back it up and with negative impacts for policy. Many warn of a forthcoming *apocalypse* brought about by *catastrophic terrorism* perpetrated by Al Qaeda with weapons of mass destruction (WMD) (e.g., Emerson 2002; Ferguson and Potter 2004; Schell 2007). These warnings about a *new terrorism*, religiously inspired and aimed at causing mass-casualty attacks, have been mirrored by similar catastrophic announcements on the front page of newspapers:

> AL-QAEDA: ALIVE AND TICKING
> Where it's building new training camps
> What's behind the CIA's warnings
> How the U.S. is fighting back
>
> (The cover included a picture of a ticking time bomb with Osama bin Laden's face on it)
>
> ***Time* (2003)**

> TERROR NOW
> A plot against airlines.
> Bin Laden at large.
> Iraq in flames.
> Five years after 9/11,
> Are we any safer?
> LESSONS OF A GLOBAL WAR
>
> ***Newsweek* (2006)**

> Al-Qaeda's terrifying vision of a devastated America in the wake of a nuclear attack
>
> ***Daily Mail* (2008)**

and in the political sphere:

> Not a conventional fear about a conventional threat but the fear that one day these new threats of WMD, rogue states and international terrorism combine to create a catastrophe to our world and then the shame of knowing that I saw that threat day after day but did nothing to stop it.
>
> **Tony Blair (BBC 2005)**

> The biggest threat we face now as a nation is the possibility of terrorists ending up in the middle of one of our cities with deadlier weapons than have ever before been used against us – biological agents or a nuclear weapon or a chemical weapon of some kind to be able to threaten the lives of hundreds of thousands of Americans.
>
> **Dick Cheney (AP 2004)**

These predictions have turned out to be far from the truth. Terrorism has proved to be an important problem to be managed, rather than an existential threat. Overall, it has posed a marginal risk in the world, especially in Western countries.* Between 2002 and 2012, 36 people have died in the United States because of terrorist attacks, 57 in the United Kingdom, 12 in France, and 1 in Canada according to the Global Terrorism Database (GTD). These 106 deaths are 106 too many, and these estimates might underestimate the scope of terrorist activities in these three countries. However, they do not come anywhere near the figures commentators and politicians had predicted in the aftermath of 9/11 (GTD 2013). Worldwide, over 65,000 people have died in terrorist attacks in the decade following 9/11 with an average of 7,258 deaths per year (national consortium for the Study of Terrorism and Responses to Terrorism [START] 2011). This figure is on the rise, with an estimated 17,958 killed in terrorist attacks in 2013, a 61% increase from 2012 (Institute for Economics & Peace 2014). However, to put things into perspective, deaths related to illicit drug use were estimated at 211,000 for the single year of 2011 United Nations Office on Drugs and Crime (UNODC 2013), while annual death rates related to the use of alcohol and tobacco worldwide, respectively, amount to 2.5 million and nearly 6 million (WHO 2013).

A counterargument often used in response to suggestions that terrorism has been overestimated is that terrorism fatalities have been low precisely because of counterterrorism efforts, with little further explanation of the links between the two. In 2008, economists Linda Bilmes and Joseph Stiglitz estimated the cost of the U.S. response to the 9/11 terrorist attacks at $3–5 trillion (Stiglitz 2011). While the methodology of this estimate can be criticized, it is clear that the cost of counterterrorism efforts in the United Stated and some other Western countries has been overwhelming. In the meantime, while over 65,000 people died in terrorist attacks between 2001 and 2010 worldwide, with an average of 7,258 deaths

* The terms *risk* and *threat* are often used interchangeably. According to the U.S. Department of Homeland Security (DHS), *risk* can be defined as the "potential for an unwanted outcome resulting from an incident, event, or occurrence, as determined by its likelihood and the associated consequences" and *threat* as a "natural or man-made occurrence, individual, entity or action that has or indicates the potential to harm life, information, operations, the environment and/or property" (DHS 2008). Other definitions point to the differences of policy goals, between threat eradication and risk management or mitigation. One Chatham House report notes: "risk can be defined as a compound of threat (or natural hazard), vulnerability and impact… Risk must be understood in the broadest possible sense, and at the level of society as a whole." As a result, "the goal of risk management is to reduce risk to an acceptable level (by mitigating, excluding, transferring or accepting risk) and by doing so to improve the prospects for security" (Cornish et al. 2009, pp. 17–18).

per year, the figures for the preceding decade are similar: 61,000 terrorist fatalities around the world, or 6,825 deaths per year (START 2011).

Counterterrorism policies are arguably designed to manage a low risk with potentially devastating impact. However, an overfocus on worst-case scenarios and attempts to minimize the risks almost at all costs have created a number of negative impacts, including wide-ranging opportunity costs and a disproportionate sense of fear that have often played into the hands of terrorists.

This is not to say that terrorism is not a problem. Countries such as Iraq, India, Pakistan, Afghanistan, and Thailand have been most particularly affected in the last decade, with a combined 15,500 terrorist incidents between 2002 and 2010, 46% of which were carried out in Iraq (START 2011). The recent rise of the so-called Islamic State in Iraq and Syria (ISIS) is certainly a serious challenge. Beyond the number of incidents, fatalities, and injuries, security is also a subjective and psychological concept as "perceptions" of crime tend to matter as much as actual numbers. Indeed, there is often a disconnect between personal experiences and public opinion regarding many social and security issues (Gomis 2013). Governments and commentators have the responsibility to manage expectations and concerns, reassure populations when fears do not match reality, refrain from using terrorism as a political or electoral tool, and instead look for the most effective ways to tackle the risk.

This book does not claim that there is no risk or that governments should do nothing to address the challenges posed by terrorism. Rather, it argues for more proportionate, evidence-based, and accountable responses, not only from governments but also from the media and analysts. As David Rapoport put it, "terrorist tactics invariably produce rage and frustration, often driving governments to respond in unanticipated, extraordinary, illegal, and destructive ways" (Rapoport 2002). Knee-jerk reactions have proved ineffective and counterproductive. We hold the tools to respond to terrorist attacks and the risk posed by terrorism in a more appropriate and effective manner while keeping a sense of perspective. As George Kassimeris noted, "America's biggest enemy after 9/11 was not Bin Laden and his followers but [the country's] inability to maintain a realistic sense of the threat they posed" (Kassimeris 2007).

Counterterrorism policies have of course differed from one country to another. For instance, the United Kingdom has opted for a response focused on criminal justice, treating terrorism as a risk to be managed, while the United States has leaned toward an approach more heavily centered on the military, considering terrorism as a threat to be eradicated.

Differences between the United States, the United Kingdom, and France in particular will be further examined throughout this book.

Over the years that have passed since 9/11, counterterrorism policies and discourses have become more measured, focusing on the broader issue of preventing and countering violent extremism and the need to build more resilient societies. President Obama's remarks after the Boston marathon bombings seem to suggest a move in that direction: "That's why a bomb can't beat us. That's why we don't hunker down. That's why we don't cower in fear. We carry on. We race. We strive. We build, and we work, and we love—and we raise our kids to do the same. And we come together to celebrate life, and to walk our cities, and to cheer for our teams" (Obama 2013).

The overall lesson of the first decade of the counterterrorism experience in the twenty-first century, though, is that governments and societies have often overreacted to the marginal risk posed by terrorism in the West, which has led to a number of unintended, yet foreseeable and damaging, consequences that are still visible today. In addition, governments and commentators have often oversimplified political, ethnic, and security challenges in other parts of the world. Labeling them as "terrorism" has too often led to a one-size-fits-all response that ignores the gravity, complexity, and nuances of these situations.

The revelations by former National Security Agency (NSA) contractor Edward Snowden have highlighted the size and scope of U.S. intelligence measures put in place in the months and years following 9/11—measures that remain and continue to extend today, primarily for counterterrorism purposes. The U.S. administration's use of combat drones in Pakistan and Yemen, in particular, has proved very controversial as well—to name only two of the most contentious facets of current counterterrorism policies. In addition, while some progress has been made toward more sensible counterterrorism policies in several Western countries, there is still a widespread tendency to overreact to terrorist attacks and stories of uncovered terrorist plots, regardless of how small and marginal these may be.

With this in mind, how do we sustain and expand improvements of the past few years while addressing remaining challenges? How can we ensure that government and society responses to terrorism are effective and proportionate to the actual risk terrorists pose, not the attention they aim to attract?

This book aims to serve as a reference guide for policy makers, commentators, and researchers. Its primary goal is to challenge conventional wisdom on terrorism and counterterrorism, currently marked by threat inflation and overreaction. In particular, it will aim to reassess the threat posed by terrorism; review current counterterrorism policies and provide guidance to policy makers, researchers, and students; highlight the responsibility of nongovernment actors in defining the threat and informing policy responses; and emphasize the opportunities and challenges of technological advances for counterterrorism. The book is divided into three sections:

I. *Defining the Threat of Terrorism*—which looks into definitional issues, demonstrates why terrorism matters, and shows that terrorism is a complex yet often overestimated problem.
II. *Dangers of Overreaction*—which explores the negative consequences of overreacting to the risk of terrorism.
III. *How to Break the Cycle? Rethinking the Policy Response*—which focuses on the importance of challenging counterterrorism policies and provides recommendations toward a more measured and comprehensive response.

REFERENCES

AP (Associated Press). 2004. Cheney: Terrorists may nuke U.S. cities. *Infowars*, October 19, 2004.

Bakker, E. 2014. Terrorism and counterterrorism: Comparing theory and practice. University of Leiden online course, January–February 2014.

BBC. 2005. The power of nightmare: The rise of the politics of fear, episode 3: The shadows in the cave. BBC 2 Documentary, January 2005.

Cornish, P., Hughes, R., and Livingstone, D. 2009. Cyberspace and the national security of the United Kingdom: Threats and responses. Chatham House Report. Chatham House, London, March 2009.

Daily Mail. 2008. Al-Qaeda's terrifying vision of a devastated America in the wake of a nuclear attack, May 31, 2008.

DHS. 2008. DHS risk lexicon. Risk Steering Committee, September 2008.

Emerson, S. 2002. *American Jihad: The Terrorists Living Among Us*. New York: Free Press.

Ferguson, C. and Potter, C. 2004. *The Four Faces of Nuclear Terrorism*. London: Routledge.

Global Terrorism Database (GTD)—Run by the National Consortium for the Study of Terrorism and Responses to Terrorism (START), a Center of Excellence of the U.S. Department of Homeland Security, University of Maryland, College Park, MD. http://www.start.umd.edu/gtd/. Accessed on January 15, 2014.

Gomis, B. 2013. Port in a storm: Drug trafficking and organised crime in Marseille. *Jane's Intelligence Review*, November 2013, 44–47.

Guardian. 2007. The rise and rise of terrorism studies, July 3, 2007.
Institute for Economics and Peace. 2014. *Global Terrorism Index 2014*.
Kassimeris, G. (ed.). 2007. *Playing Politics with Terrorism: A User's Guide*. London: Hurst Publishers Ltd.
Newsweek. 2006. Terror now. Front cover, August 28, 2006.
Obama, B. 2013. Transcript: Obama's remarks at Boston Marathon memorial. *Los Angeles Times*, April 18, 2013.
Rapoport, D. 2002. Four waves or rebel terror and September 11. *Antropoethics* 8, Spring/Summer 2002.
Schell, J. 2007. *The Seventh Decade: The New Shape of Nuclear Danger*. New York: Metropolitan Books.
Schmid, A. 2011. 50 Un- and under-researched topics in the field of (counter-) terrorism studies. *Perspectives on Terrorism* 5(1), 76–78.
Schmid, A. and Jongman, A. 1988. *Political Terrorism: A New Guide to Actors, Authors, Concepts, Databases, Theories and Literature*. Amsterdam: North Holland Publishing Company.
Silke, A. 2008. Research on terrorism: A review of the impact of 9/11 and the global war on terrorism. In *Terrorism Informatics: Knowledge Management and Data Mining for Homeland Security, Integrated Series in Information Systems*, Vol. 18, eds. H. Chen, E. Reid, J. Sinai, A. Silke, and B. Ganor. New York: Springer.
START. 2011. Background report: 9/11, ten years later, September 2011.
Stiglitz, J. 2011. The price of 9/11. *Project Syndicate*, September 1, 2011.
Time. 2003. Al-Qaeda: Alive and ticking. Front Cover, October 28, 2003.
UNODC. 2013. World drug report 2013. http://www.unodc.org/unodc/secured/wdr/wdr2013/World_Drug_Report_2013.pdf
World Health Organization (WHO). 2013. Tobacco, Fact Sheet No. 339. Alcohol, Facts and Figures.

Section I

Defining the Threat of Terrorism

Terrorism draws a lot of attention from the media, politicians, academics and others, and yet much confusion remains as to what the term actually means and which particular organizations and activities it refers to. This section will explore some of these challenges. Chapter 1 will look into definitional issues; Chapter 2 will provide a brief historical overview of terrorism and examine some of the key contemporary organizations and trends; Chapter 3 will study the often-neglected right-wing terrorism, and demystify two widely used terms, *narco-terrorism* and *cyber terrorism*. Finally, Chapter 4 will explain how and why the terrorism threat has often been exaggerated.

1

Definitional Issues

> Increasingly questions are being raised about the problem of the definition of a terrorist. Let us be wise and focused about this: terrorism is terrorism... What looks, smells, and kills like terrorism is terrorism.
>
> **Sir Jeremy Greenstock**
> *British Ambassador to the United Nations, in post–September 11, 2001, Speech* (Schmid 2011, p. 39)

There is no universal definition of terrorism. The term is very subjective, political, and dependent on personal experiences and perspectives. As the famous saying goes, "one man's terrorist is another man's freedom fighter." Mia Bloom noted, it is telling that "more former terrorist leaders than American presidents have won the Nobel Peace Prize" (Bloom 2012, p. 18). The absence of a globally shared definition is often considered problematic for comparative research, transnational political cooperation, and international legal prosecution.

Perhaps too much time has already been spent trying to establish the most accurate and objective definition of terrorism—although the author would not go as far as Sir Jeremy Greenstock in his description of the current situation. In 1987, Walter Laqueur argued "it can be predicted with confidence that the disputes about a detailed, comprehensive definition of terrorism will continue for a long time, that they will not result in a consensus, and that they will make no noticeable contribution towards the understanding of terrorism" (Laqueur 1987, p. 72). With this in mind, the following section will highlight the main differences between definitions, and the broader challenges the lack of definitional consensus poses in terms of public perception and policy making.

LEGAL AND ACADEMIC DEFINITIONS

A number of definitions already offer a valuable contribution to the field, as analyzed by eminent terrorism expert Alex Schmid in the very comprehensive *Routledge Handbook of Terrorism Research,* where he notably provides a selection of more than 250 academic definitions—an indication of the impressive number of attempts to define terrorism to date (Schmid 2011, pp. 99–157).

The Study of Terrorism and Responses to Terrorism (START) Consortium at the University of Maryland uses the following definition for the Global Terrorism Database (GTD)—currently the most widely used global database on terrorist incidents: "the threatened or actual use of illegal force and violence by a non-state actor to attain a political, economic, religious, or social goal through fear, coercion, or intimidation" (GTD 2014). It also provides three main criteria:

1. "The act must be aimed at attaining a political, economic, religious, or social goal.
2. There must be evidence of an intention to coerce, intimidate, or convey some other message to a larger audience (or audiences) than the immediate victims.
3. The action must be outside the context of legitimate warfare activities." (GTD 2014)

Boaz Ganor, a well-respected scholar on the issue, defines terrorism as "a form of violent struggle in which violence is deliberately used against civilians in order to achieve political goals (nationalistic, socioeconomic, ideological, religious, etc.)." He asserts that the use of *deliberate* targeting of civilians in order to achieve political objectives is what distinguishes a terrorist act from guerrilla warfare, where military units are targeted (Ganor 2005, p. 17, as quoted in Schmid 2011, p. 47).

In her book *What Terrorists Want,* Louise Richardson lists seven key criteria to define terrorism. First, a terrorist act is "politically inspired, if not, it is simply a crime." Second, "if the act does not involve violence or the threat of violence it is not terrorism." Third, "the point of terrorism is to communicate a message." Fourth, "the act and the victim usually have symbolic significance." Fifth, terrorism is "the act of sub-state groups, not states."

Sixth, "the victim of the violence and the audience the terrorists are trying to reach are not the same." Seventh, "the most important characteristic of terrorism is the deliberate targeting of civilians" (Richardson 2006, pp. 19–21).

In terms of legal definitions of terrorism—as defined by states and used for policy making and judicial processes, the United States has revised the State Department definition of terrorism several times since its inception in 1983. The U.S. code (18 U.S.C. § 2331) now states the following:

"*International terrorism* means activities with the following three characteristics:

- Involve violent acts or acts dangerous to human life that violate federal or state law
- Appear to be intended (i) to intimidate or coerce a civilian population, (ii) to influence the policy of a government by intimidation or coercion, or (iii) to affect the conduct of a government by mass destruction, assassination, or kidnapping
- Occur primarily outside the territorial jurisdiction of the United States or transcend national boundaries in terms of the means by which they are accomplished, the persons they appear intended to intimidate or coerce, or the locale in which their perpetrators operate or seek asylum

Domestic terrorism means activities with the following three characteristics:

- Involve acts dangerous to human life that violate federal or state law
- Appear intended (i) to intimidate or coerce a civilian population, (ii) to influence the policy of a government by intimidation or coercion, or (iii) to affect the conduct of a government by mass destruction, assassination, or kidnapping
- Occur primarily within the territorial jurisdiction of the United States

18 U.S.C. § 2332b defines the term *federal crime of terrorism* as an offense that

- Is calculated to influence or affect the conduct of government by intimidation or coercion, or to retaliate against government conduct
- Is a violation of one of several listed statutes, including § 930 (c) (relating to killing or attempted killing during an attack on a federal facility with a dangerous weapon) and § 1114 (relating to killing or attempted killing of officers and employees of the United States)" (FBI 2014)

Under the Terrorism Act 2000, the United Kingdom defines terrorism as "the use or threat of action designed to influence the government or an international governmental organisation or to intimidate the public, or a section of the public"; "made for the purposes of advancing a political, religious, racial or ideological cause"; and which involves:

- Serious violence against a person;
- Serious damage to a property;
- A threat to a person's life;
- A serious risk to the health and safety of the public; or
- Serious interference with or disruption to an electronic system."

The Terrorism Act 2006 inserted the words "or an international government organization," and the Counter-Terrorism Act 2008 added the word "racial" (Legislation.gov.uk 2014). Further edits may be made in the near future, as the Supreme Court has recently been considering potential changes to the definition. In particular, judges are exploring whether the current definition "includes military attacks by non-state armed groups against national or international armed forces in a non-international armed conflict" (UK Human Rights 2013).

The Council of the European Union defines terrorism as "intentional acts that were committed with the aim of seriously intimidating a population, or unduly compelling a Government or international organisation to perform or abstain from performing any act, or seriously destabilizing or destroying the fundamental political, constitutional, economic or social structures of a country or an international organisation" (EU Council 2014).

The United Nations attempted to come up with a unifying definition of the term in 2004, an initiative led by Secretary General Kofi Annan and aforementioned expert Alex Schmid. Their efforts did not lead to any general agreement on a single definition, given the range of difficulties and political obstacles the next section will explore further (Bakker 2014). However, a few definitions received much support and served as useful starting points. The first one is the academic definition suggested by Alex Schmid and Albert Jongman in 1988: "Terrorism is an anxiety-inspiring method of repeated violent action, employed by (semi-) clandestine individual, group, or state actors, for idiosyncratic, criminal, or political reasons, whereby—in contrast to assassination—the direct targets of violence are not the main targets. The immediate human victims of violence are generally chosen randomly (targets of opportunity) or selectively (representative or symbolic targets) from a target population, and serve as message generators. Threat- and violence-based communication processes between terrorist (organization), (imperiled) victims, and main targets are used to manipulate the main target (audience(s), turning it into a target of terror, a target of demands, or a target of attention, depending on whether intimidation, coercion, or propaganda is primarily sought" (Schmid and Jongman 1988, pp. 5–6). Alex Schmid offered the second one in 1992, when he suggested that acts of terrorism are "peacetime equivalents of a war crime." The Supreme Court of India in fact adopted this definition in a 2003 ruling in the case *Madan Singh vs. State of Bihar* (START 2011).

The latest—and still debated—UN text defining terrorism is contained in article 2 of the UN Comprehensive Convention on International Terrorism and goes as follows:

"Any person commits an offence within the meaning of this (the present) Convention if that person, by any means, unlawfully and intentionally, causes:

a. Death or serious bodily injury to any person; or
b. Serious damage to public or private property, including a place of public use, a State or government facility, a public transportation system, an infrastructure facility or to the environment; or
c. Damage to property, places, facilities or systems referred to in paragraph 1 (b) of this [the present] article, resulting or likely to result in major economic loss; when the purpose of the conduct, by its nature or context, is to intimidate a population, or to compel a Government or an international organization to do or to abstain from doing any act." (Schmid 2011, p. 51)

Given the failed attempts of the Ad Hoc Committee on Terrorism of the Sixth (legal) Committee of the General Assembly to come up with a common legal definition, perhaps the most complete definition to date is the revised academic consensus definition of terrorism, whose core component states: "Terrorism refers, on the one hand, to a doctrine about the presumed effectiveness of a special form or tactic of fear-generating, coercive political violence and, on the other hand, to a conspiratorial practice of calculated, demonstrative, direct violent action without legal or moral restraints, targeting mainly civilians and non-combatants, performed for its propagandistic and psychological effects on various audiences and conflict parties" (Schmid 2011, pp. 86–87).

ON THE IMPORTANCE OF A COMMON DEFINITION

In the end, how much does this matter? As we have seen, there are numerous definitions of the concept of terrorism and not a single universally accepted one. Academic and legal debates have raged on for decades over seemingly small details of vocabulary and grammar; full books and extensive reports have been written on the topic; and yet countries cannot agree on common wording. There are several specific points academics, officials, and others usually disagree on.

Whether states should be included as potential perpetrators of terrorism is occasionally a point of contention, although the majority of academic and legal definitions tend to exclude states, as other laws already exist on the matter of state actions, including international law, international human rights law, and the law of war. However, according to some definitions, states can also employ terrorist *tactics* or *sponsor* terrorism.

Furthermore, there is often disagreement as to whether attacks against politicians and military personnel should be included in the definition, as the former could be treated instead as a case of political assassination, and the latter as a matter of military conflict or war—both of which could in theory fall outside the terrorism remit.

Many also consider that groups fighting for independence or self-determination, such as within the decolonization era following World War II, should not be treated as terrorists, regardless of the tactics employed. This was one of the main sticking points in the 2004 negotiations, when Kofi Annan and his colleagues unsuccessfully attempted to rally all UN member states around one common definition.

As illustrated by the previous examples, two further definitional elements are contested, with clear implications for current developments around the world. The first one is whether the use of violence or the threat thereof should be a core element of any definition of terrorism. Louise Richardson, for instance, thinks it should be. Therefore, as she points out, the term *cyber terrorism* is not useful, because it does not directly or indirectly involve violence (Richardson 2006, p. 20). Regardless, politicians, academics, and commentators have used the term extensively in recent years. In November 2012, Peter W. Singer of Brookings estimated that over 31,300 magazine and journal articles had been written on cyber terrorism (Singer 2012). The last contested element is whether acts perpetrated for economic or socioeconomic purposes can be considered as terrorism, instead of crime or organized crime. In Mexico, a number of organized crime groups and drug cartels in Mexico, including Los Zetas, have used torture and gruesome killings as way to spread fear and intimidate law enforcement and government authorities. Should these actions be considered terrorist attacks as well?

The lack of consensus on a definition of terrorism has been deemed problematic for a number of reasons, including the following five. First, it is important to have a common definition for judicial purposes. Fundamental disagreements over what constitutes terrorism cannot serve as a sound basis for prosecution, especially given that terrorism sentences are often harsher than any other criminal sanctions. As a number of researchers have found, "offenders who are investigated, and prosecuted, under a terrorist label receive harsher sentences than offenders who commit similar criminal acts, but who are not identified as terrorists" (Amirault 2014, referring to Bradley-Engen et al. 2009; Shields et al. 2006; Smith and Damphousse 1996, 1998).

Second, with doubts and hesitations over the definition of terrorism, it is more likely that interpretations will change according to political circumstances, as has been the case with the U.S. Department of State definition of 1983, reviewed and reinterpreted multiple times since its inception (Schmid 2011, p. 49). In the United Kingdom, definitions have also been revised a number of times, as part of new legislations—the United Kingdom is second to South Africa in the world for the highest number of enacted laws on terrorism, with respectively 51 and 63 (Shor 2011, as referred to in Amirault 2014, p. 5). Independent reviewer of Terrorism Legislation David Anderson QC recently noted that "the current law allows members of any nationalist or separatist group to be turned into terrorists by virtue of their participation in a lawful armed conflict, however great the provocation and however odious the regime which they have attacked" (Anderson 2012, p. 37).

Recent developments in Syria certainly back up that argument. Bachar Al-Assad has repeatedly qualified opponents as *terrorists* since the beginning of the popular uprising:

> The unrest is caused by terrorists who spread riots and disorder under the guise of freedom and democracy.
>
> **(UPI 2011)**

> We have to fight terrorism for the country to heal… We will not be lenient. We will be forgiving only for those who renounce terrorism.
>
> **(AP 2012)**

> You have terrorists coming with very sophisticated armaments, nearly all kinds of armaments that they can carry with them and started killing people, destroying infrastructure, destroying public places, everything.
>
> **(*New York Times* 2013)**

Jihadi groups, including Jahbat al-Nusra (al-Nusra front), Jaish al Mujahireen wal-Ansar (Army Emigrants and Helpers), Sukur al-Sham (The Falcons of the Levant), and Al-Dawla al-Islamiyya (Islamic State of Iraq and Syria), have now reportedly infiltrated opposition factions in Syria (Bakker et al. 2013). These groups have emerged in response to the Syrian government crackdown of the uprising, which began in March 2011. The government has cracked down on the local populations with violent and indiscriminate tactics, including torture and the widespread killing of civilians, which has contributed to an overall toll estimated at over 191,000 deaths in August 2014 (*BBC News* 2014), 6.5 million internally displaced people, and more than 3 million having fled to neighboring countries, including Turkey, Lebanon, Jordan, and Iraq (Syrian Refugees 2014). Many opponents to the regime are now widely considered to be *radicalized*, because of the violent tactics used against the government. However, the language used by Bachar Al-Assad demonstrates clear willingness early on in the conflict to delegitimize the opposition and relieve the government from its own responsibility, attempting to portray the situation as a Manichean struggle between good—the state and its government—and evil—the said *terrorists*, while the reality is very different.

Third, counterterrorism cooperation between several countries and organizations can be achieved only if the partners agree on what they are fighting against. Indeed how can the European Union, for instance, aim to increase cooperation between its member states on matters such as information sharing and operational cooperation if there is disagreement on who should be considered a terrorist and what should be considered terrorism in the first place?

Fourth, without a commonly accepted definition of what terrorism is and is not, political statements on the issue can appear confusing and misleading. Following the murder of a soldier in Woolwich, a neighborhood in the southeast of London in the United Kingdom, Prime Minister David Cameron, London Mayor Boris Johnson, Home Secretary Theresa May, and others publicly warned that further information was needed in order to find out whether the attack was a terrorist incident. For instance, Boris Johnson said it was "extremely likely" that the attack was a "terrorist attack" (*BBC News* 2013). In addition, some media reported early on that it was "unclear...whether this was a terrorist attack or criminality"; that "if the attack is determined to be terrorist then it exposes a gap in efforts by police and the domestic security service MI5 to keep track of potential violent extremists"; and that the emergency committee *Cobra* (Cabinet Office Briefing Room A) meeting was told "there are strong indications that it was a terrorist incident" (*Guardian* 2013). However, it remains unclear which specific questions needed to be answered at the time to determine whether the attack was a terrorist incident. Questions could include among some of the following: Was the attack perpetrated with the purpose of advancing a "political, religious, racial, or ideological cause?" Was the action "designed to influence the government" or "intimidate the public?" Is there a link between the alleged conspirators and a broader terrorist organization such as Al Qaeda? Was the victim a member of the British military or a civilian? Is this murder part of a larger and sustained campaign of terrorist activities? In addition, there was a clear lack of clarity as to who should decide whether an attack is a terrorist incident—for example, the police, the judiciary, the government?

Fifth, disagreements over how to define terrorism have often led to vague and all-encompassing definitions that fail to account for the complexities and nuances of situations on the ground. In February 2005, the Subcommittee on the Social, Behavioral, and Economic Sciences of the National Science and Technology Council in the White House noted that using the term *terrorism* "may over-simplify different types of actors, warfare and motivations, encapsulating them in a single group or act so that critical variables are overlooked" (NSTC 2005, p. 7, in Sinai 2004, p. 1).

In sum, defining terrorism is an arduous task. A significant amount of time and energy has already been spent trying to resolve an unresolvable debate. Legal definitions of terrorism have important ramifications for counterterrorism efforts, investigations, trials, international cooperation, the rule of law, and respect of human rights. However, further lengthy academic debates on a common definition of terrorism will not solve the more profound issues at stake. The definition of terrorism has too often become a red herring or even worse contributed to the overall sense of fear and perceptions of threat. Disagreements over definitional matters do not *cause* but rather *reflect* more fundamental differences of views on the problem itself, which will not be reconciled through legal and academic definitions. Furthermore, the priority following any crime should not be to figure out whether it can be labeled *terrorism* but rather to find out what happened and why and provide an effective and proportionate law enforcement and political response to the incident (Gomis 2013).

REFERENCES

Amirault, J. 2014. Timing is everything: The role of contextual and terrorism specific factors in the sentencing outcomes of terrorist offenders, Chapter 4. In *Criminalizing Terrorism: The Impact of Context and Cohort Effects on the Sentencing Outcomes of Terrorist Offenders*. Dissertation. Simon Fraser University, Burnaby, Canada, Summer 2014.

Anderson, D.Q.C. 2012. The terrorism acts in 2011. Report of the independent reviewer on the operation of the Terrorism Act 2000 and Part 1 of the Terrorism Act 2006, June 2012.

AP. 2012. Bachar al-Assad: Syrian regime not to blame for Houla massacre. *Guardian*, June 3, 2012.

Bakker, E. 2014. Terrorism and counterterrorism: Comparing theory and practice. University of Leiden online course, January–February 2014.

Bakker, E., Paulussen, C., and Entenmann, E. 2013. Dealing with European foreign fighters in Syria: Governance challenges and legal implications. ICCT Research Paper, December 2013.

BBC News. 2013. Boris Johnson: Likely that attack was a "terrorist incident," May 22, 2013.

BBC News. 2014. Syria death toll "more than 191,000," August 22, 2014.

Bloom, M. 2012. *Bombshell: Women and Terrorism*. Philadelphia, PA: University of Pennsylvania Press.

Bradley-Engen, M.S., Damphousse, K.R., and Smith, B.L. 2009. Punishing terrorists: A re-examination of U.S. federal sentencing in the postguidelines era. *International Criminal Justice Review* 19(4): 433–455.

EU Council. 2014. Europa summary of EU legislation: Terrorist offences. Accessed on January 29, 2014.

FBI. 2014. Definition of terrorism in the U.S. code. *Terrorism*. http://www.fbi.gov/about-us/investigate/terrorism/terrorism-definition. Accessed on January 23, 2014.

Ganor, B. 2005. *The Counter-Terrorism Puzzle: A Guide for Decision Makers*. New Brunswick, NJ: Transaction.

Gomis, B. 2013. Woolwich attack: Managing fear. Expert Comment, Chatham House, May 24, 2013.

GTD. 2014. Data collection methodology. START, Accessed on January 29, 2014.

Guardian. 2013. Woolwich attack: Aftermath and reaction to killing on London street—As it happened, May 22, 2013.

Laqueur, W. 1987. *The Age of Terrorism*. London: Weidenfield & Nicolson.

Legislation.gov.uk. 2014. Terrorism Act 2000. Accessed on January 29, 2014.

New York Times. 2013. Assad denies starting war in new interview. The Lede: Blogging the news with Robert Mackey, February 20, 2013.

NSTC. 2005. Combating terrorism: Research priorities in the social, behavioral and economic sciences. Social, Behavioral, and Economic Sciences Working Group. URL: https://www.ncjrs.gov/App/Publications/abstract.aspx?ID=209523

Richardson, L. 2006. *What Terrorists Want: Understanding the Terrorist Threat*. Eastbourne: Gardners Books.

Schmid. A. (ed.). 2011. *The Routledge Handbook of Terrorism Research*. London: Routledge.

Schmid, A. and Jongman, A. 1988. *Political Terrorism: A New Guide to Actors, Authors, Concepts, Databases, Theories and Literature*. Amsterdam: North Holland Publishing Company.

Shields, C.A., Damphousse, K.R., and Smith, B.L. 2006. Their day in court: Assessing guilty plea rates among terrorists. *Journal of Contemporary Criminal Justice* 22(3): 261–276.

Shor, E. 2011. Constructing a global counterterrorist legislation database: Dilemmas, procedures and preliminary analyses. *Journal of Terrorism Research* 2(3): 49–77.

Sinai, J. 2008. How to define terrorism. *Perspectives on Terrorism* II(4), 9–11.

Singer, P.W. 2012. *The Cyber Terror Bogeyman*. Washington, DC: Brookings Institution, November 2012.

Smith, B.L. and Damphousse K.R. 1996. Punishing political offenders: The effect of political motive in federal sentencing decisions. *Criminology* 34(3): 289–321.

Smith, B.L. and Damphousse, K.R. 1998. Terrorism, politics and punishment: A test of structural-contextual theory and the "liberation hypothesis." *Criminology* 36(1): 67–92.

START. 2011. Alex P. Schmid: Biography. Accessed on January 29, 2014.

Syrian Refugees. 2014. A snapshot of the crisis—In the Middle East and Europe. A project by European University Institute, Robert Schuman Centre for Advanced Studies, and the Migration Policy Centre. Accessed on December 17, 2014.

UK Human Rights Blog. 2013. Supreme Court considers definition of "terrorism," October 23, 2013.

UPI. 2011. Assad says terrorists causing Syria unrest, June 20, 2011.

2

Why Does Terrorism Matter?

> When I was coming up, it was a dangerous world, and we knew exactly who they were. It was us versus them, and it was clear who them was. Today we are not so sure who they are, but we know they're there.
>
> **George W. Bush**
> *Speech at Iowa Western Community College, January 21, 2000* (*Guardian* 2000)

Terrorism remains one of the primary concerns on government agendas, and many citizens believe that terrorism poses one of the biggest threats to our societies. Reports of terrorist attacks or plots being uncovered remind us that terrorism remains a problem that needs to be dealt with. Like many security challenges we face today, it has evolved over the past few decades. The following chapter will look at the history of terrorism and analyze current trends, looking in particular at Al Qaeda since 9/11 and the emergence or reemergence of *lone wolves*.

BRIEF HISTORY OF TERRORISM

The term *terror* first emerged following the French revolution to qualify the period between 1792 and 1794, which was marked by mass executions and arbitrariness under the revolution government led by Robespierre. It is interesting to note that the initial meaning thus included the actions of a state actor, while today's definitions often exclude them.

It is difficult to trace back the origins of terrorism as such, but many name the Order of Assassins of the eleventh century in the Middle East, who killed political and military leaders, as the first terrorists (Bakker 2014). Terrorism is a multifaceted phenomenon that has taken many different forms across many different countries in modern history. However, David Rapoport has divided the global history of terrorism into four different waves (Rapoport 2002): first the *Anarchist Wave*, which appeared in the 1880s and lasted approximately 40 years. The most visible attack perpetrated at the time was the assassination of U.S. President William McKinley in Buffalo in 1901, although it was not qualified as a *terrorist* attack by commentators at the time. The movement started in Russia and later on spread to other parts of the world, including the United States. In contrast to most terrorist organizations of today, anarchists did indeed call themselves terrorists, often referring to their historical origins (of the French revolution or even the Order of Assassins). They targeted political figures, with a view to shock the public and ultimately reshape societies in a fundamental manner and carried out bank robberies in order to finance their operations.

Second, the *Anti-Colonial Wave* began in the 1920s and lasted until the 1960s. This wave comprised the struggle for self-determination and independence from colonial empires such as France and Britain. Instead of political assassinations, the organizations resorted to guerilla tactics and did not call themselves *terrorists* but *freedom fighters*. Examples of organizations of the Anti-Colonial Wave include the Irish Republication Army, the Front de Libération Nationale (National Liberation Front) in Algeria, and Irgun in Israel (Ha-Irgun Ha-Tzvai Ha-Leumi be-Eretz Yisrael or "The National Military Organization in the Land of Israel"). The July 22, 1946, bombing of the King David Hotel—then the British headquarters for Palestine—is perhaps the most significant attack of the era, killing 91 people.

Third, the *New Left Wave* started in the 1960s, and groups which included the Weather Underground from the United States, Action Directe from France, the Red Army Faction from Germany (Rote Armee Fraktion), the Japanese Red Army, and the Italian Red Brigades (Brigate Rosse), largely dissipated in the 1990s. Resentment against the Vietnam War was a key driver of these left-wing movements—many of whom acted both locally and internationally on behalf of Third World countries. Tactics included not only hijackings and hostage takings such as during the 1972 Olympic Games in Munich, but also political assassinations, as Italian Prime Minister Aldo Moro was kidnapped and murdered by the Red Brigades in 1979.

Fourth, the *Religious Wave* began in 1979, a year marked by the Islamic revolution in Iran, Russia's invasion of Afghanistan, a new century according to the Muslim calendar, and the occupation by the Sunni Muslims of the grand mosque in Mecca, which resulted in hundreds of fatalities. In addition to political assassinations and hijackings, suicide bombings—a tactic once used by the Assassins—were reintroduced. This has included Christian sects (such as Aum Shinrikyo, responsible for the sarin gas attack on the subway in Tokyo in 1995), Islamic organizations (e.g., Hezbollah, Al Qaeda), and Sikh groups (especially against Indian authorities). It is important to note that religious organizations may also have political, territorial, or self-determination aspirations, in a way similar to the organizations of the *Anti-Colonial Wave.*

A history of terrorism is bound to be politically and culturally biased and subjective, just like any definition of such a contested and controversial concept. Different degrees of political violence have been used or attempted throughout history, from the failed Gunpowder Plot of 1605 in England to the actions of the military branch of the African National Congress (Umkhonto we Sizwe or MK) in South Africa and the many popular uprisings in response to oppressive governments across the world—many of which are not considered terrorism as such, and rightfully so.

TERRORISM TODAY

More than a decade after 9/11, terrorism persists around the world. Over 65,000 people died in terrorist attacks between 2001 and 2011, with an annual average of 7,258 deaths, an increase from the previous decade when approximately 61,000 deaths were caused by terrorism, or 6,825 per year (START 2011). An estimated 6,771 terrorist attacks were carried out worldwide in 2012, resulting in more than 11,000 deaths, more than 21,600 injuries, and more than 1,280 people being kidnapped or taken hostage (U.S. State Department 2013).

Terrorism trends over the so-called 9/11 decade also point toward more geographically concentrated terrorist attacks around the world. Between 1991 and 2001, 51 countries experienced at least one large terrorist attack. This number went down to 34 for the period 2002–2010, as Iraq alone accounted for almost half of the 394 large attacks recorded. In 2013, 82% of all fatalities from terrorist attacks occurred in only five countries, namely, Iraq, Afghanistan, Pakistan, Nigeria, and Syria, countries that face a range of political challenges that cannot be merely described as terrorism (Institute for Economics and Peace 2014).

The terrorism situation in the Middle East and South Asia is arguably getting worse in recent years, with problems also increasing in African countries such as Nigeria (1,386 killed in 2012), Yemen (365 in 2011), and Somalia (323 in 2012) (U.S. State Department 2013). Meanwhile, the terrorism threat has diminished in Western Europe and North America (START 2013).

In the United States, there were approximately 41 attacks per year between 1991 and 2000, resulting in 217 fatalities. The bombing carried out by Timothy McVeigh on the Alfred P. Murrah Federal Building in Oklahoma City on April 19, 1995, alone left 168 people dead and more than 680 injured. In the decade following 9/11, 16 terrorist attacks were perpetrated every year on average in the United States. These caused 25 fatalities in total. The fatality rate per terrorist attack also decreased after 9/11, with respectively 0.42 fatalities in the years preceding 2001, and 0.24 deaths between 2002 and 2010 (START 2011).

The largest terrorist attack in North America excluding 9/11 was carried out on June 23, 1985, when Air India Flight 182 was blown up over the Atlantic Ocean, and 329 people were killed, including 268 Canadians (Public Safety Canada 2014). Between 9/11 and the end of 2013, terrorism in Canada has led to the death of only one person according to the Global Terrorism Database. However, some have questioned the reliability of the estimates related to terrorism in Canada, or involving Canadian citizens, which has led to a new initiative—the Canadian Incident Database—which aims to collect information on all terrorist incidents since 1960 with a Canadian connection (including those occurring overseas involving Canadian perpetrators and/or victims) (TSAS 2014). This initiative is partly funded by the Kanishka Project, run by Public Safety Canada. The project, named after the *Emperor Kanishka*, nickname given to the Boeing 747-237B that was bombed in 1985, was launched in June 2011 to fund and foster research on "pressing questions for Canada on terrorism and counterterrorism, such as preventing and countering violent extremism" (Public Safety Canada 2011).

The terrorism landscape in Europe has a long and diverse history. Many countries have been affected by terrorism since the emergence of the term *terreur* in France. A number of countries in particular have experienced far more terrorism than others. Between 1970 and 2007, Northern Ireland, Spain, Turkey, and Italy ranked in the top 20 of the most frequently attacked countries in the world, respectively, 5th, 6th, 8th, and 20th with

3,762, 3,165, 2,691, and 1,487 terrorist attacks. Turkey and Northern Ireland were also the 12th and 20th countries with the highest numbers of fatalities worldwide, with 4,674 and 2,842 (LaFree 2010). Every year, the European Police Office (Europol) produces the EU Terrorism Situation and Trend Report (TE-SAT), which offers facts and figures regarding terrorism in the EU.* In 2012, it reported that 17 people died as a result of 219 failed, foiled, or completed terrorist attacks in the EU's 27 Member States, down from 249 in 2010 but up from 174 in 2011.† In addition, 537 individuals were arrested in the EU for terrorist-related offenses, which is lower than in 2010 when 611 people were arrested on terrorism charges, but higher than in 2011 (484). France alone accounted for approximately 57% of attacks in the EU and 35% of arrests (Europol 2013).

AL QAEDA

Since 9/11, Al Qaeda has been the most notorious terrorist group in the world. Created in 1988, it only gained international attention in the late 1990s with the bombings of the U.S. embassies in Dar es Salaam and Nairobi in August 1998 and the attack on the *USS Cole* in October 2000. The September 11, 2001, attacks made Al Qaeda the most prominent terrorist organization in the world as it carried out the deadliest series of terrorist attacks in modern history, causing almost 3,000 fatalities.

A decade later, Al Qaeda remains high on security agendas. It is often qualified as an international franchise or network, with global connections and aspirations, and significant resources. It features high on the list of organizations posing the biggest threat in most countries around the world. The 2010 U.S. National Security Strategy uses the word *Al-Qa'ida* 25 times in only 60 pages (U.S. White House 2010). In the 2010 UK National Security Strategy, the section on the "Security Context" starts with the following sentence: "We face a real and pressing threat from international terrorism, particularly that inspired by Al Qaeda and its affiliates" (UK HMG 2010, p. 13). The 2013 French White Paper on Defence and National Security notes that "more than ten years after the attacks of September 11 and in spite of the important progress made by the fight against terrorism

* Europol uses the following definition of terrorism for data collection and analysis: "acts which aim to intimidate populations, compel states to comply with the perpetrators' demands and/or destabilize the fundamental political, constitutional, economic or social structures of a country of international organization" (Europol 2013).

† The EU now has 28 member countries, with the accession of Croatia on July 1, 2013.

internationally, the threat level remains very high" and adds that "there are no signs that the terrorist threat could decrease in the short- or mid-term" (France 2013, p. 44).

However, as David Rapoport noted, "since Al Qaeda achieved none of its objectives and the early attacks produced virtually no response, the September 11 attacks could be understood as a desperate attempt to rejuvenate a failing cause by triggering indiscriminate American reactions" (Rapoport 2002). Has Al Qaeda succeeded in its rejuvenation efforts?

On 9/11, the attacks perpetrated by Al Qaeda led to the death of almost 3,000 people and the destruction of the World Trade Center and parts of the Pentagon. In the following decade, groups allied with Al Qaeda were reportedly responsible for over 12,000 deaths worldwide (START 2011). Crucially, if one of the key elements of a terrorism strategy is to spread fear among the public and lead to disproportionate reactions from governments, one could argue that Al Qaeda has succeeded. As the 9/11 Commission Report noted, Al Qaeda, Bin Laden, and even terrorism in general were not an important topic of discussion in American politics prior to September 2001: "As best we can determine, neither in 2000 nor in the first eight months of 2001 did any polling organization in the United States think the subject of terrorism sufficiently on the minds of the public to warrant asking a question about it in a major national survey. Bin Ladin, al Qaeda, or even terrorism was not an important topic in the 2000 presidential campaign. Congress and the media called little attention to it" (National Commission on Terrorist Attacks upon the United States 2004, p. 341).

In the years following 9/11, the United States and some of its partners engaged in a financially and humanly costly global war on terrorism, while the media highlighted the salience of the threat of Al Qaeda, and the public reported high levels of fear of terrorism. For example, 85% of Americans considered there would be acts of terrorism in the United States over the next several weeks in late 2001. This figure overall decreased throughout the following decade, to 38% in September 2011, but particular events or reports have also led to sudden spikes in fear—for example, 62% feared terrorist attacks would soon occur in May 2011, following the death of Osama bin Laden (Gallup 2011).

Al Qaeda is often reported to have changed in form since 9/11, progressively turning into a less hierarchical organization with an expanded geographical outreach. Its central leadership—often referred as the *Al Qaeda Core*—is much weaker than it once was, and Al Qaeda's capacity to launch international attacks with a massive impact has been diminished. Counterterrorism operations of the past decade or so have contributed to this trend, through the targeted killing or capture of a number of senior leaders including Osama bin Laden on May 2, 2011. However, two other factors have played a significant role in the weakening of the organization. Indiscriminate killings of Muslims across South Asia and the Middle East, especially in 2005 and 2006, led to a sharp decrease in confidence for Osama bin Laden and Al Qaeda (Kurth Cronin 2011; Moeckli 2011; Pew Research Center 2011). Jason Burke, for instance, notes: "Muslims across the world have shown themselves to be revolted by violence when they see it up close... When, early on, the violence was in America or a long way away, it was much easier for communities to feel supportive of what was going on" (The Browser 2011b). In addition, Al Qaeda has offered no positive outlook and has thus struggled to appeal to significant parts of the population. In other words, "Al Qaeda offers no economic blueprint, no political vision" (Gerges 2011). This absence of a positive message became even more problematic for Al Qaeda with the emergence of the Arab Spring, which demonstrated that peaceful movements could overthrow long-standing regimes (Moeckli 2011) (Figure 2.1).

Al Qaeda has become more decentralized. Its main regional affiliates include Al Qaeda in the Arabian Peninsula (AQAP), based in Yemen;

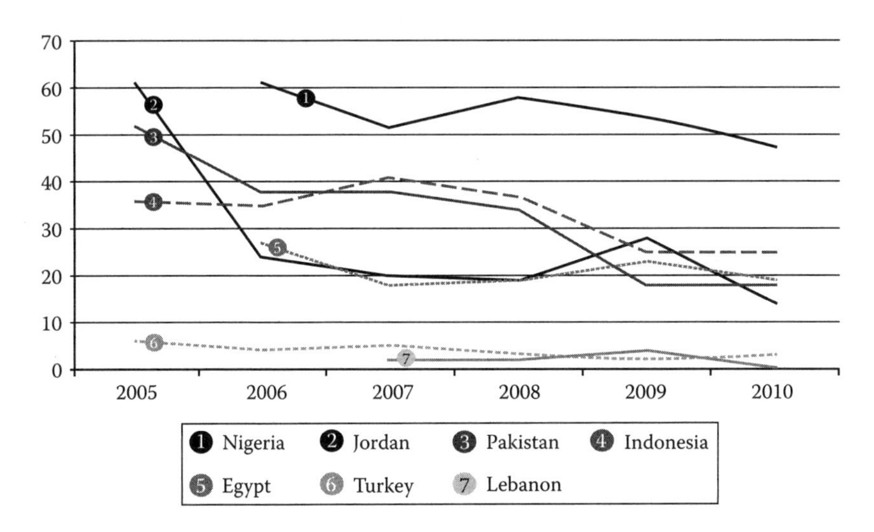

Figure 2.1 Confidence in Osama bin Laden. (From Moeckli, D., 9/11 ten years on: Terrorism as a manageable risk, Strategic trends 2011: Key developments in global affairs, Center for Security Studies, ETH Zürich, Chapter 3, pp. 67–88, 2011.)

Al Qaeda organizations in Iraq, including the Islamic State of Iraq and Syria (ISIS), also known as Al-Dawla al-Islamiyya, the Islamic State in Iraq and the Levant (ISIL), and the Islamic State or Daesh (also spelt *Daech*)—which we will study in greater detail later; Al Qaeda in the Islamic Maghreb (AQIM), previously called the Salafist Group for Preaching and Combat, which originated in Algeria in the 1990s and changed its name to AQIM in 2006; and Al-Shabaab, who formally allied with Al Qaeda in 2010. Other regional groups have also emerged, including Jabhat al-Nusra, a spin-off of Al Qaeda in Iraq (AQI), which has been very active in Syria. The UK Foreign & Commonwealth office (FCO) even suggests that the term *Al Qaeda Core* no longer reflects the current devolved hierarchy. The report notes that the appointment of AQAP's Nasir al-Wuhayshi as deputy leader of Al Qaeda reflects a geographical spread of its leadership, mirroring the geographical spread of the threat posed by Al Qaeda (UK FCO 2013). In sum, Al Qaeda could be qualified today as an *alliance hub* (Tricia Bacon, in Tankel 2013) (Figure 2.2).

It is easy to exaggerate how much cohesion there is within Al Qaeda. The words *franchise, network,* and *organization* describe a well-designed,

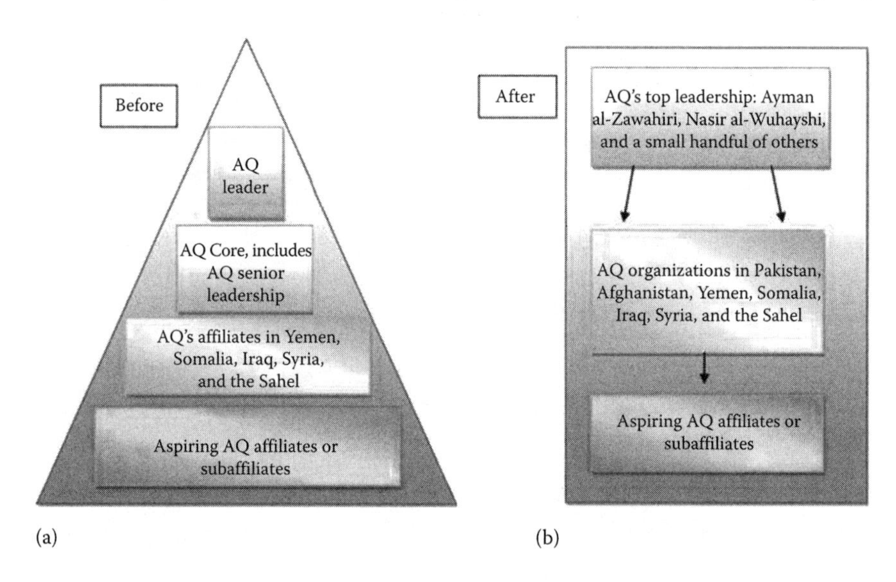

Figure 2.2 Our previous understanding of the AQ Movement's leadership structure (a) and the current, more fluid structure (b). (From The Changing Structure of Al Qaida, Foreign Office Research Analyst Papers. Foreign & Commonwealth Office [UK FCO], November 12, 2013.)

robust structure with a business-like division of responsibilities between different units. However, the reality is much more nuanced. Smaller terrorist groups often claim allegiance to Al Qaeda to boost their image and credibility. In a sense, as Peter Taylor has noted, "Al Qaeda has become a revolutionary idea rather than a strictly regimented organization" (The Browser 2011a). Accordingly, militants and groups often join the cause of their own will and for their own interests rather than through top-down recruitment from Al Qaeda leadership. When former chief investigative reporter for Al-Jazeera Arabic Yosri Fouda was interviewed about the 9/11 conspirators, he suggested "I don't think al Qaeda recruited Mohammed Atta. I think Mohammed Atta recruited al Qaeda. It suited him and he needed an umbrella for his frustration" (The Browser 2009). Security expert Bruce Schneier even considers that Al Qaeda "isn't a well-organized global organization with movie-plot-villain capabilities; it's a loose collection of people using the same name" (Schneier 2010).

The threat posed by Al Qaeda is in fact very local. Grievances of affiliates are often related to specific local contexts, and their operations are rarely transnational (Moeckli 2011; *Guardian* 2011). Based on personal research, Jason Burke has noted that a "vast proportion, 95% perhaps, of violent attacks have occurred within a couple of hours' travel, at most, from where the perpetrators lived or grew up" (*Guardian* 2011). The trend is similar in Europe, as Lorenzo Vidino has found: "There is little evidence suggesting that AQ and affiliated organizations operating outside of Europe conduct direct efforts to recruit European Muslims... The absorption of jihadist ideology by European Muslims is an independent process, taking place individually or, most often, within a small group of friends" (Vidino 2011). Organizations like AQAP have attempted to conduct operations outside Yemen, through to the notorious Christmas bomb plot and the cargo plane plots, and their attempts to attract more jihadists are also aimed beyond the country's borders. However, the organization has been far from successful to date, and other affiliates such as Mali-based AQIM only pose a marginal direct threat to Western countries.

ISLAMIC STATE

In 2014, this terrorist organization became a great source of concern. The name itself is important to decipher. *Islamic State* is a misnomer in the sense that it is not officially recognized by international law or any other actual *state* within the international community. Furthermore, it only represents the views of an extremely tiny proportion of Muslims, not the religion of Islam as a whole. The term is part of the organization's branding strategy, which has proved effective. In 2012, the group, a spin-off of AQI, began to call itself ISIS or ISIL, to reflect broader territorial ambitions than just Iraq (CFR 2014). After gaining control of the city of Mosul in June 2014, the group renamed itself the *Islamic State* (Lister 2014). Most commentators or government officials have referred to the organization by the names that include the words *Islamic State* or their acronym, for example, ISIS, ISIL, or IS. In September 2014, the French government began to call them *Daesh* or *Daesh cutthroats* with a view to delegitimizing their actions and existence. Foreign Minister Laurent Fabius explained: "This is a terrorist group and not a state. I do not recommend using the term Islamic State because it blurs the lines between Islam, Muslims and Islamists. The Arabs call it 'Daesh' and I will be calling them the 'Daesh cutthroats.' The move has reportedly angered some of the organizations' members, although 'Daesh' is merely the Arab acronym of 'ISIL,' i.e., al-Dawla al-Islamiya al-Iraq al-Sham" (France 24 2014).

This group is different from most terrorist organizations for five main reasons. First, although prone to exaggerated reports, it has managed to gather substantial amounts of funding in a short period of time. Initially, financial support came from a number of wealthy businessmen in the Gulf including Qatar, Kuwait, and Saudi Arabia, some of whom have direct or indirect links with state officials (*BBC News* 2014). In late October 2014, the U.S. Treasury Department's Under Secretary for Terrorism and Financial Intelligence Daniel Cohen suggested that ISIS revenues from oil sales stand at approximately $1 million per day, with others suggesting that the amount might be three times higher (PBS 2014). However, a more careful and realistic assessment seems to suggest that actual figures are around $270,000–360,000 per day (Belli et al. 2014). Similarly, the widely reported news that ISIS had stolen more than $400 million from financial institutions in Mosul in June 2014 turned out to be false (FT 2014). ISIS has reportedly made at least $25 million in ransom money in 2014, a considerable amount (Belli et al. 2014). Second, the organization has managed to acquire a significant amount of military equipment, especially from the Iraqi Army itself. Third, ISIS has vast territorial claims over the whole Levant region and has acted upon them effectively, which makes the organization more of a militant group than a traditional terrorist group. Fourth, they have skillfully used social media to convey their messages, amplify their importance, document their successes, romanticize what ISIS membership might entail for foreign fighters, and spread fear across the world.

Ultimately, the threat posed by the Islamic State is a serious one. However, it is not the sort of invincible monster it is often made out to be. An investigation by German newspaper *die Zeit* notes: "The fact is, the caliphate bears greater resemblance to a failing state than an aspiring one" (Belli et al. 2014). Exaggerating their strengths and overlooking their limits are likely to play into their hands and prevent the establishment of an objective, rational, and effective response. At the heart of the issue, ISIS has capitalized on the implosion of the states of Syria and Iraq, and the reluctance of Western powers to engage in the region. In other words, addressing the political and socioeconomic failures of Syria and Iraq should be the policy priority, not only to reduce the appeal and damaging impact of ISIS, but also to pave the way for peace and resilience in these countries.

LONE WOLVES

The threat from *lone wolves* has emerged as one of the priority issues on national counterterrorism agendas in Western Europe and North America. In 2011, President Obama noted: "the risk that we're especially concerned over right now is the lone wolf terrorist, somebody with a single weapon being able to carry out wide-scale massacres of the sort that we saw in Norway recently… You know, when you've got one person who is deranged or driven by a hateful ideology, they can do a lot of damage, and it's a lot harder to trace those lone wolf operators" (AP 2011). After the attacks carried out by Mohammed Merah in Toulouse and Montauban, then French President Nicolas Sarkozy declared: "He was a lone wolf. He was a terrorist, a monster" (Sarkozy 2012). David Cameron has also warned of the continuous threat posed by lone actors: "Of course, there is always the risk of a radicalized individual acting alone, a so-called lone-wolf attack" (Cameron 2011).

What is a *lone wolf* terrorist? The term itself originates from the extreme right in the United States. In the early 1990s, Louis Beam, a former Ku Klux Klan and Aryan Nations member, preached the strategy of leaderless resistance, whereby "all individuals and groups operate independently of each other, and never report to a central headquarters or single leader for direction or instruction" (COT/TTSRL 2007; Bakker and de Graaf 2011). In 1998, the U.S. Federal Bureau of Investigation (FBI) launched an investigation targeted at white supremacist Alexander James Curtis and several of his associates. The investigation was named *Operation Lone Wolf*, referring to the term used by Curtis to encourage other white supremacists to engage in *lone wolf* activism, in other words to commit criminal acts in small groups or *cells* in order to evade law enforcement (FBI 2014).

There are several definitions and typologies of *lone wolves,* also known as *lone actors* (e.g., Europol 2012; UK Security Service 2014) or *stray dogs* (Jenkins 2011). Stewart and Burton define a lone wolf as "a person who acts on his or her own without orders from – or even connections to – an organization" (Stewart and Burton 2008), which Bakker and de Graaf expand to include "individuals that are inspired by a certain group but who are not under the orders of any other person, group or network" (Bakker and de Graaf 2011). Europol defines "lone actors" as "single terrorists operating in isolation from any other organisation or other associates" and "solo terrorists" as "individuals executing acts of terrorism without others but who are actively supported and assisted by a wider terrorist organisation" (Europol 2012).

Raffaello Pantucci has offered a typology of Islamist lone wolf terrorists, dividing the concept into four categories. According to Pantucci, a "Loner" is an "individual who plans or attempts to carry out an act of terrorism using the cover of extreme Islamist ideology"; "Lone Wolves" are "individuals who, while appearing to carry out their actions alone and without any physical outside instigation, in fact demonstrate some level of contact with operational extremists"; a "Lone Wolf Pack" is "similar to the Lone Wolves, except rather than there being a single individual who becomes ideologically motivated; it is a group of individuals who self-radicalise using the Al Qaeda narrative." Finally, "Lone Attackers… operate alone, but demonstrate clear command and control links with actual Al Qaeda core or affiliated groups" (Pantucci 2011a). Gill, Horgan, and Deckert distinguish between "individual terrorists" who "operate autonomously and independently of a group (in terms of training, preparation, and target selection, etc.)"; "individual terrorists with command and control links" who "are trained and equipped by a group—which may also choose their targets—but attempt to carry out their attacks autonomously"; and "isolated dyads" that "include pairs of individuals who operate independently of a group" (Gill et al. 2013).

Examples of *lone wolf* terrorists include Ted Kaczynski, also known as the "Unabomber" (referring to "UNABOM," the name of the FBI investigation—university and airline bombings). Kaczynski was an American mathematician who studied at Harvard University and the University of Michigan. He became an assistant professor of mathematics at the University of California, Berkeley, at 25 and resigned 2 years later, in 1969, to live in a remote area of Montana. From 1978 to 1995, he planted or mailed numerous homemade bombs, killing three people and injuring 23. Kaczynski justified his attacks as protests against the "industrial-technological progress" he resented for its denial of human nature and destruction on individual freedom, as he outlined in a 35,000-word essay shortly before his arrest. He was caught in 1995 and now serves a life sentence in Colorado (FBI 2008; McCauley et al. 2013).

In May 14, 2010, Roshonara Choudhry repeatedly stabbed British Labour MP Stephen Timms in the stomach with a three-inch kitchen knife at his constituency surgery. She was immediately arrested and during subsequent police interviews declared: "I've fulfilled my obligation, my Islamic duty to stand up for the people of Iraq and to punish someone who wanted to make war with them," and stated she "wanted to be a martyr" (*Guardian* 2010). Choudhry had been an excellent student at the prestigious university of King's College, London, from where she had just dropped out. She reportedly conducted research online and watched videos of American Yemeni preacher Anway al-Awlaki before carrying out the attack (Pantucci 2011a).

Between March 11 and 19, 2012, Mohammed Merah killed three paratroopers, a Rabbi, and three Jewish children in Toulouse and Montauban in the South West of France. Merah claimed the attacks were intended as revenge for the war in Afghanistan and the conflict in Palestine. The French authorities identified him, and the antiterrorist unit Recherche Assistance Intervention Dissuasion moved to arrest him on March 22. He showed resistance and fought back for 32 hours, as a result of which he was shot and killed. Merah's name had already been on the intelligence services' radar: he was reportedly on the U.S. no-fly list and was also being watched by the French Central Directorate of Interior Intelligence (Direction central du renseignement intérieur) (Garavelli 2012).

On July 22, 2011, Anders Behring Breivik detonated a bomb near government buildings in downtown Oslo, killing 8 people, and later shot and killed 69 people, mostly teenagers, at a camp organized by the Workers' Youth League (the youth wing of the Labour party) on the island of Utøya. Hours before the attacks, he uploaded a document on the Internet entitled "2083: A European Declaration of Independence," in which he calls himself a "crusader warrior" fighting for Christendom and against "advancing hordes of Muslims" on the European continent and describes what his perfect society and army would look like. On August 24, 2011, he was sentenced to 21 years in prison, the longest possible term in Norway (Pantucci 2011b).

These examples highlight the range of personalities (mathematician, student, young and unemployed adult, etc.), motivations (technology, foreign policy, etc.), targets (from people to buildings), tactics (bombing, shooting, etc.), locations (United States, Norway, France, United Kingdom), and impacts (from an attempted murder to 77 deaths) lone wolf terrorism may have. The difficulty of predicting such attacks has led to high levels of fear around this type of threat, often considered the most worrying development in terrorism. However, research has shown that terrorist attacks planned within networks with operational ties to groups operating outside Europe tend to be more elaborate, professional, and lethal. For example, between 1990 and 2010, plots by actors who have received formal training in explosives were four times more likely to be successful than those by perpetrators without training (Sageman 2007). Most lone wolf terrorist attacks use low technological tools and have limited impact. The Oslo attacks of 2011 are often shown as an example of how much physical impact lone wolves can have. However, it is worth noting that it took Breivik approximately 9 years of preparation to carry out his attack and that he needed a significant amount of luck, as Norwegian intelligence services did indeed come across his name when he purchased a substantial amount of fertilizer during the planning phase.

Lone wolf attacks are a rare occurrence. As summarized by McCauley et al. (2013), Ramon Spaaij lists only 88 lone wolf terrorism cases across 15 countries including the United States between 1968 and 2010, and Charles Eby identifies 53 lone wolf terrorists in the United States between 2001 and 2011. Finally, according to a study by COT (the Dutch Instituut voor Veiligheids-en Crisismanagement, an Aon company), "a total number of 72 lone wolf terrorist incidents accounted for only 1.28 percent of the total number of terrorist incidents in the U.S., Germany, France, Spain, Italy, Canada and Australia" between January 1, 1968, and May 1, 2007 (COT/TTSRL 2007; Baaker and de Graaf 2011).

As Michael Clarke, director general of the Royal United Services Institute (RUSI), put it, international terrorism is "a problem, but not an overwhelming strategic challenge unless we let it be so" (RUSI 2011). Suggesting that the threat posed by terrorism is often overestimated does not mean that the threat does not exist or that nothing should be done to counter it. Terrorism has been an important problem for many decades and will remain a threat for decades to come. Therefore, there is a need for relevant researchers and policy makers to rethink the assumptions that were formed around 9/11 and explore the nuances and complexities of terrorism today.

REFERENCES

AP. 2011. *Obama: Lone Wolf Terror Attack Biggest Concern*. New York: Associated Press, August 17, 2011.

Bakker, E. 2014. Terrorism and counterterrorism: Comparing theory and practice. University of Leiden online course, January–February 2014.

Bakker, E. and de Graaf, B. 2011. Preventing lone wolf terrorism: Some CT approaches addressed. *Perspectives on Terrorism* 5(5–6): 43–50.

BBC News. 2014. Islamic State: Where does jihadist group get its support, September 1, 2014.

Belli, O.B., Böhm, A., Bühler, A., Kohlenberg, K., Meining, S., Musharbash, Y., Schieritz, M. et al. 2014. The business of the Caliph. Zeit Online, December 4, 2014.

The Browser. 2009. Yosri Fouda on 9/11. Five Books Interview, September 28, 2009.

The Browser. 2011a. Peter Taylor on Al-Qaeda. Five Books Interview, June 24, 2011.

The Browser. 2011b. Jason Burke on Islamic militancy. Five Books Interview, August 22, 2011.

Cameron, D. 2011. Prime Minister: "While Bin Laden is gone, the threat of Al Qaeda remains." Announcement to the House of Commons. UK FCO, May 3, 2011.

CFR. 2014. Islamic State in Iraq and Syria. Backgrounders, August 8, 2014.

COT/TTSRL. 2007. Lone-wolf terrorism. Transnational Terrorism, Security and the Rule of Law, July 2007.

Cronin, A.K. 2010. The evolution of counterterrorism: Will tactics trump strategy? *International Affairs* 86(4): 837–856, July 2010.

Europol. 2012. TE-SAT 2012: EU terrorism situation and trend report, April 25, 2012.

Europol. 2013. TE-SAT 2013: EU terrorism situation and trend report, April 25, 2013.

FBI. 2008. FBI 100: The Unabomber, April 24, 2008.

FBI. 2014. Operation Lone Wolf. FBI San Diego Division. History. Accessed on February 13, 2014.

France. 2013. Livre Blanc sur la Défense et la Sécurité Nationale (White Paper on defence and national security). Président de la République, April 2013.

France 24. 2014. French govt to use Arabic "Daesh" for Islamic State group, September 18, 2014.

FT. 2014. Biggest bank robbery that "never happened"—$400 million ISIS heist, July 17, 2014.

Gallup. 2011. Americans' fear of terrorism in U.S. is near low point, September 2, 2011.

Garavelli, D. 2012. Most lone wolves are high on motivation but low on skills. Mohammad Merah was high on both. *Scotland on Sunday. The Scotsman*, March 25, 2011.

Gerges, F.A. 2011. Al-Qaeda's existential crisis. *Washington Post*, May 2, 2011.

Gill, P., Horgan, J., and Deckert, P. 2013, December 6. Bombing alone: Tracing the motivations and antecedent behaviors of lone-actor terrorists. *Journal of Forensic Sciences* 59(2): 425–435.

Guardian. 2000. Bush, in his own words. Special report: The U.S. elections, November 4, 2000.
Guardian. 2010. Roshonara Choudhry: Police interview extracts, May 14, 2010.
Guardian. 2011. Twin Towers and terrorism: The impact 10 years on, September 11, 2011.
Institute for Economics and Peace. 2014. *Global Terrorism Index 2014*.
Jenkins, B.M. 2011. Stray dogs and virtual armies: Radicalization and recruitment to jihadist terrorism in the United States since 9/11. Occasional Paper. RAND Corporation, Santa Monica, CA.
LaFree, G. 2010. The global terrorism database: Accomplishments and challenges. *Perspectives on Terrorism* 4(1): 24–46.
Lister, C. 2014. Profiling the Islamic State. Brookings Doha Center Analysis Paper. Brookings Institution, Washington, DC, December 1, 2014.
McCauley, C., Moskalenko, S., and Van Son, B. 2013. Characteristics of lone-wolf violent offenders: A comparison of assassins and school attackers. *Perspectives on Terrorism* 7(1): 4–24.
Moeckli, D. 2011. 9/11 ten years on: Terrorism as a manageable risk. Strategic trends 2011: Key developments in global affairs. Center for Security Studies, ETH Zürich, Chapter 3, pp. 67–88.
National Commission on Terrorist Attacks upon the United States. 2004. The 9/11 commission report: Final report of the National Commission on Terrorist Attacks upon the United States. Chapter 11: Foresight—and hindsight, p. 341.
Pantucci, R. 2011a. A typology of lone wolves: Preliminary analysis of lone islamist terrorists. Developments in radicalisation and political violence. The International Centre for the Study of Radicalisation and Political Violence (ICSR), London, March 2011.
Pantucci, R. 2011b. What have we learned about lone wolves from Anders Behring Breivik? *Perspectives on Terrorism* 5(5–6): 27–42.
PBS. 2014. Islamic State group earning $1 million per day in black market oil, U.S. says, October 23, 2014.
Pew Research Center. 2011. Osama bin Laden largely discredited among Muslim publics in recent years. Pew Global Attitude Project, Pew Research Center, Washington, DC, May 2, 2011. http://www.pewglobal.org/2011/05/02/osama-bin-laden-largely-discredited-among-muslim-publics-in-recent-years/
Public Safety Canada. 2011. Kanishka project, June 23, 2011.
Public Safety Canada. 2014. Remembering Air India Flight 182, Last updated on April 3, 2014.
Rapoport, D. 2002. The four waves of rebel terror and September 2011. *Anthropoetics* 8(1), Spring/Summer 2002. http://www.anthropoetics.ucla.edu/ap0801/terror.htm
RUSI. 2011. The 9/11 Decade and the challenges ahead. RUSI Online. YouTube, September 1, 2011.

Sageman, M. 2007. Radicalisation of Global Islamist Terrorists. Testimony before the U.S. Senate Committee on Homeland Security and Governmental Affairs, June 27, 2007.
Sarkozy, N. 2012. Interview on Radio France Bleu, March 22, 2012.
Schneier, B. 2010. Where are all the terrorist attacks? Schneier on Security, May 4, 2010.
START. 2011. Background Report: 9/11, Ten Years Later, September 2011.
START. 2013. Despite fewer attacks in Western world, global terrorism is increasing, December 19, 2013.
Stewart, S. and Burton, F. 2008. The Lone Wolf Disconnect. Stratfor, January 30, 2008.
Tankel, S. 2013. Not Another Al Qaeda article. War on the Rocks, August 6, 2013.
TSAS (The Canadian Network for Research on Terrorism, Security and Society). 2014. TSAS Awarded Funds to Create the Canadian Incident Database (CIDB). TSAS Announcements, February 2014.
UK FCO 2013. The changing structure of Al Qaida. Foreign Office Research Analyst Papers, Foreign & Commonwealth Office, November 12, 2013.
UK HMG (Her Majesty's Government). 2010. *A Strong Britain in an Age of Uncertainty: The National Security Strategy*. London: HMG, October 2010.
UK Security Service (MI5). 2014. Lone Actors. Accessed on February 13, 2014.
U.S. State Department. 2013. Country Reports on Terrorism 2012, May 30, 2013.
U.S. White House. National Security Strategy, May 2010.
Vidino, L. 2011. Radicalization, Linkage, and Diversity: Current Trends in Terrorism in Europe. Occasional Paper. RAND National Defence Research Institute, July 6, 2011.

3

A Multifaceted Problem

Terrorists are made by local experience, not grand ideology.

Jason Burke (*Guardian* 2011)

Following 9/11, much of the focus of counterterrorism policies has been on Al Qaeda. The inability of the U.S. government and its intelligence agencies to foresee and disrupt the attacks was widely criticized, leading to a situation where Al Qaeda and its allies had to be destroyed in order to prevent further attacks on American soil.

Al Qaeda's attacks have tended to be more lethal than attacks carried out by other terrorist organizations. Looking at data from the Terrorism Knowledge Database of the Memorial Institute for the Prevention of Terrorism, James Piazza noted that between 1998 and 2005, attacks perpetrated by Al-Qaeda-affiliated groups caused a mean number of 36.1 victims per attack, compared with 9.7 victims for all terrorist attacks during the same period (Piazza 2009). In addition, between 1970 and 2010, Al Qaeda carried out attacks in 21 countries, more than any other terrorist organization, and bore responsibility for less than 0.5% of terrorist attacks between 1998 and 2010, but more than 5% of fatalities (START 2011).*

However, Al Qaeda is not the only existing Islamist terrorist organization, and Islamic extremism is far from being the only form of extremism in the world. In its annual TE-SAT report, Europol divides terrorism into five main categories: religiously inspired terrorism (including Al Qaeda and its affiliates), ethno-nationalist and separatist terrorism, left-wing

* Other terrorist organizations such as Shining Path have caused more fatalities than Al Qaeda (as of 2006) (see Table 3.2).

Table 3.1 Arrests in 2013 per EU Member State and per Affiliation

Member State	Religiously Inspired	Left-Wing	Right-Wing	Separatist	Single Issue	Not Specified	Total 2013
Austria	1	2	0	0	0	0	3
Belgium	19	0	0	1	0	0	20
Bulgaria	12	0	0	2	1	0	15
Croatia	0	0	0	0	0	1	1
Czech Republic	1	0	0	0	0	0	1
France	143	1	3	77	0	1	225
Germany	5	6	0	0	0	0	11
Greece	0	18	0	0	0	5	23
Ireland (Republic of)	0	0	0	41	0	0	41
Italy	5	7	0	0	2	0	14
The Netherlands	3	0	0	3	0	0	6
Romania	7	0	0	1	0	0	8
Spain	20	15	0	55	0	0	90
The United Kingdom	—	—	—	—	—	77	77
Total	216	43	3	180	3	84	535

Source: Europol. TE-SAT 2014: EU Terrorism Situation and Trend Report, May 28, 2014.

and anarchist terrorism, right-wing terrorism, and single-issue terrorism (Europol 2014). This typology illustrates the complex and multifaceted, yet often oversimplified, nature of terrorism (see Table 3.1).

One particular category—right-wing extremism—is worth expanding upon, as it demonstrates that Islamic extremism should not be the only worry of governments and intelligence agencies. In 2012 in Europe, only two right-wing terrorist attacks were reported and 10 individuals were arrested (Europol 2013). No such attack was reported in 2013 (Europol 2014). However, these figures underestimate the importance of the issue. As Europol points out: "for the period of 2013 no attacks classified as right-wing terrorism were reported by European Union (EU) Member States. However, a series of terrorist attacks in the United Kingdom were motivated by right-wing extremist ideology" (Europol 2014, p. 39). Some instances of right-wing violence or threat thereof have surprisingly not been considered *terrorism* as such.

Table 3.2 Ten Most Active Terrorist Groups in Terms of Attack Frequency and Fatalities between 1970 to 2006 (as per GTD Estimates)

	Most Frequent Perpetrators		Most Fatalities	
Rank	**Organization**	**Frequency**	**Organization**	**Fatality Count**
1	Shining Path (SL)	2,817	Shining Path (SL)	6,057
2	Basque Fatherland and Freedom (ETA)	1,378	Liberation Tigers of Tamil Eelam (LTTE)	4,038
3	Farabundo Marti National Liberation Front (FMLN)	1,249	Al Qaeda	3,460
4	Irish Republican Army (IRA)	1,165	Hutus	3,222
5	Revolutionary Armed Forces of Colombia (FARC)	1,066	Mozambique National Resistance Movement (MNR)	2,247
6	National Liberation Army of Colombia (ELN)	784	Farabundo Marti National Liberation Front (FMLN)	1,856
7	Hamas (Islamic Resistance Movement)	608	Revolutionary Armed Forces of Colombia (FARC)	1,791
8	Liberation Tigers of Tamil Eelam (LTTE)	569	Tanzim Qa'idat al-Jihad fi Bilad al-Rafidayn	1,646
9	Manuel Rodriguez Patriotic Front (FPMR)	568	Nicaraguan Democratic Force (FDN)	1,342
10	Kurdistan Workers' Party (PKK)	535	National Union for the Total Independence of Angola	1,151

Source: LaFree, G., *Perspect. Terror.* 4(1), 2010.

For instance, a 20-year-old Briton, supporter of the English Defence League (EDL), the Ku Klux Klan, and the British National Party, who built a nail bomb with 181 pieces of shrapnel and vowed to "drag every last immigrant into the fires of hell" avoided terror charges. During the trial, Prosecutor Roger Smart noted that the accused was not a "terrorist" but an "immature teenager" (*Guardian* 2014a). This highlights the significant issue of *double standards*, whereby Islamic extremists are often more readily considered *terrorists* than other types of extremists. More broadly, extreme right-wing ideas are increasingly resonating in parts of the world today, especially in Europe. While these ideas might not necessarily lead to acts of political violence, they are significant in themselves, as they greatly contradict some of the key values of modern society, including equal rights, fraternity, freedom, and multiculturalism.

RIGHT-WING TERRORISM AND VIOLENT EXTREMISM

The terms *terrorism* and *violent extremism* are used here as synonyms. However, as we explored in Chapter 1, it is important to note that the latter term can serve as a useful substitute to the still hotly debated term *terrorism*. The use of *violent extremism* also highlights an ongoing shift from the war on terror, focusing on military tools, to *countering violent extremism*, an approach centered on noncoercive instruments (Schmid 2012).

Officials in several countries have recently warned of the rising threat posed by right-wing extremists. In the United Kingdom, Commander Shaun Sawyer of the London Metropolitan Police's counterterrorism command (SO15) expressed his concern at a Muslim Safety Forum event in 2009: "I fear that [right-wing extremists] will… carry out an attack that will lead to a loss of life or injury to a community somewhere. They're not choosy about which community" (*Telegraph* 2009). More recently, Home Office Minister James Brokenshire claimed that "the far-right appeals to people who share many of the same vulnerabilities as those exploited by Al Qaeda-inspired extremism. It feeds off the same sense of alienation and questions around identity… It has the same ambition to reshape the world in an impossible way. The threat is real, and our response must be effective" (*BBC News* 2013a). In Germany, then interior minister Hans-Peter Friedrich warned in 2011 that the core of extremely violent neo-Nazis and nationalist anarchists had increased to about 1,000 individuals: "The problem is not the ones we can watch but those who radicalize in hiding" (UPI 2011a). In 2014, EU Commissioner for Home Affairs Cecilia Malmström noted: "the biggest threat right now comes from violent right-wing extremism... for example in Greece and in Bulgaria, but also in Hungary" (*Local* 2014).

In the United States, the Department of Homeland Security (DHS) issued a report on right-wing extremism in 2009. It indicated that the situation resembled the early 1990s, in the sense that "right-wing extremists may be gaining new recruits by playing on their fears about several emergent issues," including the economic climate and the proposed imposition of firearms restrictions and weapons bans. In addition, returning military veterans—"disgruntled, disillusioned, or suffering from the psychological effects of war"—may be subject to recruitment and radicalization (DHS 2009). The report caused uproar among the right-wing political class and media. In a public statement, House Majority Leader John Boehner protested: "To characterize men and women returning home after defending our country as potential terrorists is offensive and unacceptable... The Department of Homeland Security owes our veterans an apology" (*The Washington Post* 2009). Republican Representative Lamar Smith accused the report of "political profiling" and said that the DHS was "using people's political views to assess an individual's susceptibility to terror recruitment" (*Washington Post* 2009). Conservative journalist Michelle Malkin called the report a "hit job on conservatives" and noted it was "one of the most embarrassingly shoddy pieces of propaganda I'd ever read out of DHS" (*CBS News* 2009). Fox News added: "the government considers you a terrorist threat if you oppose abortion, own a gun or are a returning war veteran" (*Fox News* 2009).

Beyond the understandable widespread political and public support for veterans, the backlash against the 2009 DHS report can be analyzed in light of three developments. First, the 9/11 attacks and the subsequent response by the United States have led to an overwhelming political and law enforcement focus on Islamic terrorism. This has often meant that discriminations and suspicions against Muslims were deemed justified in the face of the overall pressing threat. As a result, it is fair to consider that the environment of the 9/11 decade proved less difficult for right-wing extremists than the second half of the 1990s, as authorities then cracked down on groups in the aftermath of the 1995 Oklahoma City bombing. Second, the increased emphasis on Islamic extremism has come at the expense of other threats. Although the FBI continued to investigate right-wing extremist groups, overall intelligence efforts, resources, and political attention devoted to this type of extremism were hampered in the process. In addition, a huge majority of research funding was dedicated to Islamic extremism and prevented enough monitoring and analysis of other risks. Third, the reaction to the DHS report also reflects how the political landscape in the United States has become extremely polarized, increasingly leading to knee-jerk reactions, systematic oppositions to the government irrespective of the policies put forward, and government shutdowns.

Nonetheless, a number of recent cases show that the threat posed by war veterans indeed exists. On November 5, 2009, Nidal Malik Hasan, a U.S. army major who had been in the military since 1995, killed 13 people and injured more than 30 others in a shooting at Fort Hood, a U.S. military base in Texas (*New York Times* 2009). Five years later, an Iraq war veteran named Ivan Lopez killed three people and wounded 16 others at the same post (*Guardian* 2014b). On August 5, 2012, six people were killed in a shooting at the Wisconsin Sikh temple in Oak Creek, near Milwaukee. The perpetrator, Wade Michael Page, served in the U.S. Army from 1992 to 1998 and was associated with a number of white supremacist groups (*New York Times* 2012). On September 16, 2013, Aaron Alexis, a civilian contractor who had formerly served in the navy, shot and killed 12 people and injured 3 others at the Washington Navy Yard in Washington, DC (CNN 2013).

In Europe, there has also been much research into Al Qaeda, Islamic terrorism and extremism, and in comparison a relative lack of attention on the drivers and motives of violence and terrorism motivated by extreme right narratives and ideologies. However, the attacks carried out in Oslo in July 2011 and the ensuing trial of perpetrator Anders Behring Breivik have led to a growing interest in the issue (Briggs and Goodwin 2012). Other recent events in Europe have also highlighted the threat posed by the far right in Europe: In October 2013, Pavlo Lapshyn was convicted of racial murder and for plotting a series of attacks against mosques in the United Kingdom. In May 2013, the trial of Beate Zschäpe, the supposedly last standing member of the National Socialist Underground (NSU) began. The NSU is a far-right terrorist group, which "has been linked to murders of immigrants, the murder of a policewoman and the attempted murder of her colleague, the 2001 and 2004 Cologne bombings and 14 bank robberies" (Ramalingam 2014). In 2011, 17 people were incarcerated in the United Kingdom for terror offenses associated with right-wing extremism, including one individual found with 50 explosive devices and more than 30 guns in a concealed room in his home (*BBC News* 2013a). Four years before, a British national had been convicted for stockpiling chemical explosives due to his fears over *uncontrolled immigration*. In Russia, an estimated 600 attacks were racially motivated and 80 murders linked to neo-Nazi and racist movements in 2007 (Briggs and Goodwin 2012).

Beyond these figures and incidents, a worrying trend is the increasing presence of the far right in European societies, which manifests itself in three different ways. First, right-wing extremists rarely carry out spectacular attacks with high impact, and the "high-frequency lower level acts of violence, which cumulatively are having a serious impact on communities" are therefore less likely to get much media coverage (Briggs and Goodwin 2012).

Second, far-right parties have been on the rise in recent years. Across Europe, parties such as the UK Independence Party, the Austrian Freedom Party, the National Front in France, the Danish People's Party, the Dutch Freedom Party, the Finns Party, Alternative for Germany, and the Sweden Democrats have seen their support increase in the past few years (Quartz 2014) (see Figure 3.1).

Golden Dawn, a neo-Nazi party in Greece, entered the domestic political scene by winning 21 seats in parliament in May 2012 (reduced to 18 the following month) (*The Guardian* 2012). Through a racist and xenophobic narrative drawing on concerns over mainstream politicians, immigration, unemployment, austerity measures, and the economy, it received 7% of the votes in the 2012 national election, thereby winning 21 seats in a 300-seat parliament. Far-right parties across Europe do not represent a homogeneous movement. Ramalingam divides them into five categories: extremist subcultures (e.g., Sweden Democrats, British National Party), nationalist foundations (National Front in France, Austrian Freedom Party), protest movements or party transformations (e.g., Danish People's Party, Finns Party), postcommunist authoritarian and militant politics (Central and Eastern European variety, e.g., National

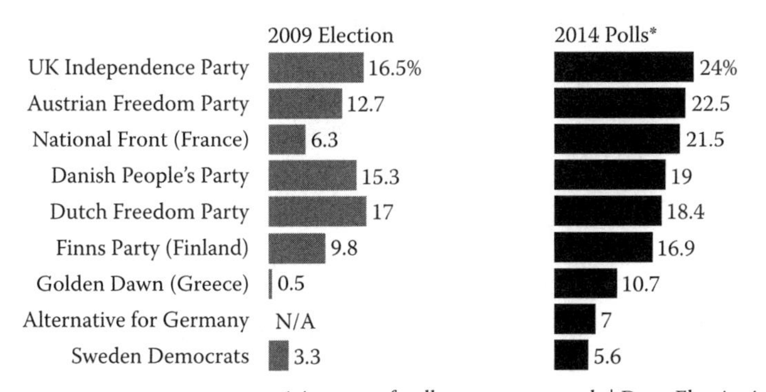

Figure 3.1 Support for Euroskeptic right-wing parties in the European parliament. (Courtesy of Quartz, http://qz.com/.)

Union Attack in Bulgaria, Movement for a Better Hungary), and new parties (Party for Freedom and List Pim Fortuyn in the Netherlands) (Ramalingam 2012). Grassroots movements outside the political arena, such as the EDL, have also seen their visibility and membership increase in recent years.

The support far-right parties and groups currently enjoy is volatile and has fluctuated in the past two decades. Since the onset of the economic crisis, their popularity has risen, but it would be naïve to narrow down the motivations of members to the economy. Studies have shown that despite national differences, common characteristics between members of extreme right groups include the following: these are often young males, with average or low levels of education and qualifications, a long history of criminality and/or alcohol and drug abuse, a deep mistrust of mainstream politicians, and who are xenophobic, profoundly hostile toward immigration, and pessimistic about economic prospects (Briggs and Goodwin 2012; Goodwin 2013). In addition, their grievances do not only pertain to recent developments. As Matthew Goodwin notes, "The Eurozone crisis may have enlarged their political space, but these challengers were already well on their way" (Goodwin 2012).

Third, extreme right ideas have entered the mainstream political discourse. Center-right parties across Europe such as the *Union pour un Mouvement Populaire* (UMP) in France and the Conservatives in the United Kingdom have co-opted far-right issues such as immigration, the European Union, gay rights, and Islam and national identity in order to appeal to this part of the electorate. These issues have become of major concern for European populations. In France, for instance, 67% of the population consider that there are too many immigrants (49% in 2009), 50% are in favor of reinstating the death penalty (32% in 2009), and 34% trust Marine Le Pen, the head of the National Front (second of a list topped by former President Nicolas Sarkozy with 36%) (Opinion Way 2014).

Despite the earlier considerations, it is important not to overestimate the importance of the extreme right. Center-right or center-left parties are still in power in a very large majority of countries across Europe and North America. In the United States, the two-party system largely prevents the emergence of an extreme party, although it may also lead to a more polarized political environment. Incidents of violence, whether they can be defined as terrorism or more broadly violent extremism, remain rare. Nonetheless, the increased appeal of extreme right-wing ideas, illustrated by the rise of radical parties and groups, and growing discontent with mainstream political parties among the public certainly add to the complexity of the extremism landscape.

NARCO-TERRORISM

Terrorism has also been linked to other threats and challenges including drug trafficking and cyber security, demonstrating how intricate the problem is. In the aftermath of 9/11, the links between international terrorism and the international drug trade became a source of much activity in U.S. law enforcement and government. The term *narco-terrorism*, often used then, was in fact not new: it emerged in the 1980s to describe the activities of organizations involved in both drug trafficking for financial and territorial gain and the use of violence against civilians for political purposes in South America, by groups such as the Revolutionary Armed Forces of Colombia (FARC) and the National Liberation Army (ELN) in Colombia, and the Shining Path (*Senderoso Luminoso*) in Peru (see Figure 3.2).

Following September 2001, the American government was keen to use every possible tool against Al Qaeda and international terrorism as a whole, especially in Afghanistan. As early as October 3, 2001—only 3 weeks after the attacks—the U.S. House of Representatives Subcommittee on Criminal Justice, Drug Policy and Human Resources of the Committee on Government Reform held a hearing entitled "Drug Trade and the Terror Network." Committee Chairman Mark Souder then declared that "the Afghan drug trade has given direct financial support for the Taliban regime to harbor international terrorists and at least indirectly assisted

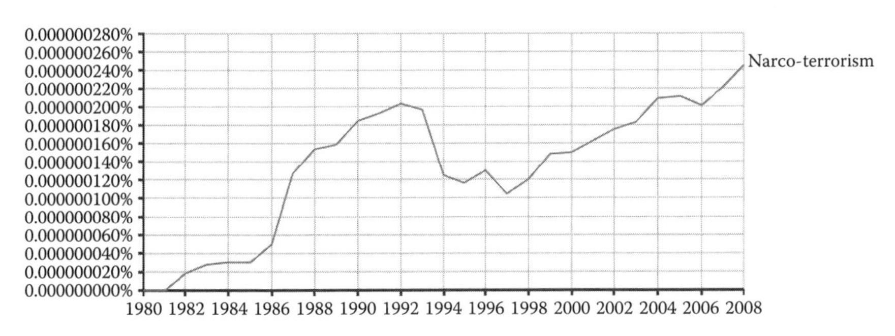

Figure 3.2 Percentage of books published with the word *narco-terrorism* in their title between 1980 and 2008. (From Google Books Ngram Viewer, accessed March 6, 2014.)

Osama bin Laden and the al-Qaeda terrorist network to grievously attack the United States of America" (Shanty 2011, p. 47). Asa Hutchinson of the Drug Enforcement Administration (DEA) added that "the very sanctuary enjoyed by Bin Laden is based on the existence and control of the Taliban, whose modest economy is dependent upon opium. This connection defines the deadly symbiotic relationship between the illegal drug trade and international terrorism" (Shanty 2011, p. 47). In the United Kingdom, then Prime Minister Tony Blair was quick to establish the connection as well, referring to a British intelligence report: "The Taliban regime... has provided Bin Laden with a safe haven within which to operate, and allowed him to establish terrorist training camps. They jointly exploit the Afghan drugs trade. In return for active Al Qaida support the Taliban allow Al Qaida to operate freely, including planning, training and preparing for terrorist activity. In addition they provide security for the stockpiles of drugs" (*Guardian* 2001). Two years later, U.S. Democratic Representative Joe Biden assuredly noted: "Afghanistan: the connection between the warlords, drugs and terror is as clear as a bell" (U.S. Senate 2003, p. 4), while Republican representative Mark Kirk went as far as saying that "bin Laden is one of the world's largest heroin dealers" (Shanty 2011, p. 57).

A decade later, military officials, policy makers, and analysts from many countries across the world continue to affirm the existence of systematic links between terrorism and drug trafficking, beyond Afghanistan's borders. In 2009, Admiral James Stavridis, then commander of the U.S. European Command and NATO's Supreme Allied Commander Europe, pointed to the increasingly dangerous nexus between illicit drug trafficking, "including routes, profits, and corruptive influence" and "Islamic radical terrorism" (*Washington Times* 2009). Only weeks prior to France's military intervention *Opération Serval* in Mali, French Foreign Minister Laurent Fabius warned of the "rise of narcoterrorism" in Mali, where "several hundreds of people very heavily armed are linked to trafficking of hostages and drugs." He added that without any action, "the whole of Africa, Eastern and Western, and Europe would be threatened... If we want to avoid that in the next few months our countries are under the influence of narco-terrorism, we must act" (Le Figaro 2012). In addition, analysts often refer to violence perpetrated by drug trafficking organizations in Mexico as narco-terrorism, highlighting the killing and intimidation of civilians for political and territorial purposes.

The global drug trade is a significant challenge for international security. The United Nations Office on Drugs and Crime (UNODC) estimates the value of the global retail market for illicit drugs at $320 billion

(UNODC 2005, p. 2). The value of the illicit drugs market, like other criminal markets, is extremely difficult to estimate, for obvious reasons, but its impact in terms of homicides, violence, corruption, and pressure on state institutions is evident.

However, the links between the drug trade and terrorism are in fact far from systematic. Cooperation does take place between some groups at the local level, but more often than not, activities involve broader organized crime activities, and not just drug trafficking. Field research and quantitative data reveal that there is no strong sign of automatic integration between terrorism and drug trafficking and that terrorist organizations and drug trafficking organizations are in no way merging—as we will explore further. Part of the reason why these threats seem to be converging and increasingly dangerous, as pointed out by Vanda Felbab-Brown, may be that there has been more attention devoted to them in recent years than in the 1990s (Felbab-Brown 2013a). Moreover, she notes that "these marriages of convenience [between terrorist and criminal groups], to the extent that they emerge at all, might very easily unravel, and the divorces might be far more common than the marriages staying together" (Felbab-Brown 2013b).

Afghanistan, Mali, and Mexico have been under media spotlight and government scrutiny in recent years, partly because of the alleged links between terrorism and drug trafficking. A closer look at these three case studies proves illuminating.

Afghanistan

In Afghanistan, U.S. officials were quick to claim a direct link between Bin Laden and the drug trade after 9/11. However, studies have found that the reality on the ground was much more nuanced. The opium trade out of Afghanistan is a substantial source of revenue for the country. Afghanistan produces approximately 90% of the world's opium (UNODC 2013a). Production decreased sharply in 2000/2001, largely as a result of the Taliban ban on harvest completed in August 2001, but increased again drastically from 2002 onward, with average production soon surpassing the levels of the 1990s (Gomis 2014, p. 6). Taliban commanders have been reported to collect agricultural taxes (*ushr*) from poppy farmers and roadside taxes (*zakat*) from traffickers. Taliban commanders are also reportedly involved in the drug trade through facilitating migrant flows toward poppy farms, providing security to traffickers, protecting labs and shipments of precursor chemicals, and preventing poppy eradication efforts, while local Taliban commanders may also engage more directly in drug trafficking activities for additional revenues (Rollins and Wyler 2013, p. 11). However, research has found that Bin Laden in fact never was "one of the world's largest heroin producers" nor had he played any major role in heroin production at all. Jason Burke notes that "there has never been any evidence that Bin Laden has ever been involved in narcotics production, and everyone involved in the trade in Pakistan, Afghanistan and elsewhere, from farmers through to the UN experts monitoring drugs production, denies the allegation" (Burke 2003, p. 19; Shanty 2011, p. 45). The 9/11 Commission itself found no evidence linking Bin Laden and the drug trade: "While the drug trade was a source of income for the Taliban, it did not serve the same purpose for al Qaeda, and there is no reliable evidence that Bin Ladin was involved in or made his money through drug trafficking" (9/11 Commission 2004, p. 171).

The Taliban have been involved with the drug trade as a marginal player, and Al Qaeda has been an even more remote player. Looking at UN data released in 2009, University College Dublin researcher Julien Mercille found that the Taliban collected only 3% of the proceeds of the drug trade, while 75% of revenues in fact benefited state officials, the police, various power brokers, and traffickers (Mercille 2012; Comolli and Hofmann 2013). As Mercille points out, the UNODC estimated in 2009 that between \$200 and 400 million of drug-related funds ended up in the hands of *insurgents and warlords* and that the Taliban had an annual opium-related revenue of \$90–160 million—an important sum, yet one that represents only roughly 3% of an estimated \$4bn harvest and only 10–15% of the Taliban's revenue (UNODC 2009; Mercille 2012). In a report for the Center on International Cooperation, Caulkins, Kulick, and Kleiman note that the Taliban take somewhere between "2 [and] 12% of a \$4bn industry," while "farmers, traffickers, smugglers, and corrupt officials collectively earn much more" (Caulkins et al. 2010, 2011). With this in mind, assertions made in the immediate aftermath of 9/11, directly linking Al Qaeda and the Taliban and the drug trade, can be qualified as overstatements not supported by quantitative and qualitative analysis.

Mali

In Mali, a similar dynamic has emerged in recent years. Mali has become a regional and international security priority because of reported links between the drug trade and terrorist groups in the country and the broader regions of West Africa and the Sahel. This led to declarations such as those made by French Foreign Minister Laurent Fabius—qualifying security challenges in the area of *narco-terrorism* (Le Figaro 2012). The country's security problems have caused significant concerns, particularly in France, due to historic and strategic ties between the two countries*. On March 21–22, 2012, military officers carried out a putsch against then President Amadou Toumani Touré. Their main grievance was the lack of resources devoted to the military campaign in the north of the country, against the Tuareg rebels of the National Movement for the Liberation of Azawad. Other extremist groups, including Al Qaeda in the Islamic Maghreb (AQIM), had been causing much disruption as well (Melly 2012). This instability led France to launch an intervention in the country in January 2013, with the support of a number of partner countries.

Mali and West Africa have become parts of an increasingly important drug trafficking route in recent years, especially for cocaine originating in Colombia and the broader Andean region, largely as a result of tightened law enforcement measures in Europe in the early 2000s (UNODC 2007, 6; European Monitoring Centre on Drugs and Drug Addiction—EMCDDA—and Europol 2013, p. 45). The UNODC estimates the annual value of cocaine trafficked through West Africa at $1.25 billion (UNODC 2013b, p. 17). Countries like Guinea-Bissau have been particularly affected, and Mali has become a major transit point for cocaine going to Europe and the Gulf, seen by traffickers as a crucial emerging market (FCO 2013). In addition, smuggling of Moroccan cannabis resin through Mali has also reportedly increased in the past decade (Lacher 2012).

However, officials and analysts often oversimplify the relationship between the drug trade and terrorist groups in the region and the importance of drug-related revenues for these organizations. The situation on the ground is much more complex, with various types of relationships between multiple stakeholders, but it is clear that there is no automatic merging between terrorists and drug traffickers. A 2013 FCO paper notes that "the term 'narco-terrorism' does not accurately describe a reality: terrorists are usually not the same as drugs traffickers. But they are useful to each other for political and social power, access to resources and for personal connections" (FCO 2013).

Based on extensive field research, Wolfram Lacher has debunked the myths of the so-called drug-terror nexus in the region, noting that (1) the evidence presented to suggest the existence of a nexus is often flaky or impossible to verify; (2) AQIM and the Movement for Oneness and Jihad in West Africa (commonly referred to through its French acronym MUJAO, which

* Mali was a French colony between 1892 and 1960.

stands for *Mouvement pour l'unicité et le jihad en Afrique de l'Ouest*) are far from being unitary organizations with clear objectives and consistent tactics, and their members are "driven by multiple, and at times, conflicting motivations"; (3) terrorist groups are part of a long list of actors playing an equally or more important role in drug smuggling; (4) the focus on the connections between drug trafficking and terrorism in the region often serves as a distraction from the much more important role played by state actors in organized crime; and (5) kidnapping, and more precisely kidnap for ransom (often referred to as Kfr), is a much more lucrative business for AQIM and MUJAO (Lacher 2012, 2013)—AQIM is reported to have gained at least $40 million in ransoms between 2003 and 2013 according to the FCO, with other estimates putting the figure as high as $90 million (FCO 2013; Aronson 2014).

Other types of organized crime activities also provide revenues for Mali and its broader region, historically well known as a smuggling route for various kinds of licit and illicit items, including weapons and cigarettes. Mokhtar Belmokhtar, an Algerian terrorist operating in the region and leader of MUJAO, earned the nickname of "Mr. Marlboro"* for his predominant role in cigarette smuggling in the region. He was charged for playing a central part in the attack on a gas processing facility in a remote part of the east of Algeria, near the border with Libya, in January 2013, during which over 800 people were taken hostage and at least 40 hostages were killed (*Guardian* 2013).

What is less often reported is the role of official actors in organized crime in the region, including state actors, as Lacher points out. There are numerous relevant examples of low-, mid-, and high-level officials' involvement in drug trafficking throughout West Africa in recent years. In Guinea-Bissau, top military and government officials have been actively participating in drug trafficking, including President João Bernardo "Nino" Vieira, Armed Forces Chief Batista Tagme Na Wai, Navy Chief Rear Admiral José Americo Bubo Na Tchuto, and Air Force Chief of Staff Ibraima Papa Camara (Sun Wyler and Cook 2010; U.S. Department of Treasury 2010; Gberie 2013; *New York Times* 2013). In Sierra Leone, Mohamed Bashil Besay (also known as Ahmed Sesay), cousin of former Minister of Transport and Aviation Kemoh Sesay, was found to be directly involved in a cocaine trafficking scheme (Gberie 2013, pp. 14–16).

* Not to be confused with "The Marlboro Man," Santander Lopesierra. The former Liberal Party Senator of Colombia was one of Philip Morris's main smugglers in the country and played a key role in a large money-laundering scheme of so-called *narco dollars* (*BBC News* 2003; Campaign for Tobacco-Free Kids 2003).

In Mali, the most infamous drug trafficking case revolves around the Boeing 727 dubbed "Air Cocaine," which crashed in the northern part of the country in November 2009. This incident highlights three key elements: first, the transnational nature of the business. The cocaine is said to have been produced in Colombia, shipped by plane to Mali, for it to be then smuggled overland by individuals from Spain, France, Morocco, Mali, and Senegal to Morocco and likely later dispatched throughout Europe (Lebovich 2013; West Africa Commission on Drugs—WACD 2014, p. 24). Second, the government has often encouraged drug trafficking. According to numerous sources, Malian government officials and soldiers have been directly involved and actively participated in smuggling operations, facilitating the flow of drugs through the country, at best ignoring evident signs of ostentatious wealth related to smuggling (a lavish neighborhood of Gao with expensive villas has been dubbed "Cocainebougou" or "Cocaine Town"—Dreazen 2013), and ensuring that the prosecution against top officials involved in drug trafficking would eventually falter (WACD 2014, p. 24). Third, unsanctioned corruption has fuelled tensions and resentment in Mali. In February 2013, a crowd of protesters nearly lynched two officials suspected of an active role in the "Air Cocaine" case. Mohamed Ould Awainatt, an alleged billionaire drug trafficker, is reportedly a close friend to former President Amadou Toumani Touré and was released from prison in February 2012 in exchange for his militia's support to the Malian army's operations against Tuareg rebels in the north of the country (Toumast Press 2012). The second individual, Baba Ould Cheikh, is the mayor of Tarkint, a village in the Gao region (Maliweb.net 2013).

Private companies have also been taken part and facilitated criminal activities. British American Tobacco (BAT), among other transnational tobacco companies, has been actively involved in the contraband and smuggling of cigarettes across Africa. Through an extensive study of internal documents and industry publications, LeGresley et al. demonstrated in 2008 that BAT had "relied on illegal channels to supply markets across Africa since the 1980s," noting that "smuggling has been an important component of BAT's market entry strategy in order to gain leverage in negotiating with governments for tax concessions, compete with other transnational tobacco companies, circumvent local import restrictions and unstable political and economic conditions and gain a market presence" (LeGresley et al. 2008).

In sum, there is some overlap between organized crime groups and extremists in the region. Field research suggests that MUJAO is directly involved in smuggling, while AQIM has provided protection to drug convoys in exchange for a fee and facilitated and financially benefited from smuggling in general (FCO 2013; Lacher 2013). However, actors in the region are largely connected through loose, local, and evolving relationships, rather than robust regional networks. Moreover, drug trafficking constitutes only a source of revenue among many others for smugglers and extremists of the region. What is often ignored or underestimated is the central role that governments and private companies play in the region. The most important common feature between drug trafficking and terrorism in Mali, West Africa, and the Sahel is in fact not the nexus between the two types of threat, but their close collusion with governments. Weak governance, and the inability of the state to control their territories due to rampant corruption and low resources, should be considered the most urgent priority for the region.

Mexico

According to UNODC data, over 120,000 people died in homicides between 2007 and 2012 in Mexico. Some reports noted that over 70,000 of these homicides were "drug-related" (*BBC News* 2014). These figures should be taken with precaution: Mexico's National Institute for Statistics and Geography (Instituto Nacional de Estadística y Geografía [INEGI]) itself estimated that in 2013 over 90% of crimes were in fact not reported and almost 94% were not investigated (Cawley 2014). In other words, with so little police investigation, how could one confidently put forward a reliable estimate of the proportion of these killings that were drug-related? The surge in violence follows a crackdown on so-called drug cartels under President Calderón (2006–2012), increased competition between the drug trafficking organizations, and an increase in the flow of weapons coming from the United States (*BBC News* 2013c). This latter point, often ignored, is worth expanding upon—a study by Arindrajit Dube of the University of Massachusetts and NYU researchers Oeindrila Dube and Omar Garcia-Ponce found that the 2004 expiration of the U.S. Federal Assault Weapons Ban "exerted a spillover on gun supply" in Mexican municipalities across the border and a subsequent increase in homicides: "homicides rose by 60% more in *municipios* at the non-California entry ports" (California retained a preexisting state ban) (Dube et al. 2013, p. 416). Up to 80% of the guns in circulation in Central America come from the United States, and roughly 253,000 guns are smuggled from the United States to Mexico annually (McDougal et al. 2013, Mélendez (2011)).

Over the last decade, the number of firearms being smuggled into Mexico has tripled (Institute for Economics and Peace 2013).

In this context, Mexico's homicide rate almost tripled between 2007 and 2012—from 8.1 per 100,000 to 23.7 per 100,000 (UNODC 2013c). It is worth noting that degrees of violence vary substantially from one region to another: the state of Chihuahua has a rate of 194 homicides per 100,000 inhabitants, while Yucatán, Mexico's safest state, has a rate of 1.74 (United Nations Development Programme [UNDP] 2013, p. 4). Eighty percent of drug trafficking–related homicides between December 2006 and July 2010 occurred in 162 of the country's 2,456 municipalities (less than 7%) (Beittel 2013, p. 30). In addition, despite the recent spike in violence, Mexico remains more peaceful than some of its closest neighbors. Honduras, El Salvador, and Guatemala have much higher homicide rates, with respectively 91.6, 70.2, and 38.5 homicides per 100,000 inhabitants in 2011 (UNODC 2013c). These countries rarely receive the same kind of media attention as Mexico, partly because rates have not increased as dramatically as in Mexico in recent years, but also because these countries rarely produce any data on deaths related to drug trafficking. Mexico is of course a direct neighbor and a close partner in trade, energy, and security matters to the United States, which has made the violence there all the more important in the eyes of United States and international media.

The violence related to drugs and organized crime in Mexico has also had a negative impact on the economy. The country has performed rather well in recent years, with GDP growth of 3.9% in 2012 (UK Trade and Investment 2013). Nonetheless, the Institute for Economics and Peace estimates that the direct and indirect costs of drug-related violence amounted, respectively, to 3.8% and 15.8% of the country's GDP in 2012 (Institute for Economics and Peace 2013). Mexican analysts have criticized these figures, pointing instead to national studies that seem more reliable. The 2013 National Survey on Victimization and Perception of Public Safety (ENVIPE), for instance, estimated the overall cost of crime in Mexico at $16.3 billion or 1.34% of GDP in 2012 (INEGI 2014). Beyond economic estimates, the Mexican population's perception of insecurity is high—72.3% in 2013—and increasing—up from 66.6% in 2012 (INEGI 2014).

Violence related to drugs and organized crime in Mexico is a significant issue, which has had a negative impact in human, financial, social, and institutional terms. In business language, a cartel can be defined as "a group of similar, independent companies which join together to fix prices, to limit production or to share markets or customers between them" (European Commission 2014). It is misrepresentative to imply that criminal organizations in Mexico form an association to control the illicit drug market, given the violent competition between those groups. They are perhaps more accurately defined as *organized crime groups*, given the scope of their activities including extortion, human trafficking, racketeering, armed robbery, money laundering, *milking*—that is, oil theft, an activity recently on the rise in the states of Tamaulipas, Nuevo Leon, and Coahuila in particular (Reuters 2011)—and kidnapping: Mexico is now the country with the highest kidnapping rate in the world (Brookings 2014), as kidnappings reportedly increased by 188% between 2007 and 2013 (Beittel 2013). It is fair to assume that official kidnapping figures are likely to vastly underestimate the reality, as individuals and families affected rarely report occurrences for fear of reprisal.

Some analysts and officials suggest that these organizations should be considered terrorists, given their use of violence against civilians for territorial means. In April 2011, Michael McCaul, U.S. Republican Representative of Texas and Chairman of the Homeland Security Oversight and Investigations Subcommittee, introduced a bill to add Mexico's six main "cartels" (then listed as Arellano Felix, Los Zetas, Beltran Leyva, Familia Michoacana, Sinaloa Cartel, and the Gulf Cartel) to the U.S. State Department foreign terrorist organizations list, arguing that "the [Mexican] cartels use violence to gain political and economic influence." The unsuccessful bill would have increased U.S. law enforcement powers in Mexico, including easier access to the criminal organizations' finances and tougher sanctions against organizations and individuals providing them support. Arturo Sarukhan, then Mexican ambassador to the United States, provided a powerful counterargument: "if you label these organizations as terrorist, you will have to start calling drug consumers in the U.S. 'financiers of terrorist organizations' and gun dealers 'providers of material support to terrorists'" (CNN 2011). The Mexican government has been adamant that organized crime-related violence in Mexico should not be considered terrorism, perhaps largely because of concerns over the wide-ranging consequences any legal move of the sort might have, including greater law enforcement, intelligence, and financial involvement from the United States.

Facts on the ground also seem to validate the Mexican government's official stance not to consider "drug cartels" as terrorist organizations. They indeed lack political or ideological motivations that would characterize them as terrorist groups according to a large majority of definitions of the term, as seen in Chapter 1 of this book. Their motivations are primarily economic, and violence often remains localized between "cartels" fighting for territorial control, and between "cartels" and law enforcement forces. Even the START Consortium's GTD, which defines terrorism as "the threatened or actual use of illegal force and violence by a non-state actor to attain a political, *economic* [emphasis mine], religious, or social goal through fear, coercion, or intimidation," only lists 16 terrorist attacks in Mexico in 2012, leading to 17 fatalities (GTD 2014).

That is not to say that innocent civilians are not affected by the violence in Mexico: Businesses and other parts of local populations have been extorted, kidnapped, or intimidated, and gunfights between organized crime groups have caused civilian casualties. Civilians have also been more directly targeted. In 2011, members of Los Zetas burned down a casino in Monterrey, in the northeast state of Nuevo León, and 52 people, including a majority of women, died as a result. It was later revealed that the attack was meant to scare the owners of the casino, who had refused to pay the cartel a weekly extortion fee, and the situation grew out of control (*Los Angeles Times* 2011). Los Zetas have been particularly brutal in their tactics, often publicly displaying bodies or body parts. Other attacks carried out by the cartel have been particularly deadly, as part of a violent struggle against rival Gulf cartel: these include the San Fernando massacre of August 2010, where the bodies of 72 undocumented immigrants were found; in December 2010, there was a large explosion and subsequent fire at a pipeline in Puebla, which led to the deaths of 29 people including 13 children, and was thought to be the result of Los Zetas members stealing oil; the San Fernando massacre of April 2011, when members of Los Zetas intercepted several buses and kidnapped many on board and executed an estimated 193 people; the Apodaca prison riot, where 44 inmates died and 30 cartel members escaped; in May 2012, 49 decapitated bodies were dumped on a highway outside the city of Monterrey (*Global Post* 2013). In 2013, "cartels" in Mexico also carried out a record high of 22 violent political acts, including five assassinations of candidates running for local government posts (National Institute for Statistics and Geography 2014).

Vanda Felbab-Brown has offered a compelling argument about the motivations of Mexican cartels: "What is a more political act than controlling bullets and money on the street? If you are the Sinaloa Cartel and you determine how much violence takes place within a territory, and you—directly or indirectly, through illegal economies and their spillovers into the legal economy—provide income for 20% of the population, are you not a political actor" (Felbab-Brown 2013b). In early August 2010, then President Calderón noted that drug trafficking organizations in Mexico represent "a challenge to the state, an attempt to replace the state." President Calderón thereby implied political motives, even though he refused to call cartels terrorist organizations (Beittel 2013, p. 5).

Nonetheless, Alex Schmid's revised academic definition notes that terrorism involved "direct violent action without legal or moral restraints, *targeting mainly civilians and non-combatants* [emphasis mine]" (Schmid 2011, pp. 86–87). Civilians and noncombatants in Mexico have very largely been collateral victims of fights between cartels, not primary targets.

More importantly, officials and analysts too often use the terrorism label as a way to demonstrate the severity of the threat. However, violence related to organized crime in Mexico is significant in its own right and should be considered an urgent priority, even though it is not *terrorism* as such and despite the absence of links between drugs and organized crime and terrorism.

In sum, the links between the drug trade and terrorism are far from systematic and are often complex, dependent on the local context, and much more loose and volatile than often stated in public speeches and reports. This does not mean that organized crime groups and terrorist groups do not cooperate. Tamara Makarenko has argued that since the end of the Cold War and the decline in state sponsorship of terrorism, terrorists and organized criminals have increased their collaboration in Europe, in four main ways, namely, (1) alliance (e.g., Balkans, Corsica, AQIM, Al Qaeda, ETA), (2) appropriation of tactics (e.g., Provisional Irish Republican Army, Ulster Defence Association, Red Army Faction, Kurdistan Workers' Party [PKK]), (3) hybrids (no current examples, but the Russian and Albanian mafias of the 1990s are historical examples), and (4) transformation (no example) (Makarenko 2012). The examples, or lack thereof, provided within each category, demonstrate that in Europe, alliances and appropriation of tactics are by far the most common mechanisms of cooperation between organized crime and terrorist groups, who in fact very rarely transform from one type of entity to another (i.e., organized crime group to terrorist organization or vice versa), or even simultaneously display both economic and political motivations. The situation is of course different, as we previously examined, depending on the country or region affected.

If the drug-terror nexus is not as systematic as was once thought, why has there been this urge to amalgamate terrorism and drug trafficking after 9/11? Three related motivations can be identified. First, the terrorist attacks on U.S. soil on September 11, 2011, led to a much more forceful and wide-ranging counterterrorism strategy by the United States and its international partners. This included more efforts devoted to tracking down terrorist finances, also known as the *follow the money* approach (Shanty 2011, p. 44). While terrorist organizations do indeed receive funding from a range of sources, including donations, extortions, and kidnappings, establishing a connection between the drug trade and international terrorism was perhaps seen as an easier measure to implement politically. Being *tough on drugs* has been widely considered as a powerful political and electoral move since the beginning of the *War on Drugs*—an expression first used by President Richard Nixon during a speech on June 17, 1971, in which he declared that drug abuse had become America's *number one enemy* (Nixon 1971). More importantly, linking the international drug trade to terrorism has meant that a more simple counternarcotics strategy—focused on heavy-handed, reactive, and coercive measures—could be implemented and indeed appeals to a larger part of the population.

Second, merging counter-narcotics and counterterrorism policies led to an increase in law enforcement capacity to deal with the two ends of the spectrum. As Csete and Sanchez point out, the U.S. Criminal Code (Title 1 U.S.C. § 960a) "authorizes U.S. agencies to pursue and prosecute drug offences outside the U.S. if a link to terrorism is established" and gives the DEA "extraterritorial jurisdiction over drug offenses with some link to the U.S., even if there is no actual entry into U.S. borders by the drugs at issue" (Title 1 U.S.C. § 959) (Csete and Sanchez 2013, pp. 10–11).

Finally, increased political attention to the links between drug trafficking and terrorism after 9/11 also meant more funding was available for research on this issue. This led to further focus on the problem, at the expense of other perhaps more relevant studies including on corruption, development, and weak governance. In addition, terrorism often helps raise awareness and attract attention, which many media outlets have arguably used to capture a broader audience.

CYBER TERRORISM

Progress in and broader access to modern technology seem to have increased the complexity of the threat posed by terrorism. Media reports regularly warn readers of the rising danger of cyber terrorism. Less than 2 weeks after 9/11, the French newspaper *Le Monde* already suggested that cyber terrorists were always *a step ahead* of law enforcement

(*Le Monde* 2001). Many presaged devastating attacks. The *Washington Post* front page once stated: "Cyber-Attacks by Al Qaeda Feared, Terrorists at Threshold of Using Internet as Tool of Bloodshed, Experts Say" (2002). Even the *New Yorker*, not otherwise known for hyping up threats, noted in May 2001: "sophisticated terrorists (or hostile governments) now have the ability to crash satellite systems, to wage economic warfare by unplugging the Federal Reserve system from Wall Street, even to disrupt the movements of ships at sea" (in Conway 2005, p. 17). Paul Vixie of *Newsweek* went so far as to suggest: "[Cyber terrorism] isn't so much a threat to national security as a threat to civilization" (Conway 2005, p. 1).

Years later, similar media coverage of cyber terrorism goes on: In a *UPI* article titled "Cyberterrorism: A Threat that won't go away," the opening line announced that "[t]he greatest security threat looming for industrialized societies may not be a terrorist armed with a bomb but an enemy with a keyboard and Internet connection" (UPI 2011b). PolicyMic, noting that "Cyber attacks will be the greatest national security threat in the 21st Century," added: "Cyber-terrorism is all-pervasive, like an ethereal Rubik's cube; you can't touch it and it keeps resetting itself… When the intent is there, a cyber hacker may take your information at will to disrupt and generate fear comparable to traditional terrorism" (PolicyMic 2011). In the United Kingdom, the *Daily Mail* attempted to examine "Why Britain is desperately vulnerable to cyber terror" (*Daily Mail* 2010), while the *Guardian* asked "Is Armageddon on the cyber horizon?" (*Guardian* 2013).

Beyond these consistent hyperbolic headlines, the mainstream media is obviously not the only actor discussing the topic of cyber terrorism. As Peter W. Singer noted, roughly 31,300 magazine and journal articles have been written to discuss the phenomenon of cyber terrorism (as of November 2012—Singer 2012). Academics and policy analysts play an important role in describing and analyzing threats, and therefore in shaping the media and policy debate around them. "Our nation is at grave risk of a cyberattack that could devastate the national psyche and economy more broadly than did the 9/11 attacks," warned Carnegie Mellon University computer scientist Roy Maxion in a letter to President George W. Bush, which was cosigned by 50 computer scientists (Weimann 2005, p. 130). Terrorism expert Walter Laqueur wrote as early as 1999: "The electronic age has now made cyberterrorism possible. A onetime mainstay of science fiction, the doomsday machine, looms as a real danger. The conjunction of technology and terrorism make for an uncertain and frightening future" (Laqueur 1999, p. 254; Conway 2005, p. 12).

Last but not least, government officials have described the threat posed cyber terrorism in striking terms as well. This includes U.S. Democratic Senator Charles Schumer, who described "the absolute havoc and devastation that would result if cyberterrorists suddenly shut down our air traffic control system, with thousands of planes in mid-flight" (Weimann 2005, p. 144). Richard Clarke, then former Special White House Adviser for Cyberspace Security, noted a year after 9/11 that cyber terrorism is "much easier to do than building a weapon of mass destruction. Cyberattacks are a weapon of mass disruption, and they're a lot cheaper and easier" (Conway 2005, p. 24). Tom Ridge, while in position as director of the DHS, affirmed: "Terrorists can sit at one computer connected to one network and can create worldwide havoc" (Weimann 2004, p. 3). However, former U.S. Defense Secretary Leon Panetta likely drew most attention when he recently warned of a "cyber Pearl Harbor," which "could be as destructive as the terrorist attack on 9/11" and "could virtually paralyze the nation" (Panetta 2012). "Cyber Pearl Harbor" is only one in a long list of colorful metaphors that have been used by officials and commentators to describe how substantial the threat posed by cyber terrorism is and the overwhelming impact an attack could have. The list also includes "cyber Katrina," "cyber Armageddon," and even "cyber Waterloo" (similar allegories include the prefix "digital" or "electronic" as well) (see Figure 3.3).

The term *cyber terrorism* has been used extensively and increasingly so in recent years—as Figure 3.3 demonstrates. However, the term encompasses a wide range of different realities depending on who is using the

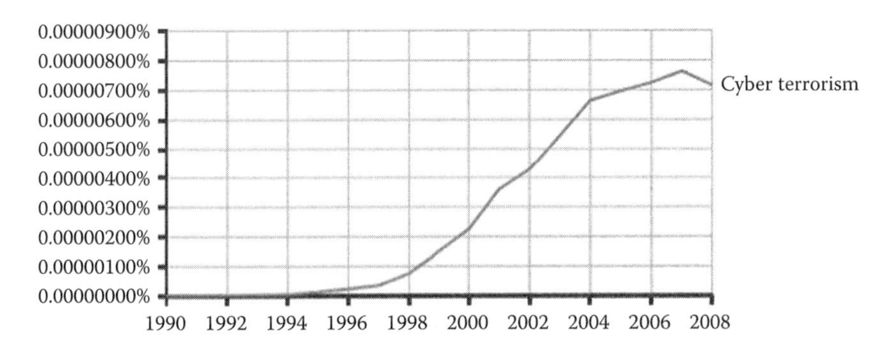

Figure 3.3 Percentage of books published with the word *cyber terrorism* in their title between 1990 and 2008. (From Google Books Ngram Viewer, accessed March 1, 2014.)

term. Conway has noted that "some unlikely acts of computer abuse" have been qualified as cyber terrorism in the press, including "sending pornographic e-mails to minors, posting offensive content on the Internet, defacing Web pages, using a computer to cause $400 worth of damage, stealing credit card information, posting credit card numbers on the Internet, and clandestinely redirecting Internet traffic from one site to another" (Conway 2005, p. 32). This disparate list is likely to lead to an understandable question: What does cyber terrorism even mean?

The term is perhaps older than one might think. It was coined in the 1980s by Barry Collin. The two most widely accepted definitions of cyber terrorism are the following. Dorothy Denning considers that "Cyberterrorism is the convergence of cyberspace and terrorism. It refers to unlawful attacks and threats of attacks against computers, networks and the information stored therein when done to intimidate or coerce a government or its people in furtherance of political or social objectives. Further, to qualify as cyberterrorism, an attack should result in violence against persons or property, or at least cause enough harm to generate fear" (Denning 2000). Stark defines cyber terrorism as "the purposeful or threatened use of politically, socially, economically or religiously motivated cyber warfare or cyber targeted violence, conducted by a non-state or state-sponsored group for the purposes of creating fear, anxiety, and panic in the target population, and the disruption of military and civilian assets" (Stark 1999).

The use or threat of violence is crucial here. By definition, as Alex Schmid and many others have noted, terrorists use *violence* against civilians as a primary tool for broader political purposes. Too often, acts of cyber criminality or criminal acts using the Internet in their preparation are confusingly considered *cyber terrorism*. In addition, it is worth restating that terrorism is, by definition, carried out by non-state actors. Many commonly used examples of *cyber terrorism* would in fact be better described with other labels. For example, as Weimann points out, cyber terrorism differs from *hacktivism*, a *marriage of hacking and political activism*. According to him, hacktivism refers to "activities conducted online and covertly that seek to reveal, manipulate, or otherwise exploit vulnerabilities in computer operating systems and other software"—these are carried out for political purposes, and yet without the use of violence (Weimann 2004, p. 4).

There are several commonly cited examples of cyber terrorism. In a report on *Cyber Terror*, the FBI describes the electronic warfare activities conducted during Operation Desert Storm in 1991—these included viruses and logic bombs planted into the Iraqi Republican Guard command-and-control center systems. It adds that "attacking the largely civilian critical infrastructure is not warfare, but terrorism - cyber terror" (FBI 2011). This is a tricky case, and delimitating what falls under terrorism and what does not is rarely an objective and straightforward process. However, the attack was part of a military intervention and can therefore fall under the laws of war. In addition, if the attack was carried out with direct state involvement, it should not be considered terrorism, as per most definitions.

In 1996, a hacker disabled an Internet Service Provider (ISP) because it had attempted to stop him from sending out racist messages worldwide under the ISP's name. The hacker, allegedly associated with the White Supremacist movement in the United States, threatened: "You have yet to see true electronic terrorism. This is a promise" (Denning 2000). Once again, there was no direct violence or threat of violence in the hacking itself, which thus could very well not be considered cyber terrorism. In fact, the hacker's declaration that *true electronic terrorism* had not yet been achieved seems to validate this argument.

In 1998, the Institute for Global Communications (IGC) was bombarded by thousands of fake e-mail messages; staff and member accounts were spammed; and the IGC website was blocked. The aim of the attacks was for the IGC to stop hosting the website of the *Euskal Herria Journal*, which supported Basque independence and contained information on the terrorist group ETA (Denning 2000). In this case, there remains a strong suspicion of direct involvement of the Spanish government in these efforts—eventually successful—to force IGC to take down the website. In addition, the protesters did not aim to kill or use violence or the threat thereof in order to achieve their objectives, albeit political. Therefore, this attack is not best described as cyber *terrorism*.

In 1999, during the Kosovo conflict, NATO computers were electronically attacked in protest against the NATO bombing. This resulted in the NATO e-mail accounts not functioning for several days and the main website being repeatedly disrupted (Theiler 2011). More recently, in August 2013, the Syrian Electronic Army hacked into the websites of several media and social media outlets including the *New York Times*, Twitter, and the Huffington Post in reprisal for what they considered to be hostile coverage of the Syrian government's activities. These two cases clearly fall under the realm of hacktivism, not terrorism, given the lack of violence.

The cyber attack that has perhaps received most attention in recent history is the Stuxnet worm, a malicious computer software that targeted the Iranian nuclear infrastructure in 2010 (see, e.g., Clemente 2010). While the degree of sophistication and psychological impact was indeed significant, the physical impact was not as extensive as initially feared, although it did cause some serious damage to Iranian centrifuges (Barzashka 2013). No one died as a result of the attack, which was likely intended to disrupt and obstruct, rather than kill. Moreover, the U.S. and Israeli governments, or parts thereof, are suspected to have been involved in the attack (*Washington Post* 2012). As a result, the *cyber terrorism* label is once again not the most appropriate.

Some, including Denning, consider that if cyber attacks include "sufficient harm or frightening," they can indeed be considered cyber terrorism, although it often comes down to a "judgment call." She adds that "the threat of cyberterrorism has been mainly theoretical, but it is something to watch and take reasonable precautions against" (Denning 2000). Fourteen years after this statement, and considering that no one has reportedly died as a direct result of a cyber attack carried out for political purposes, one can indeed reiterate that the threat remains *mainly theoretical*, at best. The label *cyber terrorism* is often a misnomer, used to draw public or political attention on a particular event or threat. It does not accurately describe most events that are often much more similar to hacking, activism, protest, or military tactics.

This does not mean that terrorists do not use the Internet—they obviously do, like a large portion of the world's population—approximately 2.4bn or 34.3% of the world's population as of June 30, 2012 (Internet World Stats 2014). As Peter W. Singer notes, "what terror groups value from the Internet is the same as the rest of us – reliable service, easy terms and virtual anonymity" (Singer 2012). Terrorists tend to use the Internet in four main ways: first, to conduct research ahead of an attack, including regarding methods and targets—in 2010, AQAP's magazine *Inspire* published an article entitled "Make a Bomb in the Kitchen of Your Mom," detailing all the steps required to make a bomb with very basic items. In 2008, the perpetrators of the Mumbai attack, which killed 171 people, used Google Earth to memorize the targets and coordinate their assault. A few weeks later, three men angry with Martin Rynja, the owner of Gibson Square Books, who was due to release a novel about the private life of the Prophet Mohammed, looked up his London home address online and poured diesel fuel through its letterbox and set it alight (the three men were being followed by the police at the time of the attack and the fire was quickly put out) (Edwards and Gomis 2011, p. 12).

Second, to communicate ahead of an attack—considering the overwhelming powers of law enforcement when it comes to digital communications, this has been used less frequently in recent years. However, members of terrorist organizations have famously communicated through Internet forums, drafts of anonymous shared e-mail accounts, and other instant messaging tools. This has been particularly important for plots organized with the involvement of individuals based in different countries. In any case, face-to-face communications are very often preferred.

Third, the Internet has been used as a medium to convey ideas, either to disseminate testimonies due to be released after a terrorist attack or to discuss broader topics through written documents and videos. The individuals who perpetrated the attacks in London on July 7, 2005, recorded videos that were later released online. Anders Behring Breivik uploaded a so-called manifesto online hours before he carried out the attacks in downtown Oslo and the island of Utøya on July 22, 2011. American Yemeni preacher Anwar Al-Awlaki, before a U.S. drone killed him on September 30, 2011, was well known for his YouTube videos, blog articles, and other social media posts in which he encouraged anti-Western Islamic extremist ideas and terrorism. Roshonara Choudhry, the student who stabbed Stephen Timms, said that she had watched videos of Al-Awlaki online before attacking the British MP on May 14, 2010.

Fourth, terrorists also use the Internet in a more disruptive way, including hacking. Younis Tsouli, often considered "one of the most notorious cyberjihadists in the world" hacked into computer networks to disseminate videos of terrorist attacks and committed credit card fraud in order to fund jihadi websites (Cornish et al. 2009, p. 5).

As suggested by these few examples, terrorists very often need to preserve their access to the Internet, which makes massive attacks on "computers, networks and the information stored therein" (Denning 2000) all the more unlikely. In addition, this sort of high-impact attack requires a high degree and range of skills and knowledge, and a potentially large network of individuals. It is therefore fair to argue, as Louise Richardson points out, that "the fear of cyber-terrorism… is overblown. Terrorists rely heavily on the internet. They use it to communicate, to proselytize, to recruit, to raise funds and to research, plan and carry out their attacks. The internet is altogether too useful a tool to become a target for terrorists" (Richardson 2006, pp. 20–21).

Despite the limited threat posed by cyber terrorism, and the often-confusing nature of the term itself, it has received much attention over the past three decades, and even more so in the aftermath of 9/11. More importantly, concerns over cyber terrorism have developed at the expense of other cyber threats that are in fact causing much more damage. To illustrate this, Singer writes that nine new pieces of malicious software are discovered every second, and 97% of Fortune 500 companies have reportedly been hacked so far (*Washington Post* 2014). In the United Kingdom, the government recently reported that it faces approximately 33,000 cyber attacks each month (*Independent* 2013). In 2001, the Code Red worm alone infected approximately a million servers and caused about $2.6 billion worth of damage (Weimann 2004, p. 5). Losses due to cyber crime and cyber espionage have been roughly estimated at approximately $100 billion per year in the United States—where it is easiest to access data—and at least $300 billion worldwide, and it is highly likely that there is a significant amount of unreported information (McAfee 2013, p. 7). Cyber terrorism and terrorism in general—seemingly more spectacular threats, with much higher potential damage—are often inappropriately seen as much more urgent priorities than cyber crime and cyber espionage—more latent, long-term, and less visible phenomena.

It is worth noting that national security strategies of most Western countries, including the United States, United Kingdom, France, and Canada, in fact include very little on cyber terrorism or cyber attacks perpetrated by terrorists—in contrast with most political and media discourse on security issues. The closest example linking terrorism and cyber activity can be found in UK government documents: In its list of "the four highest priority risks" facing the United Kingdom, the 2010 National Security Strategy includes "cyber attacks, including by other states, and by organized crime and *terrorists* [emphasis mine]" (UK HMG 2010, p. 11)—the four other risks being international terrorism, international military crisis, and major accidents or natural hazards. There is only one other mention of such incident in the document: "Terrorists use cyberspace to organise, communicate and influence those vulnerable to radicalization" (UK HMG 2010, p. 30), and no further mention of cyber attacks perpetrated by terrorists. The UK Cyber Security Strategy adds: "While terrorists can be expected to continue to favour high-profile physical attacks, the threat that they might also use cyberspace to facilitate or to mount attacks against the UK is growing. We judge that it will continue to do so, especially if terrorists believe that our national infrastructure may be vulnerable" (UK HMG 2011, p. 15).

There are two main plausible explanations for the more appropriate and measured tone and analysis used in strategic documents in the United States, the United Kingdom, France, and Canada in comparison to more dramatic assessments in media reports, political declarations, and even some academic papers. First, this type of document itself is usually balanced and less assertive. Second, one can also suggest that as we get further away from 9/11, security strategies are becoming more reasonable regarding terrorism and its related components.

With this caveat in mind, cyber security policy has often been considered part of a broader counterterrorism strategy, particularly in the United States. The FBI lists cyber crime as its third main priority, following counterterrorism and counterintelligence. However, in terms of budget and capabilities, there has long been a clear gap between the first two and the third priority: as of 2007, 5987 full-time FBI employees were working on counterterrorism and 4479 on counterintelligence, but only 1151 on cyber crime (*San Jose Mercury News* 2007). Numbers have increased since then—in March 2012, then Director Robert Mueller said that the FBI now had "more than 1,000 specially trained agents, analysts, and digital forensic examiners that run complex undercover operations and examine digital evidence" (Mueller 2012)—but the FBI budget and personnel on cyber crime still compare poorly to resources devoted to counterterrorism and counterintelligence. Regarding the DHS, former Director Richard Clarke put it bluntly: "None of the senior leadership of DHS knew anything about cyber. They were all terrified about airplanes blowing up and people in body bags… They were so focused on the physical threats, cyber didn't make the cut" (*San Jose Mercury News* 2007).

In sum, online technologies have added another layer of complexity to the problems posed by terrorism and presented new challenges for law enforcement to grapple with. The term *cyber terrorism* has attracted much attention in media and political circles in recent years. As Weimann (2004) rightly points out, "two of the greatest fears of modern time are combined in the term 'cyberterrorism'… The fear of random, violent victimization blends well with the distrust and outright fear of computer technology." However, it is a confusing term, which does not describe current challenges in a useful way and has often overshadowed the more damaging related activities of cyber crime and cyber espionage.

After the terrorist attacks on September 11, 2011, terrorism was largely seen as an overwhelming Islamist issue centered on Al Qaeda, with clear links with a range of security challenges including cyber technologies and the global drug trade. Over a decade later, more informed and objective assessments paint not only a nuanced picture of the state of terrorism, an important problem, but also a multifaceted and complex one, and most importantly one that should not distract our attention from more relevant challenges for international security.

REFERENCES

9/11 Commission. 2004. *The 9/11 Commission Report*. The National Commission on Terrorist Attacks Upon the United States, July 22, 2004.
Aronson, S.L. 2014. AQIM's threat to Western interests in the Sahel. *CTC Sentinel*. Combating Terrorism Center at West Point, April 28, 2014.
Barzashka, I. 2013. Are cyber-weapons effective? Assessing Stuxnet's impact on the Iranian enrichment programme. *RUSI Journal* 158: 2.
BBC News. 2003. Colombia's "Marlboro man" extradited, August 30, 2003.
BBC News. 2013a. Far-right extremism "a real threat" says UK security minister, March 13, 2013.
BBC News. 2013b. Q&A: Mexico's drug-related violence, July 16, 2013.
BBC News. 2013c. Mexico estimates 26,000 missing since 1006, February 27, 2013.
BBC News. 2014. Who is behind Mexico's drug-related violence? Accessed at: http://www.bbc.com/news/world-latin-america-10681249. Accessed on February 10, 2014.
Beittel, J. 2013. Mexico's drug trafficking organizations: Source and scope of the violence. *Congressional Research Service*, April 15, 2013.
Bilmes, L.J. and Stiglitz, J.E. 2008. *The Three Trillion Dollar War: The True Cost of the Iraq Conflict*. New York: W.W. Norton.
Briggs, R. and Goodwin, M. 2012. We need a better understanding of what drives right-wing extremist violence. *LSE. British Politics and Policy*, June 12, 2012.
Brookings. 2014. A conversation on President Obama's trip to Mexico for the North American Leaders' Summit. Interview with Arturo Sarukhan, Alan Berube, Vanda Felbab-Brown, and Joshua Meltzer, February 14, 2014.
Burke, J. 2003. *Al Qaeda: Casting a Shadow of Terror.* London: I.B. Tauris and Co. Ltd.
Campaign for Tobacco-Free Kids. 2003. Illegal pathways to illegal profits: The big cigarette companies and international smuggling.
Caulkins, J., Kulick, J., and Kleiman, M. 2010. Drug production and trafficking, counterdrug policies, and security and governance in Afghanistan. Center on International Cooperation, New York University, New York, March 2010.
Caulkins, J., Kulick, J., and Kleiman, M. 2011. Think again: The Afghan drug trade. *Foreign Policy*, April 1, 2011.
Cawley, M. 2014. Mexico victims' survey highlights under-reporting of crime. InSight Crime, October 1, 2014.
CBS News. 2009. DHS report warns of right wing extremists, April 14, 2009.
Clemente, D. 2010. Reality approaches hype: Critical national infrastructure and the Stuxnet worm. Expert Comment, Chatham House, September 27, 2010.
CNN. 2011. Mexican drug cartels considered terrorists? April 15, 2011.
CNN. 2013. FBI: Navy Yard shooter "delusional," said "low frequency attacks" drove him to kill, September 26, 2013.
Comolli, V. and Hofmann, C. 2013. Drug markets, security and foreign aid. Modernising drug law enforcement. *International Drug Policy Consortium*, International Institute for Strategic Studies and Chatham House, September 2013.

Conway, M. 2005. The media and cyberterrorism: A study in the construction of "reality." In Paper presented at the *First International Conference on the Information Revolution and the Changing Face of International Relations and Security*, Lucerne, May 23–25, 2005.

Cornish, P., Hughes, R., and Livingstone, D. 2009. Cyberspace and the national security of the United Kingdom: Threats and responses. Chatham House Report, Chatham House, March 2009.

Csete, J. and Sanchez, C. 2013. Telling the story of drugs in West Africa: The newest front in a losing war? *Global Drug Policy Observatory (GDPO) Policy Brief 1*, November 2013.

Daily Mail. 2010. Why Britain is desperately vulnerable to cyber terror, October 19, 2010.

Denning, D. 2000. Cyberterrorism. Testimony before the Special Oversight Panel on Terrorism, Committee on Armed Services, U.S. House of Representatives, May 23, 2000.

DHS. 2009. Right-wing extremism: Current economic and political climate fueling resurgence in radicalization and recruitment. Office of Intelligence and Analysis Assessment. Extremism and Radicalization Branch, Homeland Environment Threat Analysis Division, April 7, 2009.

Dreazen, Y. 2013. Welcome to Cocainebougou. *Foreign Policy*, March 27, 2013.

Dube, A., Dube, O., and García-Ponce. 2013. Cross-border spillover: U.S. gun laws and violence in Mexico. *American Political Science Review* 107(3). American Political Science Association, August 2013, 397–417.

Edwards, J. and Gomis, B. Islamic terrorism in the UK since 9/11: Reassessing the "soft" response. Programme Paper, Chatham House, June 2011.

EMCDDA and Europol. 2013. EU drugs markets report: A strategic analysis, July 2, 2013.

European Commission. 2014. Competition—Overview. Accessed on February 23, 2015.

Europol. 2013. TE-SAT 2013: EU Terrorism Situation and Trend Report, April 25, 2013.

Europol. 2014. TE-SAT 2014: EU Terrorism Situation and Trend Report, May 28, 2014.

FBI. 2011. Cyber Terror. *FBI Law Enforcement Bulletin*. By William L. Tafoya, PhD, November 2011.

FCO. 2013. Trafficking and terrorism in the Sahel. Foreign Office Research Analyst Papers, November 12, 2013.

Felbab-Brown, V. 2013a. Gangs, slums, megacities and the utility of population-centric COIN. *Brookings Institution*, October 5, 2013.

Felbab-Brown, V. 2013b. The purpose of law enforcement is to make good criminals? How to effectively respond to the crime-terrorism Nexus. *Brookings*, November 21, 2013.

Fox News. 2009. Chorus of protest grows over report warning of right wing radicalization. *Fox News Politics*, April 15, 2009.

Gberie, L. 2013. State officials and their involvement in drug trafficking in West Africa: Preliminary findings. WACD Background Paper No. 5, p. 11.
Global Post. 2013. The 6 most infamous crimes committed by Mexico's Zetas cartel, July 16, 2013.
Gomis, B. 2014. Illicit drugs and international security: Towards UNGASS 2016. Briefing Paper, Chatham House, February 2014.
Goodwin, M. 2012. Europe's far right: Don't blame the Eurozone crisis. Expert Comment, Chatham House, August 15, 2012.
Goodwin, M. 2013. The roots of extremism: The English Defence League. Briefing Paper, Chatham House, March 2013.
GTD. 2014. Global terrorism database. START, University of Maryland. Accessed on February 27, 2014.
Guardian. 2001. Full text of Tony Blair's speech to parliament, October 4, 2001.
Guardian. 2011. Twin Towers and terrorism: The impact 10 years on the observer, September 11, 2011.
Guardian. 2012. Greece's far-right Golden Dawn Party maintains share of vote, June 18, 2012.
Guardian. 2013. Is Armageddon on the cyber horizon? April 17, 2013.
Guardian. 2014a. Soldier jailed for making nailbomb avoids terror charge, November 28, 2014.
Guardian. 2014b. Fort Hood shootings: Iraq veteran kills three people at Texas military base, April 3, 2014.
Independent. 2013. Government faces around 33,000 cyber attacks a month, reveals Cabinet Office Minister Chloe Smith, April 23, 2013.
INEGI. 2014. A panorama of Mexico: Governance, crime and justice information. Presentation to the London School of Economics, Mexico's Week 2014.
InSight Crime. 2014. Mexico victims.
Institute for Economics and Peace. 2013. Mexico Peace Index 2013.
Internet World Stats. 2014. Internet Users in the World. Accessed on March 3, 2014.
Lacher, W. 2012. Organized crime and conflict in the Sahel-Sahara Region. Carnegie Endowment for International Peace, September 13, 2012.
Lacher, W. 2013. Challenging the myth of the drug-terror Nexus in the Sahel. West African Commission on Drugs (WACD) Background Paper No. 4, August 19, 2013.
LaFree, G. 2010. The global terrorism database: Accomplishments and challenges. *Perspectives on Terrorism* 4(1): 24–46.
Laqueur, W. 1999. *The New Terrorism: Fanaticism and the Arms of Mass Destruction*. Oxford: Oxford University Press.
Lebovich, A. 2013. Mali's bad trip. *Foreign Policy*, March 15, 2013
Le Figaro. 2012. Fabius pointe la "menace narcoterroriste," December 9, 2012.
LeGresley, E., Lee, K., Muggli, M.E., Patel, P., Colin, J., and Hurt, R.D. 2008. British American tobacco and the "insidious impact of illicit trade" in cigarettes across Africa. *Tobacco Control* 17(5): 339–346.
Le Monde. 2001. Le cyber-terrorisme en avance d'une guerre? September 24, 2001.

Local. 2014. Extreme right "biggest threat to EU": Malmström. *Local—Sweden News in English*, January 14, 2014.
Los Angeles Times. 2011. Who is responsible for the casino tragedy in Mexico? August 29, 2011.
Makarenko. 2012. Europe's crime-terror Nexus: Links between terrorist and organized crime groups in the European Union. European Parliament. Directorate-General for Internal Policies, Policy Department C: Citizen's Rights and Constitutional Affairs Study, November 27, 2012.
Maliweb.net. 2013. Après la venue du narcotrafiquant Baba Ould: La jeunesse de Gao révoltée contre le maire Sadou Diallo. *Bamako Hebdo*, February 16, 2013.
McAfee. 2013. The economic impact of cyber crime and cyber espionage. With the Center for Strategic and International Studies (CSIS). *Report*, July 2013.
McDougal, T., Shirk, D., Muggah, R., and Patterson, J. 2013. The way of the gun: Estimating firearms traffic across the U.S.–Mexico border. Igarapé Institute and Trans-Border Institute, University of San Diego, San Diego, CA, March 2013.
Mélendez, J. 2011. Centroamérica, paraísos de las armas. *El Universal*, November 15, 2011.
Melly, P. 2012. Mali: Is there a route back to democratic stability? Expert Comment, Chatham House, March 23, 2012.
Mercille, J. 2012. Washington and the Afghan drug trade since 2001, Chapter 6. In *Cruel Harvest: The U.S. Intervention in the Afghan Drug Trade*. London: Pluto Press. 2012.
Moeckli, D. 2008. *Human Rights and Non-Discrimination in the "War on Terror."* Oxford: Oxford University Press.
Mueller, R. 2012. Statement before the House Appropriations Committee, Subcommittee on Commerce, Justice, Science, and Related Agencies Testimony, Washington, DC, March 7, 2012.
New York Times. 2009. Army doctor held in Ft. Hood rampage, November 5, 2009.
New York Times. 2012. Is the threat from hate groups overlooked? Room for debate, August 12, 2012.
New York Times. 2013. U.S. sting that snared African ex-admiral shines light on drug trade, April 15, 2013.
Nixon, R. 1971. Remarks about an intensified program for drug abuse prevention and control. U.S. White House, June 17.
Opinion Way. 2014. Baromètre de la confiance politique. For CEVIPOF CRNS & Sciences Po Paris, January 2014.
Panetta, L. 2012. Remarks by Secretary Panetta on cybersecurity to the business executives for national security. *New York Security*, October 11, 2012.
Piazza, J. 2009. Is Islamist terrorism more dangerous? An empirical study of group ideology, organization and goal structure. *Terrorism and Political Violence* 21(1): 62–88.
PolicyMic. 2011. Cyber attacks will be the greatest national security threat in the 21st century, February 6, 2011.

Quartz. 2014. Right turn ahead: More and more Europeans are keen on destroying the EU from the inside, February 17, 2014.
Ramalingam, V. 2012. The rise of the radical right in Europe. In The New Radical Right: Violent and Non-Violent Movements in Europe. Briefing Paper, Institute for Strategic Dialogue. February 2012.
Ramalingam, V. 2014. The European far right is on the rise. Here's how to tackle it. Comment is Free. *Guardian*, February 13, 2014.
Reuters. 2011. Mexican oil thieves rob Pemex of $251 million this year, June 16, 2011.
Richardson, L. 2006. *What Terrorists Want: Understanding the Terrorist Threat.* Eastbourne: Gardners Books.
Rollins, J. and Wyler, L.S. 2013. Terrorism and transnational crime: Foreign policy issues for Congress. *Congressional Research Service*, June 11, 2013.
San Jose Mercury News. 2007. Part III: U.S. targets terrorists as online thieves run amok. *San Jose Mercury News*, November 13, 2007.
Schmid, A. 2012. Countering violent extremism: A promising response to terrorism. *ICCT Commentaries*, International Centre for Counter-Terrorism—The Hague, June 12, 2012.
Shanty, F. 2011. *The Nexus: International Terrorism and Drug Trafficking from Afghanistan*. Westport, CT: Praeger, Chapter 3, pp. 43–63: Drugs-Terror Nexus in Afghanistan: Claims, Counterclaims, and Accusations.
Singer, P.W. 2012. The cyber terror bogeyman. *Brookings Institution*, November 2012.
Stark, R. 1999. Cyber terrorism: Rethinking new technology. Department of Defense and Strategic Studies.
START. 2011. Background Report: 9/11, Ten Years Later, September 2011.
Sun Wyler, L. and Cook, N. 2010. Illegal drug trade in Africa: Trends and U.S. policy. *Congressional Research Service*, February 26, 2010.
Telegraph. 2009. Police fear far-right "spectacular" attack to stoke racial tensions, July 7, 2009.
Theiler, O. 2011. New threats: The cyber-dimension. Ten Years: Lessons Learnt, NATO Review.
Toumast Press. 2012. Le trio Iyad ag Ghaly, Mohamed Ag Erlaf, Mohamed Ould Awainat pour libérer l'ex-Président ATT, April 3, 2012.
UK HMG. 2010. A strong Britain in an age of uncertainty: The national security strategy, October 2010.
UK HMG. 2011. The UK cyber security strategy: Protecting and promoting the UK in a digital world, November 2011.
UK Trade and Investment (UKTI). 2013. Mexico: A destination for growth, September 2013.
UNDP. 2013. Citizen Security with a Human Face: Evidence and Proposals for Latin America. Regional Human Development Report 2013–2014, Executive Summary, November 2013. (s/citizen_security_with_a_human_face_-executivesummary.pdf).
UNODC. 2005. World drug report.

UNODC. 2007. Cocaine trafficking in Western Africa.
UNODC. 2009. Afghanistan opium survey.
UNODC. 2013a. Illicit crop monitoring: Afghanistan.
UNODC. 2013b. Transnational organized crime in West Africa: A threat assessment, February 2013.
UNODC. 2013c. UNODC homicide statistics.
UPI. 2011a. Germany fears Norway massacre copycats, August 2, 2011.
UPI. 2011b. Cyberterrorism a threat that won't go away, September 16, 2011.
U.S. Department of the Treasury. 2010. Treasury designates two narcotics traffickers in Guinea-Bissau. *Press Centre*, August 4, 2010.
U.S. Senate. 2003. Narco-terrorism: International drug trafficking and terrorism—A dangerous mix. U.S. Senate Committee on the Judiciary, Washington, DC, May 20, 2003.
WACD. 2014. Not just in transit: An independent report of the West Africa Commission on Drugs, June 2014.
Washington Post. 2002. Cyber-attacks by Al Qaeda feared: Terrorists at threshold of using internet as tool of bloodshed, experts say, June 27, 2002.
Washington Post. 2009. Napolitano defends Homeland Security Report on right-wing extremism. *WP Politics*, April 16, 2009.
Washington Post. 2012. Stuxnet was work of U.S. and Israeli experts, officials say, June 2, 2012.
Washington Post. 2014. Cybersecurity and cyberwar: A Q&A with Peter Singer, January 14, 2014.
Washington Times. 2009. Hezbollah uses Mexican drug routes into U.S., March 27, 2009.
Weimann, G. 2004. Cyberterrorism: How real is the threat? Special Report, United States Institute of Peace (USIP), December 2004.
Weimann, G. 2005. Cyberterrorism: The sum of all fears? *Studies in Conflict & Terrorism* 28: 129–149.

4

Overestimated Threat

The danger is entirely different [from] the fear.

Commander Chris Hadfield
TED Annual Conference, Vancouver, Canada, March 17, 2014

Terrorism ranks high on political agendas and has often been listed as a top-tier security threat. In the aftermath of 9/11, many observers and policy officials warned that the attack was just the beginning of an impending wave of terrorist attacks to be carried out in the United States and across the West. This has largely not materialized.

In the decade following September 11, 2011, fewer than 250 American citizens were killed in terrorist attacks across the world and fewer than 50 in the United States (NCTC 2012). Of all the people killed by terrorist attacks worldwide in 2011, only 0.001% were private U.S. citizens (Zenko 2012a). In England and Wales, terrorism has led to an annual average of five deaths (Anderson 2012, p. 27). Twelve people died in terrorist attacks between 2002 and 2012 in France and one in Canada (GTD 2014). In 2012, for example, terrorist attacks caused 17 deaths in the EU in 2012, and 0 in the United States (while 10 U.S. citizens died in terrorist attacks in Afghanistan) (Europol 2013; U.S. State Department 2013). In comparison, in the same year, terrorist attacks caused 2,632 deaths in Afghanistan, 2,436 in Iraq, 1,848 in Pakistan, 1,386 in Nigeria, and 659 in Russia (U.S. State Department 2013).

Worldwide, approximately 65,000 people died in terrorist attacks between 2001 and 2010, with an average of just over 7,200 deaths per year

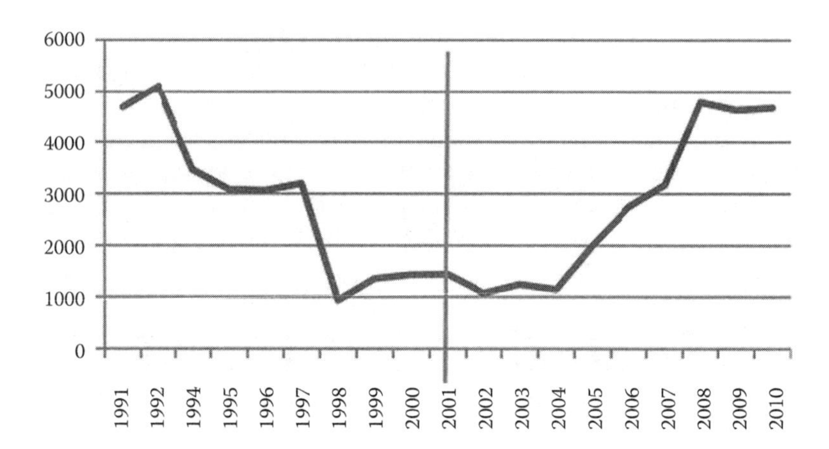

Figure 4.1 Terrorist attacks worldwide per year, pre- and post-2001. (From START Background Report: 9/11, Ten Years Later, September 2011.) *Note*: As noted on the GTD website, data is missing for 1993: "The original PGIS data, upon which the 1970–1997 GTD data are based, consisted of hard-copy index cards, which were subsequently coded electronically by START researchers. Unfortunately, the set of cards for 1993 was lost prior to PGIS handing the data over to START." (From GTD 2015, Frequently Asked Questions, accessed on April 9, 2015.)

(START 2011). This does not mark a substantial increase from previous decades. Terrorist activity increased noticeably between 2004 and 2008, as shown in Figure 4.1. However, the number of terrorist attacks perpetrated in 2010 was roughly equal to the number of attacks in 1991 (just under 4,700) (START 2011; see Figure 4.1).

Moreover, a majority of the terrorist attacks carried out in the decade after 9/11 took place in war zones, in particular in Iraq and also Afghanistan. The victims could therefore be considered victims of war, not of terrorism. Based on data collected by Steven Pinker, the Cato Institute produced the graph below (see Figure 4.2), which shows that excluding Afghanistan and Iraq—countries affected by large military conflicts—the rate of deaths from terrorism worldwide has in fact declined since the 1980s.

This graph also demonstrates that terrorism rarely kills more than 0.2 per 100,000 people annually. By comparison, the global average homicide rate was approximately 8 per 100,000 in 2013, 40 times higher than the rate of death from terrorism Institute for Economics and Peace (2014). Honduras held the world's highest homicide rate in 2011, with 91.6 homicides per 100,000 inhabitants (UNODC 2013). In contrast, in Iraq—the country most affected by terrorism in the world—there were 19.04

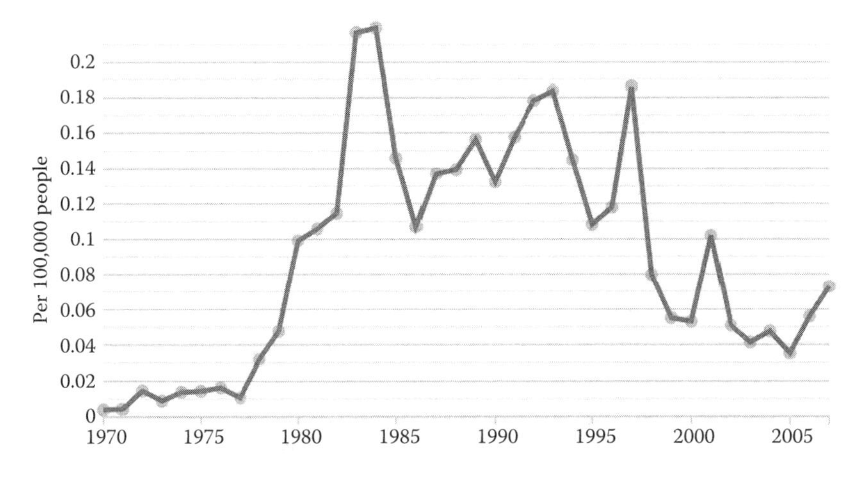

Figure 4.2 Rate of deaths from terrorism worldwide, except Afghanistan and Iraq, per 100,000 people. (From Human Progress, a project of the Cato Institute, accessed on March 12, 2014.)

terrorism-related deaths per 100,000 inhabitants in 2013 (Institute for Economics and Peace 2014; World Bank 2013). Almost 18,000 people were killed by terrorist attacks worldwide in 2013, while over half a million died in armed violence in 2011 (Geneva Declaration 2011; Institute for Economics and Peace 2014). In the United States, as Nicholas Kristof pointed out, "more Americans die in gun homicides and suicides in six months than have died in the last 25 years in every terrorist attack and the wars in Afghanistan and Iraq combined" (Kristof 2012). In 2011 alone, 7 million people died of ischemic heart disease, 6.2 million of stroke, 3.2 million of lower respiratory infections, 3 million of chronic obstructive pulmonary disease, 1.9 million of diarrheal diseases, 1.6 million of HIV/AIDS, 1.5 million of pulmonary cancers, 1.4 million of diabetes mellitus, 1.3 million of road traffic accidents, and 1.2 million of prematurity; tobacco use was responsible for approximately 1 in 10 adult deaths worldwide; and 6.9 million children died before the age of 5 (WHO 2013). Richard Jackson, among others, has gone so far as to note that things which are more likely to kill you than terrorism in the United States include bathtubs and toilets, vending machines, animals, insects, DIY accidents, alcohol, lightning strikes, and hospitals—a demonstration that "on the list of things which can kill you, and which are a real risk to human life and well-being, terrorism comes somewhere close to the very bottom" (Jackson 2011).

The killing of civilians is arguably only a means to an end for terrorists. Therefore, what ultimately matters to them is not so much how many people were killed in terrorist attacks, but whether their objectives were met. As Brian Michael Jenkins once put it, "Terrorists want a lot of people watching, not a lot of people dead" (Jenkins 1975). Multiple studies have demonstrated that terrorists very rarely achieve their goals. In a 1976 article entitled "The Futility of Terrorism," Walter Laqueur noted that "in historical perspective, [terror] has hardly ever had a lasting effect," and that although "it will always attract much publicity," "politically it tends to be ineffective." He finished his piece with a striking statement for a terrorism expert: "Compared with other dangers threatening mankind, it is almost irrelevant" (Laqueur 1976). A few years later, Martha Crenshaw corroborated Laqueur's theory, arguing that "terrorism is objectively a failure," given that terrorists do not achieve their political objectives (Crenshaw 1980; cited in Abrahms and Lula 2012, p. 47). In numeric terms, Seth Jones and Martin Libicki found that only 4% of the 648 groups they analyzed obtained their strategic demands (Jones and Libicki 2008); Audrey Kurth Cronin estimated that less than 5% of terrorist groups have been successful (Cronin 2011); and Max Abrahms has found that the 28 Foreign Terrorist Organizations as identified by the U.S. State Department achieved their objectives only 7% of the time. In addition, he noticed that terrorist groups prioritizing attacks on civilian targets over military targets "systematically failed to achieve their policy objectives." In other words, he explains, "their poor success rate is inherent to the tactic of terrorism itself" (Abrahms 2006, pp. 43–44).

Much of the media coverage and political discourse has referred to terrorist *masterminds* designing *highly sophisticated* attacks. Four decade after his famous quote, Brian Michael Jenkins himself noted: "many of today's terrorists want a lot of people watching *and* a lot of people dead" (italics added), pointing that "ethnic hatred and religious fanaticism replaced political agendas" (Jenkins 2006, pp. 118–119). It is certainly true that Al Qaeda and the Islamic State are willing to cause greater casualties than most of the terrorist groups in the 1970s. However, what is often overlooked is that over half of terrorist attacks are in fact not lethal. Since 1970, 56% of the terrorist attacks recorded in the GTD caused zero fatality, either because the immediate target was infrastructure or simply because the attack failed (LaFree 2013) (see Figure 4.3).

In addition, as illustrated by the following few examples, many of the plots uncovered in North America and Europe have proved to be very basic or amateurish. Several plots also expose clear lapses in law

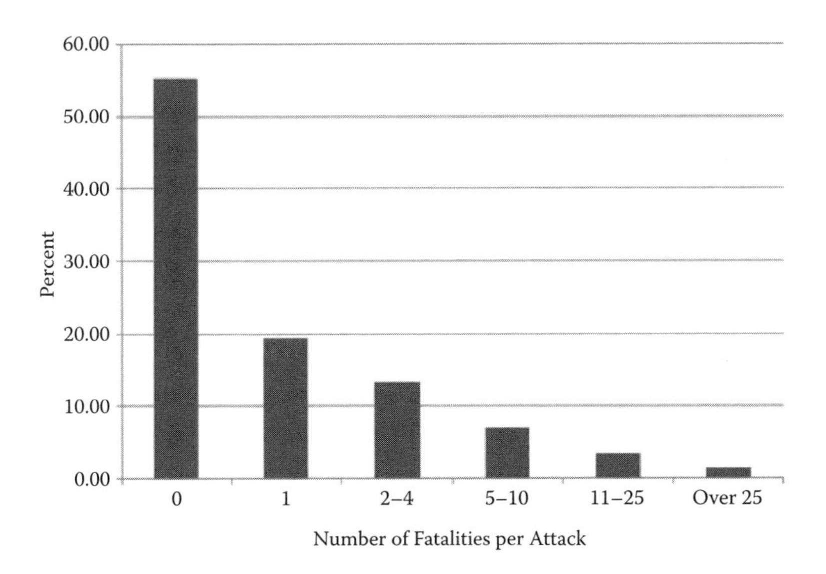

Figure 4.3 Total fatalities per terrorist attack, 1970–2007 (n = 82,910*). *Data on fatalities were missing in 8.1% of cases. (From LaFree, G., *Perspect. Terror.*, 4(1), 2010; GTD, Global Terrorism Database, START, University of Maryland, accessed on February 27, 2014.)

enforcement, or direct involvement, with FBI agents in the United States, for instance, acting as double agents:

- In September 1992, Ahmed Ajaj attempted to enter the United States with someone else's Swedish passport on which he had pasted his photo. He was arrested, and the police found bomb-making instructions, training manuals, and videos in his suitcase. From prison, he still managed to communicate with other individuals directly involved in the World Trade Center bombing of February 1993 (Radzinski 2011).
- In January 2000, a group of individuals planned to attack the U.S. Navy Destroyer *The Sullivans*, stationed in the port of Aden. However, they loaded too many explosives onto their boat and it sank. The attempt was nonetheless repeated, successfully this time, in October 2000, as they bombed the *USS Cole*, killing 17 and injuring 39 (Department of Justice [DOJ] 2003).
- In January 2003, Kamel Bourgass was arrested in Manchester, United Kingdom, for his involvement in the so-called Wood

Green ricin plot, referring to the neighborhood of London where he had been residing. In the process, he stabbed several policemen and killed detective Stephen Oake. Bourgass was found to be plotting attacks with ricin, which he aimed to spread in public places including door handles. However, ricin is only lethal when it is ingested or injected. Many questions regarding this plot remain, as no ricin was apparently found in the apartments that were raided (Oates et al. 2010, pp. 102–105).

- In November 2003, Antony Garcia ordered 600 kg of ammonium nitrate fertilizer from an agricultural retailer in Burgess Hill, Sussex, United Kingdom. The store manager joked: "I hope you're not going round bombing everything." The amount purchased that day was indeed enough for four or five football fields, and it was the wrong time of the year to apply ammonium nitrate as a fertilizer. Garcia was in fact part of a group plotting a terrorist attack. The plot was uncovered due to the plotters' carelessness: a storage unit manager eventually reported their suspicious activities to the police in early 2004 (Edwards and Gomis 2011, p. 8).
- In June 2007, Bilal Abdullah and Kafeel Ahmed attempted to bomb Glasgow Airport by driving a car carrying propane canisters through the entrance. However, they crashed onto the bollards blocking the way, as a result of which the car caught fire, and the only people injured were Abdullah and Ahmed themselves (Edwards and Gomis 2011, pp. 10–11).
- In 2006, a group referred to as *Miami 7* was arrested for plotting to blow up the then Sears Tower in Chicago (now named Willis Tower). However, as Bruce Schneier has noted, they had "no weapons, no bombs, no expertise, no money and no operational skill," and an FBI undercover agent who had infiltrated the group had in fact suggested the plot in the first place (Schneier 2007).
- In 2008, in the United Kingdom, Mohammad Rashid Saeed Alim (born Nicky Reilly) prepared three caustic soda devices in plastic bottles in the toilet of the Giraffe restaurant in central Exeter and planned to detonate the bombs in the restaurant. The bombs detonated prematurely, making a sound similar to a light bulb exploding, according to one of the customers. Alim was the only person injured. He suffered from Asperger's syndrome and had an IQ of 83, although he claimed in a suicide note: "I have not been brainwashed or indoctrinated. I am not insane" and that he was simply doing "what God wants from his mujahedeen." At his

trial, defense barrister Kerim Fuad noted: "Had his poor unsuspecting mother not handed him the £10 note that she thought was for him to purchase a CD that morning, he would simply not have had enough money for the bus fare (from Plymouth) to Exeter" (CNN 2009; Edwards and Gomis 2011, p. 11).

- In 2011, Rezwan Ferdaus was accused of planning to crash three remotely controlled planes carrying explosives into the U.S. Pentagon and Capitol. However, there were a few problems in his plan: the planes only measured 60–80 inches in length; the Al Qaeda operatives with whom he thought he was working were all undercover FBI agents and FBI informants; all of the equipment was paid for by the FBI and delivered under their watch (Sky 2011; *Guardian* 2011).

In short, there is often a significant disconnect between the reality of terrorism and how it is portrayed. The aforementioned cases are serious criminal plots. However, they can certainly be tackled by competent policing and do not pose an existential threat.

Most statements from governments and observers across Western Europe and North America, especially in the United States, do not give the impression that terrorism is in fact marginal, ineffective, and carried out by incompetent individuals. Rather, many have exaggerated the threat. The *Daily Beast* described the aforementioned plot involving Rezwan Ferdaus in the following terms: "Ferdaus posed the worst nightmare for the U.S. He aspired to kill, and appeared to have highly specialized skills" (Sky 2011). John Mueller, a political scientist at Ohio State University who has conducted substantial research on threat inflation as it relates to terrorism and nuclear terrorism in particular, has compiled a list of erroneous predictions regarding terrorism—here are a few examples:

- In November 2003, David Rothkopf from the *Washington Post* wrote that he had just recently cochaired a meeting with more than 200 senior business and government representatives, including many security and terrorism experts. In an article summarizing the meeting, he noted that "almost three-quarters of them said it was likely the United States would see a major terrorist strike before the end of 2004" and that "a similar number predicted that the assault would be greater than those of 9/11 and might well involve weapons of mass destruction" (Rothkopf 2003).
- In March and April 2006, 116 foreign policy experts were interviewed regarding, among other things, the "likelihood of a terrorist attack on the scale of the 9/11 attacks occurring again in

the United States" by the end of 2006, 2011, and 2016. As far as the 2011 time frame is concerned, for instance, only 5 considered it *very unlikely* and 16 *somewhat unlikely*, while 41 answered *somewhat likely*, 29 *very likely*, and 9 *certain* (Center for American Progress 2006, p. 17).

- In October 2006, a *senior counterterrorism source* told two *Guardian* journalists that "Britain is sitting at the receiving end of an al-Qaida campaign... It's like the old game of Space Invaders: When you clear one screen of potential attackers, another simply appears to take its place" (*Guardian* 2006).
- In a 2007 article entitled "Remember Al Qaeda? They're Baaack," terrorism expert Bruce Hoffman noted: "we have more to fear from this resilient organization, not less" (Hoffman 2007).

In line with these exaggerated assessments about Al Qaeda and the terrorism threat in general, governments have often overreacted and put in place disproportionate policies to counter what is indeed a marginal threat. The United States has spent a considerable amount of money to fight terrorism at home and abroad. The total figure is difficult to estimate, given the wide-ranging remit of counterterrorism, which includes military, homeland security, intelligence, counterradicalization programs, and traditional policing measures, among others. John Mueller and Mark Stewart assessed in 2011 that the United States had spent an additional $1 trillion dollars on counterterrorism security measures, excluding the costs of foreign wars (Mueller and Stewart 2011a, b). Bruce Schneier notes that the regulatory safety goal in the United States is of $1–10 million per life saved and argues that "in order for the $100B we have spent per year on counterterrorism to be worth it, it would need to have saved 10,000 lives per year" (Schneier 2011). In 2011, various reports have attempted to measure human and financial costs of the interventions in Afghanistan and Iraq: 137,000 civilian deaths, 7.8 million refugees, 31,000 military fatalities among the United States, the Iraqi and Afghan security forces, and their allies, and $3–5 trillion of overall spending (Bilmes and Stiglitz 2011; Brown University 2011).*

* There is no consensus as to whether the military interventions in Afghanistan and Iraq should be included in the tally of the U.S. counterterrorism spending. They were part of the overall response to the 9/11 attacks: the United States wanted to remove Afghanistan as a "safe haven" for Al Qaeda and take weapons of mass destruction off the hands of Saddam Hussein in Iraq, as alleged links between Al Qaeda and the Iraqi regime were reported in the run up to 2003. However, these also included broader strategic objectives not narrowly related to terrorism as such.

In 2010, an extensive study by the *Washington Post* revealed other striking figures: over 1,200 government agencies and almost 2,000 private companies are estimated to work on programs related to counterterrorism, homeland security, and intelligence; over 850,000 people hold Top Secret clearances; 33 building complexes for top secret intelligence work have been built after 9/11 or were being built in 2010 in Washington and its surrounding area, together occupying approximately 17 million square feet of space, as the study points out the "equivalent of almost three Pentagons or 22 U.S. Capitol buildings"; 51 federal organizations and military commands, located in 15 different cities across the United States, track flows of money funding and used by terrorist organizations; and intelligence analysts publish around 50,000 intelligence reports each year (*Washington Post* 2010).

CASE STUDY: THE UNITED KINGDOM AND FRANCE

The United Kingdom and France are two of the closest and most natural foreign policy partners to the United States in the world, and the two largest defense and security contributors in Europe. Overall, they have pursued more measured counterterrorism policies than the United States, notably building on previously existing structures. A more detailed inspection, though, shows some of the limits and flaws of programs put in place after 9/11.

The United Kingdom, a key ally of the United States in the global fight against terrorism, has spent significantly less than its transatlantic partner on counterterrorism policy. Again, it is difficult to get accurate figures, but it has been estimated that the United Kingdom has spent on average about £3 billion per year on counterterrorism in the 10 years after 9/11—in other words, about 65 times less than the United States per head of population (Chatham House 2013). However, some of the country's counterterrorism programs have proved controversial. In particular, the counterradicalization program Prevent has been criticized. Prevent is part of the United Kingdom's counterterrorism strategy named CONTEST, first released in 2003, which also includes the Pursue, Protect, and Prepare strands. Prevent is designed "to stop people from becoming terrorists or supporting violent extremism." Its main objectives are (1) "to challenge the ideology behind violent extremism and support mainstream voices," (2) "to disrupt those who promote violent extremism and support people living in the communities where they may operate," (3) "to support individuals who are vulnerable to recruitment or who have already been recruited by violent extremists," (4) "to increase the resilience of communities to violent extremism," and (5) "to address the grievances which ideologies are exploiting" (HMG 2010). The second objective has proved most problematic, as it has blurred the lines between fostering community cohesion and intelligence gathering—there have been numerous accusations of spying. The police and security services allegedly asked NGOs, sports clubs, schools, universities, and other organizations working with young Muslims to pass on information about individuals involved in initiatives funded by the Prevent program (House of Commons 2010, pp. 11–14; Edwards and Gomis 2011, pp. 16–19).

In addition, some provisions of the Terrorism Act 2000, put in place a few months before the September 11, 2001, attacks, have proved largely ineffective and discriminatory. Under Section 44, after appropriate authorization, a person can be legally stopped and searched by police officers to look for articles that could be used to carry out acts of terrorism, regardless of whether there is reasonable suspicion that these objects are being carried or that these acts of terrorism may occur in the area covered by the authorization. Between 2001 and 2010, Section 44 was used for over half a million stops that have led to only 283 terrorism-related arrests and *zero* conviction for terrorism-related offenses (Choudhury 2012, pp. 13–14).

Asian, *black*, and *other* ethnic groups are also more often stopped and searched than *white* people (Choudhury 2012, p. 39). Of the 1,221 people arrested for terrorism and the 256 charged for terrorism-related offenses between April 2005 and March 2011, 41% of those arrested and 44% of those charged defined themselves as Asian, 26% and 22% as white, and 12% and 21% as black (Anderson 2012, pp. 72–73). It is worth noting that this racial discrimination is present not only in counterterrorism policing but also in counternarcotics and immigration control policies. For instance, a study by UK Charity Release and the London School of Economics and Political Science found that in 2009/2010, black people and Asian people were respectively 6.3 and 2.5 times more likely to be stopped and searched for drugs than white people, despite the fact that drug use is lower among black and Asian people than among white people (Release and LSE 2013).

Revelations over surveillance programs run by the United Kingdom's Government Communications Headquarters, including Tempora, have demonstrated that the United States is not the only country with wide-ranging intelligence activities. Given that over three-quarters of the United Kingdom's intelligence work focuses on counterterrorism, it is worth questioning whether the digital surveillance measures put in place in recent years are in fact proportionate to the limited threat terrorism poses (Intelligence and Security Committee [ISC] 2008, p. 8).*

In France, counterterrorism spending has not reached the same heights as in the United States and has not increased substantially after 2001.† Similar to the United Kingdom, France already had a system in place, which had been designed to tackle a previous threat, while the United Kingdom was particularly affected by Irish Republican terrorism from the 1970s onward, and France suffered a series of jihadi terrorist attacks in the 1990s, in addition to separatist terrorism (e.g., FLNC, ETA), which still accounts for the bulk of terrorism activity in the country today. Therefore, neither Paris nor London felt the need to put in place a whole new infrastructure, especially as they had not been the direct targets of any attack the size of 9/11. Albeit on a smaller scale, France did increase its counterterrorism efforts, and part of its policy both before and after 9/11 has been criticized for its "overzealousness, racial bias and the abuse of civil rights" (Erlanger 2012). In 2003, two laws were passed to facilitate the deportation of foreign residents suspected (yet without tangible proof) of terrorist activities—"if there are serious reasons to believe that an individual's presence on French territory constitutes a serious threat to public order, public safety or national security" or if they are suspected of "behavior susceptible of endangering the fundamental interests of the nation, linked to terrorist activities, or incitement to discrimination, hatred or violence on the basis of ethnic origin or religion" (Camilleri 2012, pp. 23–24).

This is in contrast with the United Kingdom, where deportations are much more rare. The Immigration, Asylum and Nationality Act 2006 authorizes the UK home secretary to revoke citizenship if he or she is "satisfied that deprivation is conducive to the public good," as a result of which the person will be subject to deportation powers—if the order was made on national security grounds, it can only be appealed after the individual has in fact been deported (Moeckli 2008, pp. 168–169). Actual implementation of the measure pertaining to deportation has been more systematic in France. From the 1990s onward, the French authorities have cracked down on militant Islamist networks and have carried out up to 160 arrests

* In 2008, an ISC report noted that the British Security Service (more commonly known as MI5) allocated 70% of its total intelligence effort to international counterterrorism and planned on increasing that share to 80% (ISC 2007, p. 8).

† The French government often uses the term "*anti*-terrorisme," instead of "*contre*terrorisme." When used, the latter term often refers to the broader counterterrorism strategy as a whole, while the former more narrowly accounts for law enforcement interventions carried out as part of the overall strategy.

at once (Foley 2013, pp. 2–3). In November 2005, the then interior minister Nicolas Sarkozy boasted: "Since 1 January 2005, we have expelled nineteen Islamist fundamentalists. The preachers of hate do not have a place on the national territory" (Foley 2013, pp. 305–306)—although a government White Paper later noted that "*only* about ten fundamentalist Imams" had been deported in 2004 and 2005 (italics added) (Secrétariat général de la défense nationale 2006, p. 57). Deportations carried out by the French government have raised much criticism from the United Nations Committee Against Torture, Human Rights Watch, and other organizations that have found that these individuals, often deported for their radical Islamist and anti-Western ideas rather than incitement to violence, were being placed in situations where torture was a real threat (Foley 2013, p. 306).

Counterterrorism policies have been comparatively less debated in France than in the United States or the United Kingdom, because of the overall more limited policy debate in the country and because the country has not been hit by an attack of the size of 9/11 or 7/7—attacks that led to comprehensive reviews of counterterrorism strategies in Washington and London. However, the recent shootings carried out by Mohammed Merah in the southwest of France shed some light, in France and elsewhere, on the characteristics of the French system, including its pervasive surveillance methods. As Gary Schmitt from the American Enterprise Institute noted, "France has a very aggressive system, and before 9/11 they were centralizing the intelligence process and fixing laws to let them grab people very early to disrupt anything in advance.... They do a lot of things, including telephone intercepts, that make the Patriot Act look namby-pamby" (Erlanger 2012). However, it is apparent that although American efforts have overshadowed those of other countries, questionable counterterrorism laws and policies exist in many places outside the United States. The attacks carried out in and around Paris on January 7–9, 2015, killing 17 in addition to the three perpetrators and injuring 20, caused a profound emotional reaction throughout the country. At the time of writing, it remains to be seen what the political, legal and operational consequences of these events will be in the long term.

COUNTERARGUMENTS

Four main points are frequently raised in response to the arguments that the threat posed by terrorism is in fact limited and that current policies are disproportionate. First, it is often said that the impact of terrorism is not primarily physical but in fact psychological. Therefore, the argument goes, comparing fatality rates related to terrorism with other causes of deaths does not give justice to the pervasive effects terrorism can have beyond the mere injuries and fatalities it causes. This argument claims that the psychological effects of terrorism stem from the fact that innocent civilians are often targeted, and that although terrorists may not have been successful, they still intend to cause harm. For instance, in response to an essay by Conor Friedersdorf, Jeffrey Goldberg wrote: "The fear of terrorism isn't motivated solely by what terrorists have done, but what terrorists hope to do. Although it's true that bathtub accidents account for a too-large number of deaths, it isn't true that bathtubs are engaged in a conspiracy with other bathtubs to murder ever-larger numbers of Americans" (Goldberg 2013). It is true that terrorist attacks and terrorism in general can cause widespread psychological impact, through the indiscriminate targeting of innocent civilians. However, much of the psychological effects of terrorism are in fact often propagated and amplified by media reports and political declarations, which could indeed be altered to address this element of fear terrorists are so keen to propagate in the first place. In addition, at the individual level, a death from cancer, a car accident, or even a bathtub incident can be as equally devastating as a death from a terrorist attack—and it often strikes *innocent civilians* whose families rarely get the levels of societal emotional support and compassion they might otherwise receive in the case of a terrorist attack.

A second counterargument often raised is that while it is true that terrorism is a risk with low probability, it is also one with potentially high impact. In other words, regardless of how amateurish or incompetent terrorists may be, it only takes one successful attack to cause *terror*—as aforementioned examples demonstrate. Regarding the minuscule likelihood of an American dying from a terrorist attack (less than it would be from slipping in the shower, for example), Ambassador Benjamin Friedman, the then senior fellow at Brookings Institution and later ambassador-at-large and coordinator for counterterrorism at the U.S. State Department (2009–2012), noted that "much the same could have been said of the chance of dying in a nuclear attack at the height of the Cold War. Terrorism is not an existential threat in the sense that 150 million Americans could be wiped out in an afternoon. But the possibility of a devastating attack or series of attacks – perhaps including WMD – is real" (Friedman 2008, p. 2). However, focusing on the extremely unlikely worst-case scenarios can come at the expense of more latent, discreet trends that are as damaging or worse. In addition, even the luckiest and most damaging attack in history—September 11, 2001—has not caused as much damage as many conflicts or diseases create on a weekly basis across the world. Ultimately, the critique in this book of current counterterrorism policies, as related to the low likelihood of terrorism in Western countries, does not aim to highlight that the policy response is pointless, but disproportionate. As we will explore later, governments would do well to put less emphasis on a heavy-handed, knee-jerk, and only tactical response to terrorism and more on the political, institutional, and socioeconomic factors often leading to terrorism. Moreover, redirecting resources to some of the challenges that have been overlooked since 9/11, including organized crime and inter- and intrastate conflicts, could also prove beneficial.

Third, critics often claim that terrorism has caused such limited damage precisely because of law enforcement efforts carried out in the aftermath of 9/11. It is true that several plots have been disrupted. Nevertheless, these law enforcement successes were often the result of traditional police work instead of massive data gathering and which could have been conducted prior to the dramatic increase in counterterrorism capabilities. In addition, long-term trends show comparable numbers of terrorist attacks and terrorism-related fatalities before 9/11, when the U.S. counterterrorism efforts were much smaller, and after. As we will explore in the next chapter of this book, too much spending and excessively extensive counterterrorism efforts can have several unintended but foreseeable negative consequences that outweigh the benefits of the increased investment.

Finally, law enforcement officers, intelligence analysts, and policy makers often claim that commentators would not consider that the terrorist threat has been exaggerated if they had access to the same kind of information they (in government with high-security clearance) have. As Louise Arbour noted in a public lecture at Simon Fraser University in September 2014, we have allowed such high levels of secrecy in the aftermath of 9/11 that it is extremely difficult to have access to relevant information (which, very often, does not need to be classified) and thus any rational discussion on counterterrorism policies. While there is much NGO-led momentum for policy reform in the field of international drug policy, civil society is comparably having a much smaller impact in the counterterrorism debate, simply because the quantitative and qualitative evidence is much harder to gather (Arbour 2014). David Anderson QC, in his role as the UK government's independent reviewer of terrorism legislation, does have access to classified documents. In his 2011 annual report, he noted that "during the 21st century, terrorism has been an insignificant cause of mortality in the United Kingdom," comparing the "annualized average of five deaths caused in England and Wales over this period" with "29 people drowned in the bathtub and five killed by stings from hornets, wasps and bees" (Anderson 2012, p. 27).

WHY THE HYPE?

In spite of the evidence demonstrating the marginal nature of terrorism, especially in North America and Western Europe, governments and observers have often exaggerated the threat and overreacted to it. Why? A number of factors can help understand this apparent contradiction. To preface, it is worth noting that the post-9/11 era was not the first instance of overreaction to terrorism. For example, after anarchist attacks in the beginning of the twentieth century, President Theodore Roosevelt wanted to send all anarchists back to their countries of origin, even though many had not committed crimes and were opposed to the use of terror as a means of achieving their ends. The proposal was not implemented, but President Wilson authorized rounding up of all anarchists in 1919, including the many who had committed no crimes, in order to deport them to the Soviet Union (Rapoport 2002).

As John Mueller pointed out, many of the predictions made on the likelihood of terrorist attacks in the years after 9/11 turned out to be wrong. Philip Tetlock has shown that people, including experts, are in general bad at predicting the future. In one of his most famous studies, he gathered more than 80,000 predictions from experts about specific geopolitical scenarios, broken down into three probabilities—status quo, more, or less (e.g., of political freedom and economic growth). He concluded that "the average expert was found to be only slightly more accurate than a dart-throwing chimpanzee" and could have done better by assigning equal probabilities to each of the three potential outcomes (Tetlock 2006). As Daniel Kahneman argues, it is not necessarily the experts' fault: "errors of prediction are inevitable because the world is unpredictable." However, the people who acquire more knowledge often develop "an enhanced illusion of their skill" and become "unrealistically overconfident" (Kahneman 2012, pp. 218–221). This offers some interesting clues as to why terrorism predictions, just like many other predictions, have proved erroneous. However, it does not explain why politicians and commentators have almost systematically overestimated the threat and exaggerated its likelihood.

Once again, the field of behavioral economics and psychology of decision-making are helpful in this regard. Research has shown that terrorism induces an "availability cascade," defined as "a self-reinforcing process of collective belief formation by which an expressed perception triggers a chain reaction that gives the perception of increasing plausibility through its rising availability in public discourse" (Kuran and Sunstein 1999). Images of terrorist attacks, including blood, death, shock, and damage, can have an extremely powerful effect, especially as they are redistributed and amplified by the media and in other conversations. In other words, they become "highly accessible," and the "emotional arousal" they induce is "associative, automatic and uncontrolled" and produce an "impulse for protective action" (Kahneman 2012, p. 323). In his seminal work *Thinking Fast and Slow*, Kahneman distinguishes between two thinking systems. System 1 is *intuition*—it is fast, emotional, automatic, and often entrenched; while system 2 is *reasoning*—it is much slower, based on conscious judgment, and more volatile. He notes that the fear of terrorism is associated with system 1: "System 2 may 'know' that the probability is low, but this knowledge does not eliminate the self-generated discomfort and the wish to avoid it" (Kahneman 2012, pp. 13, 323). Basic human reactions and feelings may therefore partly explain our tendency to overreact to acts of terrorism and overestimate their likelihood. It is especially telling that the further we are from 9/11 and other major terrorist developments, the more governments and the public hold relatively more moderate and measured views on terrorism. Humans tend to be more captivated by what is happening at the moment, especially spectacular events, rather than by more complex, longer trends. The human brain is also conditioned to focus on bad news. This attracts attention faster than happy words and news (Kahneman 2012, pp. 300–309). Emotional reactions to 9/11 and other terrorist attacks matter. As George W. Bush once noted: "I don't spend a lot of time taking polls around the world to tell me what I think is the right way to act. I just got to know how I feel" (CNN 2002). In political analysis, emotions are often overlooked at the expense of evidence or political calculations, but should be included as part of a comprehensive analysis assessing motivations and implications of policy: "Rational or not, fear is painful and debilitating, and policy makers must endeavor to protect the public from fear, not only from real dangers" (Kahneman 2012, p. 144).

The threat inflation around terrorism is related to a broader trend, which wrongly claims that the world is becoming more dangerous. In the 2000s, there was an annual average of 55,000 deaths caused by war, down from 100,000 per year in the 1990s, and 180,000 during Cold War years

(Goldstein 2011). In 2010, there were 30 armed conflicts in 25 countries, down from 53 armed conflicts in 39 countries in 1992 (Zenko and Cohen 2012). All major categories of crime have fallen in the past few years in the United States, and deaths from armed violence worldwide have decreased significantly, from 740,000 in 2008 to 526,000 in 2011 (Jaffe 2012; Zenko 2012b). In other words, the world has never been safer. However, declarations by many security officials, experts, and politicians seem to suggest quite the opposite. In 2012, Republican presidential candidate Mitt Romney declared: "The world is dangerous, destructive, chaotic"; the then U.S. Defense Secretary Leon Panetta warned that the world was "more unpredictable, more volatile and yes, more dangerous," while Martin Dempsey, chairman of the joint chief of staff, noted that "the number and kinds of threats we face have increased significantly" (Jaffe 2012; Zenko 2012b). More recently, Republican Senator Lindsey Graham, in a statement that could very well be read as tongue in cheek but in fact wasn't, declared: "the world is literally about to blow up" (Huffington Post 2014). Reading threat assessments from the United States—including the 2014 Worldwide Threat Assessment of the U.S. Intelligence Community—and other countries gives little sense that conflict and violence have been decreasing worldwide.

It is of course the primary task of intelligence analysts and security agencies to focus on threats and worst-case scenarios and other bad things that might happen to their country. However, it is extremely rare to see assessments, including from politicians whose jobs are different from intelligence and security officials, putting threats into perspective, and examining longer-term developments that may usefully place these into a broader context. As Peter Feaver, a former senior official at the National Security Council under President George W. Bush, noted: "The political penalty for being wrong about the threat or underestimating it is much more severe than the penalty for overstating it" (Jaffe 2012). Politicians have a dread of appearing weak, which they perceive as very unpopular with the electorate, preferring to be seen as tough and courageous. In addition, politicians who downplay the threat days before a terrorist attack is actually carried out are likely to be regarded as disconnected with reality, complacent, and naive. On June 17, 2005, British MP Dominic Grieve, the then shadow attorney general, accused the government of deliberately overstating the threat posed by terrorism, noting in a written statement to Home Secretary Charles Clarke that the stable number of control orders issued by the government 3 months after new laws came into force appeared "to confirm our suspicion that the anti-terror bill before the general election was a cynical election ploy rather than a genuine attempt to protect British people" (FT 2005). Only 3 weeks later, on July 7, terrorist attacks were carried out in London, causing 52 fatalities and over 700 injuries.

Saying that the threat posed by terrorism is low, marginal, or decreasing is rarely seen as a vote winner or reputational boost. Research has found that there is a "general relationship between fear of external attacks and support for standing leaders"—the greater the fear, the greater the support for standing leaders (Willer 2004, p. 2). In the few days after 9/11, reported approval of President George W. Bush's performance skyrocketed, from 51% on September 10, 2001, to 86% on September 15, according to Gallup. It is telling that even the approval of his handling of the economy went up dramatically in only a few days, again based on Gallup Polls, from 54% on July 11, 2001, to 72% on October 5, 2001 (Willer 2004, p. 2). In sum, the 9/11 tragedy and the sense of fear it generated led to a substantial increase in popular support for the U.S. president. For the same reason, maintained levels of fear tend to boost support for incumbent leaders.

In addition to political considerations, there are numerous other interests that help perpetuate a system where the terrorist threat is exaggerated: in government bureaucracies often fighting for political attention and larger budgets, the mere label *terrorism* has proved very helpful, especially immediately after 9/11. Similarly, research institutes, security companies, and other organizations benefited greatly from increased counterterrorism budgets. Again, it was clearly not in their interests either to claim that the threat posed by terrorism was in fact marginal and therefore did not warrant such overwhelming policy and budgetary efforts. As David Anderson QC points out, "the threat of terrorism is, no doubt, sometimes exaggerated for political or commercial purposes. It is certainly a powerful rallying-cry for the flourishing security and surveillance industries" (Anderson 2012, p. 27). Counterterrorism is not the only field in which stakeholders would exaggerate a claim for their own purposes, whether it is raising awareness to their cause, selling products, or simply gaining attention for more power and influence—this happens regularly in our daily lives. In an effort to convince an initially reluctant American public of the need to intervene militarily in Kosovo in 1999, the then U.S. Defense Secretary William Cohen claimed that 100,000 ethnic-Albanian men "may have been murdered," and David Sheffer, U.S. Ambassador-at-Large for war crime issues, gave an even higher estimate of 225,000. The final total death toll of the civil conflict proved smaller: between 2,000 and 3,000 according to the International Criminal Tribunal for the former Yugoslavia (Chandler 2006, p. 73).

Strategically, the war on terror also filled an ideological gap in the United States, after a period of transition following the end of the Cold War. In a way, this unambiguous competition between good (the West) and evil (Al Qaeda and its sympathizers) replaced the conflict between the Western and Soviet blocs after World War II. As George W. Bush and John McCain claimed in a 2004 joint statement on the war in Iraq: "It's a fight between a just regard for human dignity and a malevolent force that defiles an honorable religion by disputing God's love for each and every soul on Earth. It's a fight between right and wrong, good and evil. It's no more ambiguous than that" (*New York Times* 2004). Therefore, in the first few years after 9/11, not only political, electoral, and financial factors, but also an ideological and moral mission, arguably began to shape the fight against terrorism, entrenching it even more deeply into policy.

Ultimately, counterterrorism policies and narratives have focused on the adage "better safe than sorry," also known as the precautionary principle (Durodié 2004). Governments often consider they should be doing everything in their power to prevent the next attack, regardless of how unlikely it may be. The attack of 9/11 had an incredibly powerful effect on the U.S. government in particular. Because the United States had been attacked once, there was an all-pervasive fear that it could very well happen again. The policy focus was therefore placed on worst-case scenarios. At first sight, the "better safe than sorry" argument seems like common sense. However, the next section of this book will explore the range of unintended, yet foreseeable negative consequences this approach has had. One could argue that it has been effective, given that the number of terrorist attacks remains low, but effectiveness should not be assumed so quickly and should be measured against the costs and impacts of policy.

REFERENCES

Abrahms, M. 2006. Why terrorism does not work. *International Security* 21(2): 42–78.

Abrahms, M. and Lula. K. 2012. Why terrorists overestimate the odds of victory. *Perspectives on Terrorism* 6(4–5): 46–62.

Anderson, D. 2012. The terrorism acts in 2011. Report of the Independent Reviewer on the Operation of the Terrorism Act 2000 and Part 1 of the Terrorism Act 2006, June 2012.

Arbour, L. 2014. From Syria to Crimea: Is global governance at a loss? Event organized by the School of International Studies, Simon Fraser University, Vancouver, September 25, 2014.

Bilmes, L.J. and Stiglitz, J.E. 2008. The Three Trillion Dollar War: The True Cost of the Iraq Conflict. New York: W.W. Norton.
Brown University, 2011. Estimated costs of post-9/11 wars: 225,000 lives, up to $4 trillion. "Costs of War" Project, Press Release, June 29, 2011.
Camilleri, R. 2012. Impact of counter-terrorism on communities: France Background Report. Institute for Strategic Dialogue and Open Society Foundations, September 2012.
Center for American Progress. 2006. Terrorism survey: Frequency questionnaire, March 8–April 21, 2006.
Chandler, D. 2006. *From Kosovo to Kabul and Beyond: Human Rights and International Intervention* (2nd Edition). London: London Pluto Press.
Chatham House. 2013. Counter-terrorism: The right response? Members Event. Speakers: Professor John Mueller and Sir David Omand; Chair: Sophie Long, September 6, 2013.
Choudhury, T. 2012. Impact of counter-terrorism on communities: UK Background Report. Institute for Strategic Dialogue and Open Society Foundations, September 2012.
CNN. 2002. Bush Talks to Press. *CNN Transcripts*, November 7, 2002.
CNN. 2009. Restaurant Bomber Jailed for Botched Plot, January 30, 2009.
Crenshaw, M. 1980. The logic of terrorism: Terrorist behavior as a product of strategic choice. In Reich, W. (ed.), *Origins of Terrorism: Psychologies, Ideologies, Theologies, States of Mind.* Washington, DC: Woodrow Wilson.
Cronin, A.K. 2011. *How Terrorism Ends: Understanding the Decline and Demise of Terrorist Campaigns.* Princeton, NJ: Princeton University Press.
DOJ. 2003. Al Qaeda associates charged in attack on *USS Cole*, attempted attack on another U.S. Naval Vessel, May 15, 2003.
Durodié, B. 2004. The precautionary principle assumes that prevention is better than cure. *Spiked*, March 16, 2004.
Edwards, J. and Gomis, B. 2011. Islamic Terrorism in the UK Since 9/11: Reassessing the "Soft" Response. Programme Paper. Chatham House, June 2011.
Erlanger, S. 2012. Fighting terrorism, French-style. *New York Times*, March 30, 2012.
Europol. 2013. TE-SAT 2013: EU Terrorism Situation and Trend Report, April 25, 2013.
Foley, F. 2013. *Countering Terrorism in Britain and France: Institutions, Norms and the Shadow of the Past*. Cambridge: Cambridge University Press.
Friedman, D. 2008. Strategic counterterrorism. *Policy Paper*. Number 7, Brookings Institution, October 2008.
FT. 2005. Threat of terrorism has been overstated, says MP, June 17, 2005.
Geneva Declaration. 2011. Global Burden of Armed Violence 2011.
Goldberg, J. 2013. What Conor Friedersdorf misunderstands about terrorism. Bloomberg, June 12, 2013.
Goldstein, J.S. 2011. Think again: War. *Foreign Policy*, August 15, 2011.
GTD. 2014. Global terrorism database. *START*. University of Maryland, College Park, MD. Accessed on February 27, 2014.

Guardian. 2006. Britain now No. 1 al-Qaida target—Anti-terror chiefs, October 19, 2006.
Guardian. 2011. Affidavit of special agent Gary S. Cacace, September 29, 2011.
HMG. 2010. Pursue, prevent, protect, prepare. HM government annual report, March 2010.
Hoffman, B. Remember Al Qaeda? They're baaack. *Los Angeles Times*, February 20, 2007.
House of Commons. 2010. Preventing violent extremism. Sixth report of session 2009–2010. House of Commons Communities and Local Government Committee, March 16, 2010.
Huffington Post. 2014. Lindsey Graham: The "World Is Literally about to Blow Up," January 29, 2014.
Institute for Economics and Peace. 2014. Global Terrorism Index 2014.
ISC. 2008. Annual report 2006–2007, January 2008.
Jackson, R. 10 Things More Likely to Kill You Than Terrorism. *Richard Jackson Terrorism Blog*, May 25, 2011.
Jaffe, G. 2012. The world is safer. But no one in Washington can talk about it. *Washington Post. WP Opinions*, November 2, 2012.
Jenkins, B.M. 1975. Will terrorists go nuclear? RAND corporation, November 1975.
Jenkins, B.M. 2006. The new age of terrorism, Chapter 8. In *The McGraw-Hill Homeland Security Handbook*. McGraw-Hill, pp. 177–130.
Jones, S. and Libicki, M. 2008. *How Terrorist Groups End: Lessons for Countering Al-Qaeda*. Santa Monica, CA: RAND.
Kahneman, D. 2012. *Thinking, Fast and Slow*. London: Penguin Books.
Kristof, N. 2012. Do we have the courage to stop this? *New York Times*, December 15, 2012.
Kuran, T. and Sunstein, C.R. 1999. Availability cascades and risk regulation. *Stanford Law Review* 51(4), 683–768.
LaFree, G. 2010. The global terrorism database: Accomplishments and challenges. *Perspectives on Terrorism* 4(1), 24–46.
LaFree, G. 2013. Public policy and (Myths About) terrorism. The International Relations and Security Network—ISN, May 22, 2013.
Laqueur, W. 1976. The futility of terrorism—The bombs seldom accomplish anything. *Harper's Magazine*, March 1976.
Moeckli, D. 2008. *Human Rights and Non-Discrimination in the "War on Terror."* Oxford: Oxford University Press.
Mueller, J. and Stewart, M. 2011a. *Terror, Security and Money: Balancing the Risks, Benefits, and Costs of Homeland Security*. New York: Oxford University Press. October 7, 2011.
Mueller, J. and Stewart, M. 2011b. Does the United States spend too much on homeland security? *Slate*, September 7, 2011.
National Counter Terrorism Center (NCTC). 2012. 2011 Annual report on terrorism, June 2012.

New York Times. 2004. The Struggle for Iraq: The President; Bush and McCain, Together, Call Iraq War a Conflict Between Good and Evil, June 19, 2004.

Oates, S., Kaid, L.L., and Berry, M. 2010. *Terrorism, Election, and Democracy: Political Campaigns in the United States, Great Britain, and Russia*. New York: Palgrave MacMillan.

Radzinski, J. 2011. Timeline Project #2: World Trade Center attack, February 26, 2011.

Rapoport, D. 2002. Four waves or rebel terror and September 11. *Anthropoetics* 8 (Spring/Summer). Accessed at: (http://www.anthropoetics.ucla.edu/ap0801/terror.htm)

Release and LSE. 2013. The numbers in black and white: Ethnic disparities in the policing and prosecution of drug offences in England and Wales. Release and The Mannheim Centre for Criminology at LSE, August 2013.

Rothkopf, D. 2003. Terrorist logic: Disrupt the 2004 election. *Washington Post*, November 23, 2003.

Schneier, B. 2007. Portrait of the modern terrorist as an idiot. *Wired*, June 14, 2007.

Schneier, B. 2011. Terrorism in the U.S. Since 9/11. *Schneier on Security*, August 26, 2011.

Secrétariat général de la défense nationale (SGDN). 2006. La France face au terrorisme—Livre Blanc du Gouvernement sur la sécurité intérieure face au terrorisme. *Livre Blanc*, Octobre 2006.

Sky, J. 2011. Useful idiots. *Gunpowder & Lead*, September 30, 2011.

START. 2011. Background Report: 9/11, Ten Years Later, September 2011.

Tetlock, P.E. *Expert Political Judgment: How Good Is It? How Can We Know?* Princeton, NJ: Princeton University Press.

UNODC. 2013. UNODC homicide statistics.

U.S. State Department. 2013. Country reports on terrorism 2012. May 30, 2013.

Washington Post. 2010. A hidden world, growing beyond control. *Part of Top Secret America: A Washington Post Investigation*, July 19, 2010.

WHO. 2013. The top 10 causes of death. Fact sheet No. 310. Updated July 2013.

Willer, R. 2004. The effects of government-issued terror warnings on presidential approval ratings. *Current Research Social Psychology* 10(1), 1–12.

World Bank. 2013. Population, total: Iraq. *Data*. Accessed on December 22, 2014.

Zenko, M. 2012a. Americans are as likely to be killed by their own furniture as by terrorism. *The Atlantic*, June 6, 2012.

Zenko, M. 2012b. America is a safe place. *Foreign Policy*, February 2012.

Zenko, M. and Cohen, MA. 2012. Clear and present safety: The United States is more secure than Washington thinks. *Foreign Affairs*, March/April 2012.

Section II

Dangers of Overreaction

Officials and experts often make the argument that *the absence of terrorist attacks demonstrates the success of existing policies*. This argument is insufficient: it fails to reflect the nuances and degrees of policy effectiveness, disregards the other internal and external factors shaping individuals' decisions not to carry out terrorist attacks, and—as we will explore in this section—ignores the negative *impact* counterterrorism policies may have when overestimating and overreacting to a problem, a crucial element that needs to be taken into consideration when assessing the *success* or *effectiveness* of a policy.

5

Negative Consequences of Overreaction

> We have to deal with this new type of threat in a way we haven't yet defined.... With a low-probability, high-impact event like this... If there's a one percent chance that Pakistani scientists are helping al Qaeda build or develop a nuclear weapon, we have to treat it as a certainty in terms of our response.
>
> **Vice President Dick Cheney**
> *November 2001 (Suskind 2007)*

As Louise Arbour points out, the term "*unintended* consequences" is misleading. It seeks to evade human responsibility and accountability—"sorry, but it wasn't our intention"—instead of focusing on the foreseeability of these consequences and the actual, negative impacts of the policies put in place (Arbour 2014). The following negative consequences will be explored in this chapter: (1) counterterrorism policies have created opportunity costs; (2) policies have tried to simplify problems that are in fact much more complex; (3) counterterrorism policies have created a disproportionate level of fear across society; (4) counterterrorism has at times been counterproductive, both leading to copycat attacks in the short term and fostering further alienation and discontent in the long term; (5) terrorism has often been used by policy officials as a political veil or tool for other purposes; (6) counterterrorism policies have infringed on privacy—as we will explore through a case study of the intelligence programs recently exposed by former National Security Agency (NSA) contractor Edward Snowden.

COUNTERTERRORISM POLICIES HAVE CREATED OPPORTUNITY COSTS

An *opportunity cost* can be defined as the "the loss of potential gain from other alternatives when one alternative is chosen" (*New Oxford American Dictionary*). In other words, it is the value of the next alternative or alternatives, or in more simple terms, "what you have to give up to get something" (Roberts 2007). When it comes to policy, opportunity costs represent the value of what could have been done had current policies not been pursued. It is important to see opportunity costs through the related concept of *trade-offs*. In microeconomics, trade-offs involve losing something in return for gaining something else. With regard to counterterrorism policy, the benefits of increased security and a diminished terrorist threat—if that is the case—must be measured against the opportunity costs implied in choosing a specific alternative at the expense of another.

Much time, energy, and money have been spent on terrorism after 9/11, especially in the United States—and all of that time, energy, and money were therefore not available to tackle other threats, risks, and broader socioeconomic strategic developments. Some tangible opportunity costs have been identified since 9/11—with more spending in one area (counterterrorism) directly leading to less spending in another. David Gold, for instance, has noted a number of them. These include more spending on security and insurance at the expense of other activities likely to generate more wealth; increased security at airports and seaports implies increased costs for travel and shipping; tightened immigration rules mean fewer skilled workers moving across borders, with negative economic repercussions (Gold cites a 2004 *Financial Times* (FT) figure attributing a 32% decline in foreign applications to American universities to a more strenuous visa application process following 9/11); and more restrictive rules regarding the transport of pathogens have hampered biomedical research. Last but not least, Gold also notes that rises in security spending have rarely been financed through taxes and have thus meant increased budget deficits, a rise in interest rates, and revenue shortfalls among U.S. states, with a broader impact on the economy (Gold 2005, pp. 3–6).

More generally, and in order to keep a sense of perspective, it is useful to explore where and how some of the money used for counterterrorism purposes could have been spent elsewhere. John Mueller and Mark G. Stewart have argued that taking a small portion of the approximately $10 billion spent every year on airline security and investing on measures with more reliable life-saving impact would be much more sensible—these include "seat belts, bicycle helmets, tandem mass spectrometry screening programs, airbags, smoke alarms, and tornado shelters" (Mueller and Stewart 2011). According to another study, an investment of $2 billion to expand immunization coverage and community-based nutrition programs could save over 1.5 million lives (Lomborg 2004, as cited in Mueller and Stewart 2011).

The policy focus on terrorism following 9/11, especially in the United States, has also meant that less attention has been devoted to other strategic challenges as a result. The graph in Figure 5.1 shows the number of books that include the words *terrorism, global warming, China, organized crime, cyber,* or *Russia* in their titles. While a large majority of these books were not indeed written by governments, they reflect an overall disproportionate societal focus on terrorism over other important issues the world has faced since 2001.

The *9/11 Decade*—as it is often referred to—saw the rise of China as an economic and strategic rival to the United States, the emergence of global warming and climate change as urgent environmental concerns with potential and actual devastating consequences across the world, Russia's assertive foreign policy and territorial claims that have led to crises in Georgia and Ukraine along other points of tension, the rise of cyber security to the top of security agendas as governments and private companies have proved ill-prepared to face this rapidly evolving challenge, and massive popular protests that have led to significant changes and turmoil in North Africa and the Middle East (often referred to as the *Arab Spring*), while organized crime has continued to cause major economic, social, and institutional damages in many parts of the world, to

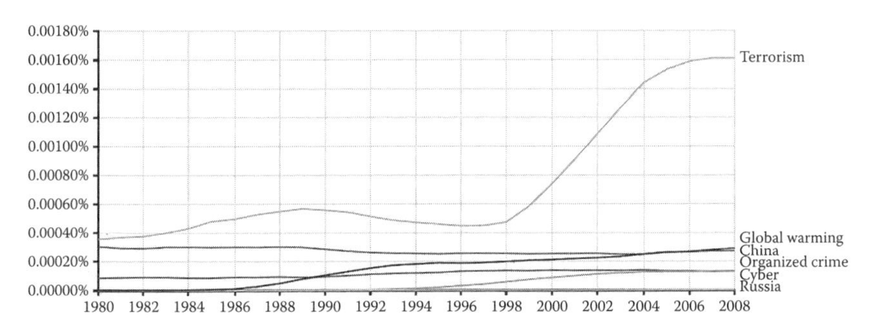

Figure 5.1 Percentage of books published with the words *terrorism, global warming, China, organized crime, cyber,* or *Russia* in their titles between 1980 and 2008. (From Google Ngram Viewer, accessed on April 10, 2014.)

name just a few pressing challenges. Perhaps even more strikingly, 7 years after 9/11, the United States and much of the Western world faced the worst economic crisis since the 1930s. These geopolitical developments have proved to be much more significant than terrorism in terms of physical and/or strategic impact.

China

Before the 2008 financial crisis, Goldman Sachs estimated that China would catch up with the United States as the world's largest economy by 2025 and would double the American economy by 2050 (Jacques 2010). However, the *Economist* readjusted their own predictions and predicted in April 2014 that China would become the world's largest economy by the end of 2014, using the GDP indicator at purchasing-power parity, which takes into account the relative value of currencies (*Economist* 2014a) (Figure 5.2).

This of course would not be the first time that China has become the world's dominant economic power. The country already held the position up until the 1890s, when the United States took the lead. However, as Martin Jacques points out, "Never before in modern history has the

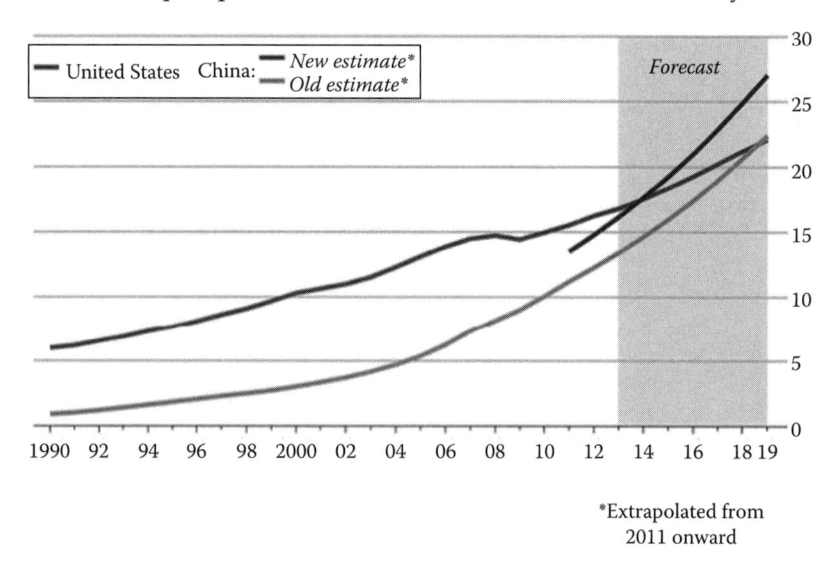

Figure 5.2 The evolution of U.S. and Chinese GDP at purchasing-power parity, (in trillions of U.S. dollars). (From the *Economist*, Crowning the dragon, Daily Chart, April 30, 2014.)

biggest economy in the world been that of a developing country rather than a developed country," which in itself represents a new challenge for the world (Jacques 2010). The economic rise of China has had some tremendously positive effects for the Chinese population, lifting over half a billion people out of poverty (World Bank 2014). It has also meant an increased strategic presence in international affairs. The mere fact that China holds more than $1.3 trillion of the U.S. debt demonstrates the significance of its role (Bloomberg 2014). In addition, while China has remained largely unwilling to get involved in recent international crises such as Syria, Libya, or Ukraine, it is heavily involved through economic, energy, and infrastructure projects in parts of Africa, has acted upon its territorial claims in the South China Sea, has participated in multilateral missions including against piracy in the Gulf of Aden, has sent combat troops to a peacekeeping mission for the first time ever (2013 in Mali), and is actively engaged in international discussions on Internet governance, cyber crime, and cyber security more broadly. The country's military budget remains far smaller than the United States: China spent $112 billion on its military in 2013, compared to the United States' $600 billion.* However, China is spending more on defense than the United Kingdom and France combined (respectively $57 billion and $52.7 billion in 2013)—these two countries are the largest military partners of the United States, two key contributors in NATO, and have played, solely or together, an instrumental role in recent conflicts including Afghanistan, Iraq, Libya, Mali, and the Central African Republic (*BBC News* 2014a). Moreover, the trends are in China's favor. While Europe is spending less on defense—over half of European countries are decreasing their budget, Asia is spending more: a 23% increase since 2010 (*BBC News* 2014a).

These few facts do not demonstrate that China should automatically be seen as a threat to the United States and the West. However, it is clear that Western countries ought to increase their understanding of China and devote more time building a relationship with it. This was partly the aim of the United States so-called pivot or rebalancing to Asia, after years of military activity in Iraq and Afghanistan (Clinton 2011). The move was certainly delayed by the overwhelming strategic focus on Al Qaeda and the war on terror of the decade following 9/11, and recent developments in Syria and Iraq have distracted from the process as well.

* In 2013, the United States spent more on defense than the next 10 countries combined (i.e., China, Russia, United Kingdom, Japan, France, Saudi Arabia, India, Germany, Italy, and Brazil) (International Institute for Strategic Studies [IISS] 2014).

Climate Change

There is overwhelming evidence that global temperatures are rising. As suggested by the following graph, the global mean temperature has been increasing steadily since the end of the nineteenth century (Figure 5.3).

Similarly, levels of CO_2 worldwide have jumped dramatically since the 1950s (Figure 5.4).

While climate change somehow remains a controversial issue or a *myth* to many, the scientific evidence is there. Crucially, there is now 95% certainty that human activity is the main cause of the current global warming, according to the Intergovernmental Panel on Climate Change (IPCC 2013).

Global warming is having a range of repercussions, including the melting and rupturing of Arctic ice. It has been estimated that, in the near future, transport between London and Tokyo could be reduced by over 4,500 miles or 10 days, and the sailing time between North America and Asia by 40% as a result of further ice melt (NATO PA 2009, 2010). In addition to these shipping opportunities, fishing, tourism, and more

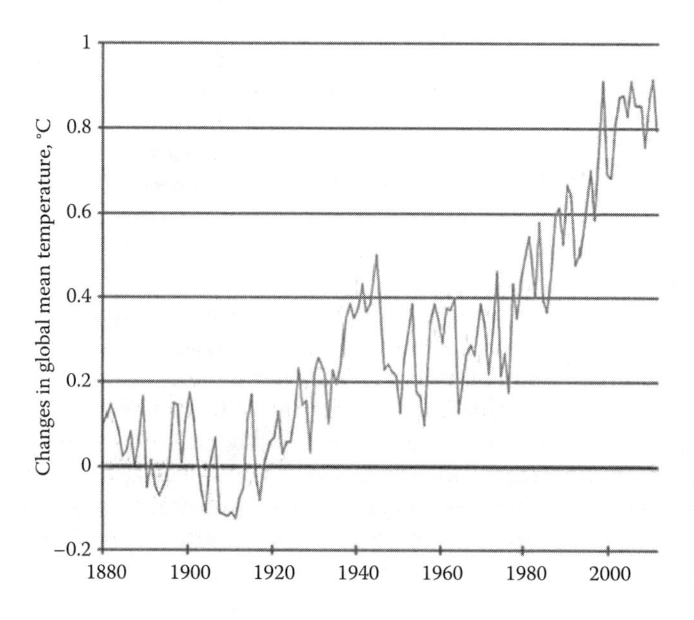

Figure 5.3 Changes in global mean temperature in degrees Centigrade between 1880 and 2010. (From Nordhaus, W., Why the global warming skeptics are wrong, the *New York Review of Books*, March 22, 2012.)

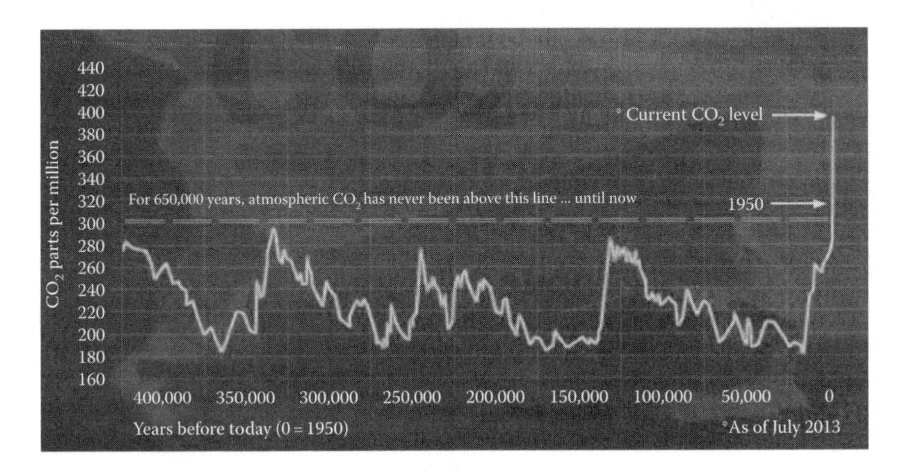

Figure 5.4 Evolution of atmospheric carbon dioxide levels in parts per million. (From NASA, Climate change: How do we know? Accessed on May 8, 2014.)

importantly energy exploration could increase as well. The Arctic may contain up to 25% of the world's oil and gas reserves. Over 90 billion barrels of natural gas liquids are located there, 84% of which could potentially be found in offshore areas (Ebinger and Zambetakis 2009, p. 1216). Although the costs of shipping through Arctic waters are so far proving dissuasive, the Arctic has become a key strategic area in recent years, one which offers both opportunities (e.g., commercial, fishing, and energy) and challenges (e.g., environmental—with a heightened risk of oil spills, for instance, and political, military—especially given the role and aspirations of Russia, which owns a majority of the Arctic coastline, and China in the region).

Global warming is also causing the sea levels to rise elsewhere, with higher risks of floods, increased vulnerability of some territories like the Republic of Maldives, more volatile and fast-changing weather conditions across the world—with more frequent cases of extreme weather, and, crucially, food and water shortages. Many countries have largely ignored the threat posed by climate change, seeking refuge behind short-term economic and political imperatives, and focusing instead on immediate concerns including as part of the war on terror. However, the costs of inaction could be very high. In economic terms alone, the cost of waiting 50 years to begin reducing CO_2 emissions has been estimated at $4.1 trillion (Nordhaus 2012).

Russia

On August 7, 2008, Georgian forces responded to attacks by secessionists in South Ossetia, whom Moscow had been supporting, by striking the region's capital Tskhinvali and attempting to regain control of the territory. Russia responded with a full-scale invasion in South Ossetia and increased its military presence in another secessionist province—Abkhazia, in the northwest of Georgia (RUSI 2008). The 5-day war led to hundreds of deaths and thousands of refugees. It also constituted one of the lowest points in U.S.–Russia relations since the Cold War and was a reminder of the fragility of borders in the former Soviet Union given the assertive presence of Russia.

The Georgia–Russia crisis can be interpreted as being in line with Russia's long-standing strategy to secure its borders, particularly in the Caucasus. However, in August 2008, Moscow circumvented traditional channels of conflict resolution and intervened militarily against another UN member state (King 2008). It is worth noting that Georgia is not immune to criticism, primarily because of its impulsive and ill-prepared moves in response to the initial attacks in South Ossetia. In addition, prior to the conflict, Georgian President Mikheil Saakashvili had already announced his intention to unify Georgia by the end of his presidency (on election night in 2004, Saakashvili declared: "My main goal is to unify Georgia, and that is what the people voted for above all" (*Los Angeles Times* 2004) and later appointed *anti-Russia hawks* in key positions (Mchedlishvili 2013). This considered further circumstances pointed toward Russian responsibility: by late July 2008, the number of Russian troops near the border with Georgia had increased significantly, and the railway in Abkhazia, which later provided armaments for Russian paramilitaries, had just been repaired (UK Parliament 2008; Mchedlishvili 2013).

More than 5 years later, and despite initial progress following the ceasefire and diplomatic efforts by the international community (including via the European Union and the Organization for Security and Co-Operation in Europe), Abkhazia and South Ossetia have not returned to full Georgian control. In a premonitory manner, Charles King perhaps put it best: "Certainly, Russia's actions have distanced the country from Western institutions. But the deeper worry is that the Kremlin and average Russians can now imagine a world in which they do not have to care" (King 2008).

During the Georgia–Russia crisis of August 2008, Western countries and institutions proved unable or unwilling to challenge Russia's territorial ambitions over some of the post-Soviet periphery countries. The crisis in Ukraine confirmed, or even solidified, this balance of power. Brushing aside official warnings from the United States, NATO, the EU, and others, military training missions designed to intimidate Moscow, and economic sanctions against key members of the Russian elite close to Vladimir Putin, Russia behaved throughout the crisis in Ukraine in an even more aggressive fashion than in 2008. The crisis began on November 21, 2013, when President Yanukovych's cabinet decided to abandon an agreement to establish closer cooperation with the EU, seeking stronger ties with Russia instead. Massive popular demonstrations followed, and only gained in strength as the police cracked down on protestors. On February 20, 2014, Kiev saw its worst day of violence since World War II, with at least 88 people killed in 2 days. The deal signed between Yanukovych and opposition leaders the following day did not lead to any peaceful and sustainable outcome. On February 27–28, pro-Russian fighters seized key buildings in Simferopol, the capital of Crimea. In March, Crimea's Parliament voted to join Russia, and a referendum confirmed the move, with 97% of votes in favor. Less than 2 weeks later, Putin signed a bill to absorb Crimea into the Russian federation, amidst international condemnations, leading to a long period of violence and instability (*BBC News* 2014b).

Just like with the gas crises of 2006 and 2009, and the Russia–Georgia crisis of 2008, Putin demonstrated the extent of his hardline nationalist approach and determination to pursue his foreign policy ambitions on his own terms. Put simply, "the current regime is not interested in international cooperation to any greater end than its own demands being met" (Nixey 2014). Through the annexation of Crimea, Russia has once again used military forces against its neighbors to achieve foreign policy objectives at little long-term cost (Giles 2014). All recent crises with Russia have come as a surprise for Western powers, uncertain on how to respond to the Kremlin's latest aggressive move. Putin knows that this type of behavior will lead to only minimal repercussions from the international community. The ceasefire negotiated in the summer of 2008 by President Sarkozy on behalf of the EU (France then held the rotating presidency of the Council of the European Union) helped tame the violence in the short term, but proved to be flawed and had little impact on Russia; only a few months later, the EU resumed cooperation talks with Russia; and in 2009, the United States announced a *reset* of relations with Russia with a resumption of military contacts (Giles 2014).

Russia became one of NATO's closest allies on countering terrorism following 9/11. Through the NATO–Russia Council Action Plan on Terrorism, cooperation was established. Official announcements have highlighted shared willingness to "improve their capabilities to deter and prevent terrorist attacks by exchanging information, supporting nonproliferation efforts and developing enhanced cooperation on armaments and technology" (NATO 2011). While several other factors have come into play, it is fair to argue that the war on terror has overshadowed relations with Russia and led the West to ignore components of Russia's hardline nationalism, in the name of counterterrorism cooperation. By disproportionately focusing on terrorism, the United States and others have arguably not paid enough attention to the threat posed by Russia to peace and stability in Eastern Europe and international affairs. In a move symptomatic of this tunnel-vision approach, amidst high tensions in Crimea in April 2014, the former UK Prime Minister Tony Blair called on Western leaders to put aside their differences with Russia in order to focus on the threat of Islamic extremism (*BBC News* 2014c).

Cyber Security

Just like *terrorism*, *cyber security* or *all this cyber stuff*, as a senior U.S. Department of Defense (DOD) official once described it (Singer and Friedman 2013, p. 10), is a very broad term, which has been defined and used in many different ways. A useful definition of *cyber space* was put forward by the U.S. DOD in 2008: "The global domain within the information environment consisting of the interdependent network of information technology infrastructures, including the internet, telecommunications networks, computer systems, and embedded processors and controllers" (Deputy Secretary of Defense Memorandum 2008). Cyber security and related terms such as cyber crime, cyber war, cyber warfare, and information security continue to be widely misunderstood. They have proved to be difficult concepts to grasp, while technology developments have enabled both problems and opportunities to spread extremely quickly over the past decade. This all occurred amidst the war on terror, which has largely overshadowed and distorted developments in cyber security.

The public Internet is approximately 20 years old, but since its birth, more than a third of the planet (almost 2.8 billion people) has been connected. It is also estimated that by 2020, the number of users worldwide will double to approximately 5 billion (Clemente 2013a). The first e-mail was sent in 1971, and by 2013, roughly 40 trillion e-mails were sent annually (although many of these, 69.6% in 2013, are spam—ZDNet 2014). The creation of the first website dates back to 1991, and two decades later, there were over 30 trillion individual web pages (Singer and Friedman 2013, p. 2). By the year 2017, it is estimated that 70% of the world's population will have a mobile broadband subscription (UNODC 2013a, p. xvii). There are now more networked devices than people, and by 2020, there is likely to be more than 50 billion *things* connected to the Internet (Clemente 2013a). These staggering numbers give an idea of the scope and scale of the Internet, and the pervasive role it plays in many people's lives. As Ben Hammersley puts it, "The Internet isn't a luxury addition to life; for most people, knowingly or not, it is life… It's where we do business, where we meet, where we fall in love" (Hammersley 2011).

Given their omnipresence, the Internet and related cyber technologies offer tools that can be used for a wide range of different positive purposes, including in business, finance, education, transport, and virtually every other sector in our societies. For instance, the increase in the number of Internet users in the least developed countries from 24 million in 2008 to 60 million in early 2013 presents significant economic, social, and political opportunities (International Telecommunication Union [ITU] 2014).

There is of course another side to the coin. As we pointed out in Chapter 3, terrorists have used the Internet in order to carry out attacks. More importantly, activities such as cyber crime, identity theft, bank fraud, credit card theft, denial of service, industrial espionage, and theft of intellectual property cause damage to our economies. In 2013, McAfee estimated the losses due to cyber crime and cyber espionage at approximately $100 billion per year in the United States and at least $300 billion worldwide (McAfee 2013, p. 7), while a 2009 study had put the latter number closer to $1 trillion. McAfee's chief technology officer Mike Fey in fact later admitted he regretted his company's estimates (Australian Financial Review 2013). Nonetheless, the mere fact that 97% of Fortune 500 companies have reported to having been hacked so far gives a sense of how widespread the problem is (*Washington Post* 2014a). Between October 2008 and April 2009 alone, the Pentagon spent approximately $100 million to recover from and repair damage caused by cyber attacks and network system issues, a figure that could even be higher given that the tracking process of these expenditures was then not as reliable and systematic as it should be (Cornish et al. 2010, p. 15). Recent examples of large-scale cyber attacks—in addition to Stuxnet, already covered in Chapter 3—include the hijacking of up to 85,000 computers to overwhelm 58 websites in Estonia, including that of the country's largest bank (Rid 2013). In 2014, the Heartbleed Bug, "a serious vulnerability in the popular OpenSSL cryptographic software library," used over two-thirds of active websites to encrypt data (The Heartbleed Bug 2014). Security expert Bruce Schneier, known for his work on the political and media inflation of terrorist threats, called it "Catastrophic… On the scale of 1 to 10, this is an 11" (Schneier 2014a). These two incidents, like many others, highlight the existence of risks in the cyber space, and much ignorance and misinformation about them.

As we previously argued, *cyber terrorism* is a very marginal threat: while the Internet is a useful tool for terrorists, cyber attacks lack physical violence and associated bloody images terrorists seek in order to maximize psychological impact. Similarly, as Thomas Rid points out, "cyberwar has never happened in the past, it is not occurring in the present, and it is unlikely that it will disturb the future" (Rid 2013). Instead of representing a new kind of war, cyber attacks are far more likely to be used as a complement to traditional military hostilities. Rid goes even further and notes that cyber attacks may indeed "diminish rather than accentuate political violence" by providing a substitute to warlike aggression (Rid 2013). Current warnings by prominent U.S. government officials of looming *cyber Armageddon* or *cyber Pearl Harbor* do not accurately describe the damage that is being done, for example, the less spectacular yet lingering economic and structural impact of sophisticated espionage, organized cyber crime, and other types of cyber attacks. These activities are often directed at the private sector who—tellingly—tend to refrain from using such hyperbolic language.

Policy makers are gradually catching up with the changes occurring in the cyber space. In 2010, the U.S. Cyber Command (Cybercom) reached full operational capability, while the UK's Strategic Defence and Security Review announced a budget commitment of £650 million over the following 4 years as part of a new National Cyber Security Programme, demonstrating the country's willingness to become a leader in the field (Cornish et al. 2010, pp. 15–16). However, much remains to be done for governments to come to grips with challenges and opportunities in cyber space. As Singer and Friedman have pointed out, in 2012, the U.S. secretary of homeland security, in charge of the country's cyber security, admitted to them: "don't laugh, but I just don't use e-mail at all." "It wasn't a fear of security, but that she just didn't believe e-mail to be useful" (Singer and Friedman 2013, p. 5). This amusing yet worrying anecdote illustrates the frequent disconnect between policy and reality when it comes to cyber space.

Policy developments in this field have arguably been negatively impacted in three main ways over the past decade. First, the focus on terrorism following 9/11 has often meant that it took governments a long time to understand the importance of technological advances in cyber space and the resulting societal implications. As the former Department of Homeland Security (DHS) Director Richard Clarke once noted: "None of the senior leadership of DHS knew anything about cyber. They were all terrified about airplanes blowing up and people in body bags… They were so focused on the physical threats, cyber didn't make the cut" (*San Jose Mercury News* 2007). Second, this resulting lack of knowledge has led to significant fear and threat inflation regarding cyber space, creating what Rid, Singer, and others have labeled *cyber anxiety* (see also Brito and Watkins 2011). And as Daniel Kahneman, among others, has pointed out, the less one knows about a problem, the more emotional their reaction is likely to be: "When you see cases in isolation, you are likely to be guided by an emotional reaction." In other words, "what you see is all there is" (Kahneman 2012). Third, overfocusing on terrorism has also meant that cyber security has too often been seen through the lens of terrorism instead of a complex societal issue in its own right, which includes not only negative elements such as crime but also significant technological and economic opportunities.

Arab Spring

In December 2010, 26-year-old Mohamed Bouazizi set himself on fire in the city of Sidi Bouzid in Tunisia, after authorities stopped him from selling vegetables on the street. Mass demonstrations ensued, and around 300 people died in the subsequent violent repression carried out by the Tunisian government. After 23 years in power, Zine al-Abidine Ben Ali was forced to resign in January 2011. These events are widely considered to have ignited a series of protests across North Africa and the Middle East, often referred to as the *Arab Spring*, the *Arab Awakening*, or *Arab uprisings*. The description of these events as a natural chain of incidents that unfolded almost seamlessly, through terms such as *waves* or indeed *Spring*, tends to mask a more complex reality, but there is no doubt that these popular movements took inspiration from one another.

Less than a month after Ben Ali's fall from power, and following 18 days of demonstrations, Hosni Mubarak was overthrown in February 2011, after 30 years in power in Egypt. In March 2011, the United Kingdom, France, the United States, and other coalition partners launched a military intervention in Libya, which included the establishment of a no-fly zone and aerial attacks against the Gaddafi regime. This followed United Nations Security Council (UNSC) Resolution 1973 authorizing the international community to "take all necessary measures, notwithstanding paragraph 9 of resolution 1970 (2011),* to protect civilians and civilian populated areas under threat of attack in the Libyan Arab Jamahiriya, including Benghazi, while excluding a foreign occupation force of any form on any part of Libyan territory" (UN 2011a). Colonel Muammar Gaddafi indeed vowed to exterminate protesters and hunt them down *house by house* as the regime forces carried out a bloody crackdown across the country (*New York Times* 2011). He was eventually killed by rebel forces on October 20, 2011, a violent ending to a 42-year reign.

In Syria, the protests that started in March 2011 have turned into a violent, protracted conflict between the Bachar Al-Assad regime and its opponents. Protesters initially demonstrated for democratic reforms, but following the violent repression, they demanded the resignation of the Syrian president. As the regime grew more and more violent, the opposition became less cohesive and more radical in its tactics and demands. It now includes a range of different groups and organizations, from the Free Syrian Army to radical jihadists including the al-Nusra front and the Islamic State. In August 2014, the United Nations estimated that over 191,000 people had been killed in the conflict, since the beginning of the protests in March 2011 (UN News Centre 2014). In addition, according to the Office of the United Nations High Commissioner for Refugees (UNHCR), over 3 million have fled to Syria's immediate neighbors and 6.5 million are internally displaced in Syria (as of October 2014—Syrian Refugees 2014). In March 2014, the United Nations Relief and Works Agency estimates that it will take at least 30 years for the economy to return at the level of 2010† (UNRWA 2014).

---

* Paragraph 9 of Resolution 1970 (2011) related to the arms embargo, including the prevention of "the direct or indirect supply, sale or transfer… of arms and related material of all types" (excluding nonlethal military equipment for humanitarian or protective use, protective clothing, or anything else approved in advance by the Committee) (UN 2011b).

† The report talks of an "economic catastrophe that saw the economy lose a total of USD 84.4 billion over the first two years of the conflict, with loss of USD 34.8 billion in GDP and USD 41.2 billion in lost capital stock, while private investment slumped by 81 per cent." It goes on to point out that "even if the conflict ceased now and GDP grew at an average rate of five per cent each year, it is estimated that it would take the Syrian economy 30 years to return to the economic level of 2010" (UNRWA 2014, p. 5).

Popular unrest has not been limited to these four countries, although they have gathered the most attention. Governments in Algeria, Bahrain, Djibouti, Iraq, Israel, Kuwait, Lebanon, Mauritania, Morocco, Oman, Palestine, Saudi Arabia, Somalia, Sudan, and Yemen have all faced demonstrations since December 2010, which led to a variety of outcomes, including governmental changes, reforms, and civil wars.

In particular, these national protests and more importantly the government responses have had significant repercussions across borders. According to the UNHCR, the number of Syrian refugees registered in Lebanon surpassed the 1 million milestone in April 2014, and this small country now has the highest concentration per capita of refugees worldwide: a quarter of Lebanon's population is now made up of Syrian refugees. As of April 2014, 668,000 Syrian refugees had also fled to Jordan, 589,000 to Turkey, 220,000 to Iraq, and 136,000 to Egypt, with untold economic, social, and political consequences (*BBC News* 2014d).

Iraq became the source of great concern in June 2014, when Islamic State rebels took control of a number of cities in the country as well as border crossings with Syria and Jordan. IS and other extremist groups are known to operate across borders and have used the chaos created by the Assad regime crackdown on protesters as an opportunity to create further instability in the region and pursue their own religious and territorial agenda.

The Arab Spring came as a strategic surprise. Very few could have predicted the spread, speed, and scale of the protests that first occurred in December 2010, the violent repression that ensued, and the tremendous human, physical, socioeconomic and political impacts it has had. The fact that Western governments, especially the United States, the United Kingdom, and France, were so focused on terrorist threats at the expense of widespread marginalization and discontent among the populations in undemocratic and repressive regimes certainly did not help in that regard.

Drugs and Organized Crime

In its 2014 World Drug Report, United Nations Office on Drugs and Crime (UNODC) estimated the number of deaths related to illicit drug use at 183,000 in 2013 (UNODC 2014).* More strikingly, many more die as a result

* According to UNODC, between 95,000 and 226,000 deaths related to drug use were reported worldwide in 2012 (UNODC 2014, p. ix).

of drug production, trafficking, and sales. In Mexico alone, between 47,000 and 65,000 people died in organized crime-related killings between 2006 and 2012 according to government data—or almost 10,000 per year, while over 26,000 disappeared over the same period (Beittel 2013). Again, these are official estimates that may vastly underestimate the scale of the violence. Honduras, El Salvador, and Guatemala hold much higher homicide rates than Mexico, with respectively 91.6, 70.2, and 38.5 homicides per 100,000 inhabitants in 2011—compared to 23.7 per 100,000 in Mexico in 2012 (UNODC 2013b). Because organized crime and drug trafficking are so prevalent in Central America, many of these homicides are assumed to be drug related. According to the United Nations Development Program (UNDP), between 2000 and 2010, more than 1 million people died in Latin America and the Caribbean as a result of criminal violence—it is in fact the only region in the whole world where homicide rates did not fall during that decade (UNDP 2013, p. 1).

These figures are striking, and terrorism-related deaths, albeit substantial, pale in comparison: for instance, while almost 10,000 people have died annually in Mexico alone in organized crime-related killings in recent years, fewer than 8,000 people have died in terrorist attacks on average per year over the decade following 9/11 worldwide (START 2011). In 2013, a year that saw a 61% increase in terrorism-related deaths, 40 times more people were still killed in homicides (Institute for Economics and Peace 2014). Additionally, organized crime is far from being merely related to drugs—other activities include extortion, human trafficking, racketeering, armed robbery, money laundering, the illicit tobacco trade, and oil theft—and it is not a phenomenon exclusively affecting Latin America. West Africa, the Gulf, Central Asia, South East Asia, and the Balkans are some of the regions often cited as key smuggling routes for drugs and other substances, as well as human trafficking—causing violence and disruption along the way. In short, while terrorism is a serious challenge with significant impact across the world, the negative effects of organized crime, including via drug trafficking, seem even greater.

There is a widespread tendency to make a distinction between people killed in terrorist attacks and those who die in killings related to organized crime. Those killed in terrorist attacks, the argument goes, are *innocent* people, while the majority of those killed in relation to organized crime are in fact *criminals*—members of gangs, organized crime groups, or drug cartels. Therefore, their deaths, however sad they might be, are deemed less worthy of compassion than those of the victims of terrorism.

The countries plagued with extreme levels of structural violence, such as Honduras and Venezuela, are conflict areas. Innocent bystanders are often victims of criminal violence, and those strong enough to confront some of the most violent organizations are often killed as well. In addition, the lines between membership, affiliation, support, or indirect links with *criminals* are often blurred, and the corruption, collusion, or direct involvement of official authorities in criminal activities further complicate the situation. In other words, in these areas, the Manichean narrative of *us vs. them* once again does not make much sense.

Drugs and organized crime indeed affect many countries around the world beyond the aforementioned fatality figures. In 2005, the UNODC estimated the retail value of the global drug trade at $320 billion—the latest attempt to quantify it (UNODC 2005). In 2009, the UNODC estimated transnational organized crime more broadly to generate as much as $870 billion per year globally (UNODC 2011). Given its very nature, it is extremely difficult to estimate the size of organized crime activities across the world. By definition, the most successful criminals are those who do not get caught, either because they evade law enforcement operations or, even better, because they do not even appear on the radars of police and intelligence forces in the first place. For instance, drug trade estimates are often based on voluntary reports from relevant national agencies around the world, some of whom simply do not have the manpower and capacity to produce the most accurate estimates and often do not have the incentive to do so: a bigger drug problem might either mean receiving more assistance (e.g., Colombia received over $8 billion from the United States through Plan Colombia [Amnesty International 2014]) or facing tougher sanctions (e.g., the prospect of EU membership or foreign aid is dependent on proof of tangible progress regarding organized crime and corruption). In addition, drug seizures or areas of illicit drug crop eradicated, on which many estimates are based, are often misleading: fewer seizures and crops eradicated might mean a decline either in the drug trade itself or in law enforcement activity.

Bearing in mind these methodological caveats, it is clear that organized crime and the illicit drug trade have impacted many different countries in various ways. At a psychological level, crime and violence have a clear restricting effect on people's movements and everyday life. In Latin America, up to 65% of people surveyed told UNDP that they have limited the number of places they go to and stopped going out at night "for fear of becoming the victim of a crime" (UNDP 2013, p. 65). While fear is a very difficult emotion to measure, it is evident that citizens have had to adjust their behavior because of the reality and perceptions of the threat of violence. This has some obvious social and economic consequences, as it creates a challenging environment, including in terms of community building, education, economic opportunities, and overall quality of life.

There is a complex relationship between crime and poverty. Indeed, Latin America, for instance, has enjoyed relatively solid economic growth in recent years (with an annual average of 4.2% between 2000 and 2010—UNDP 2013, p. 7) despite an increase in homicide rates. Reasons for this include the fact that violence has often been localized, not affecting the business districts of economic capitals, and that organized crime groups also reinvest their criminal proceeds into legitimate businesses through money laundering. However, organized crime often puts significant pressure on political institutions in countries that often have limited capacity to deliver basic services for the entire population. This pressure can take the form of additional public investments in order to tackle these challenges related not only to organized crime but also to extortion, corruption, and intimidation—all of which are structural impediments to a country's long-term development.

Perhaps more importantly, drug policies have largely been inadequate (aiming for an unrealistic *drug-free world*), ineffective (failing to reduce overall drug production, trafficking, and use; successes in one area often leading to more failures in another), and counterproductive (creating wide-ranging negative consequences via mass incarcerations, police discrimination, forced *treatment* centers, and great moral stigmatization of drug users, low-level drug offenders, and farmers) (Gomis 2014b, pp. 6–9). There has been little effort to review them until very recently, when the surge of violence in Mexico and extensive civil society pressure led to former and current heads of states, the Global Commission on Drug Policy, the Organization of American States, the West Africa Commission on Drugs, and others to challenge the current system. Importantly, the UN will hold a General Assembly Special Session in 2016, specifically devoted to the global drug problem. It is once again fair to argue that a near obsession with the challenges posed by terrorism prevented Western governments from paying enough attention to the perhaps more pressing challenges of drugs and organized crime (Figure 5.5).

Last but not least, in recent years, the United States and many other countries in the Western world were severely affected by the worst economic crisis since the 1930s. The $3–5 trillion spent on the war on terror in the decade following 9/11 could be considered a relatively low number

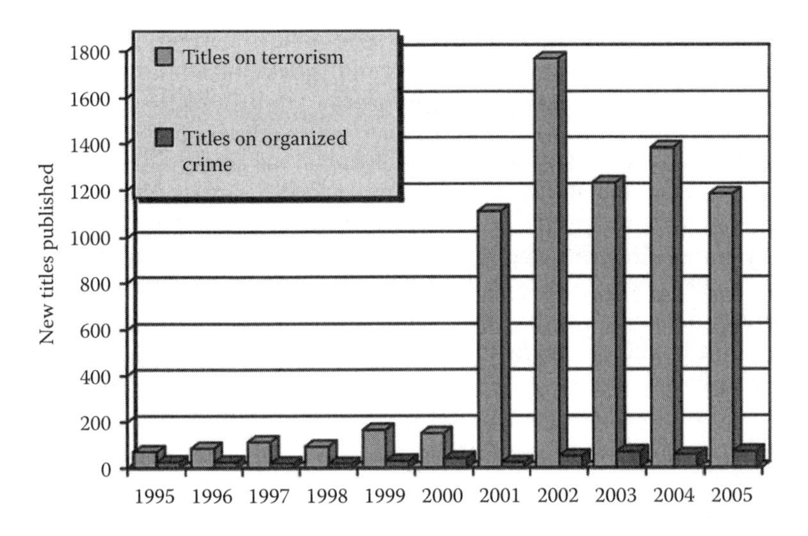

Figure 5.5 The number of books published on terrorism and organized crime between 1995 and 2005. (From Silke, A., 2008 Research on terrorism: A review of the impact of 9/11 and the global war on terrorism, in Chen, H. et al. (eds.), *Terrorism Informatics: Knowledge Management and Data Mining for Homeland Security*, Integrated Series in Information Systems, Vol 18. New York: Springer, 29.)

compared to the $3.03 trillion requested for the federal budget for the year of 2014 alone or the $18.23 trillion debt the country holds. However, it is still higher than the cost of the stimulus package for the U.S. economy (2009–2019), estimated at $830 billion (Congressional Budget Office 2014). Beyond these figures, some of the time, political attention, and energy spent on counterterrorism were indeed not spent on addressing the structural issues that led to the financial crash of 2007–2008 and the subsequent global economic downturn.

It would of course be unfair and naive to argue that all the current difficulties that Western governments are facing are a direct or indirect result of counterterrorism policies. Indeed, who could confidently guarantee that the United States and other countries would have done anything differently, paid more attention, or addressed the aforementioned issues more constructively had the war on terror been replaced by a more moderate and measured counterterrorism strategy? Nevertheless, the persistent primacy of counterterrorism in the U.S. policy in particular must be taken into consideration when analyzing other policy areas that have not received enough attention and budget in recent years.

COUNTERTERRORISM POLICIES HAVE TRIED TO OVERSIMPLIFY HIGHLY COMPLEX PROBLEMS

From the onset, the war on terror as championed by the George W. Bush administration focused on a simplistic, binary vision of the world, split between good and evil. Nine days after 9/11, President Bush noted: "Every nation in every region now has a decision to make: Either you are with us or you are with the terrorists" (CNN 2001). The complexity and nuances of international relations were seemingly replaced by a clear-cut distinction between those actively joining the fight against terrorism—who would then be considered allies, regardless of other agendas—and those not aligning their positions with the United States, who would thus be considered at best, complacent, and at worst supporters of terrorism.

Recent events in North Africa and the Middle East reveal the problems associated with this strategy. Many of the governments overthrown in the region since late 2010 were indeed allies of Western countries as part of the war on terror and considered guarantors of regional stability. As late as January 12, 2011, amidst popular protests in Tunisia and Algeria, the then French Foreign Minister Michèle Alliot-Marie announced in Parliament that Paris was offering Algiers and Tunis the "world-renowned know-how" of the French security forces in "managing security situations" (*Le Monde* 2011). These declarations caused political and media uproar, to which the then President Sarkozy later responded by acknowledging that France had *underestimated* the situation in Tunisia (Reuters 2011). Tunisia was considered a key ally against Islamic extremism, although additional historical and economic factors came into play.

France, in close cooperation with the United Kingdom as part of a newly revamped *Entente cordiale*, was then instrumental in securing UN Security Council Resolution 1973 in March 2011 to protect civilians in Libya, and both countries were at the forefront of military operations against the Gaddafi regime. A decade earlier, both France and the United Kingdom, along with other Western countries, had considered Colonel Gaddafi a key ally in the fight against terrorism in the Middle East when he began a strategy of rapprochement with the West. Following 9/11, Gaddafi had indeed opted for a more peaceful and diplomatic approach, notably renouncing Libya's nuclear weapons program, admitting responsibility of Libyan officials in the 1988 Lockerbie bombing and the UTA

Flight 722 attacks of 1989, stepping up the country's fight against illegal immigration toward Europe, and opening the country's economy to foreign companies to a greater extent.

Relations between the West and Syria have proved perhaps even more complex, notably because of heated relations with Lebanon culminating in suspicions of Syrian government involvement in the assassination of Lebanese Prime Minister Rafik Hariri in February 2005. There is no denying that relations have been considerably shaped by the war on terror. Although Damascus opposed the Iraq War in 2003, it provided intelligence assistance on terrorism after 9/11. It reportedly provided the CIA with numerous reports on Al Qaeda's presence in the Middle East and Europe, and apparently contributed to uncovering an Al Qaeda plot to attack the U.S. Fifth Fleet headquarters in Bahrain and another one in Ottawa (Reveron 2008, p. 9). In recent years, and before the civil war in Syria, Western leaders increasingly saw Bachar al-Assad as a *reformer* and a guarantor of stability and safety in the neighborhood against the threat posed by Islamic extremism, despite evident human rights abuses and the antidemocratic nature of the regime (Phillips 2010; *CNS News* 2011).

In August 2013, the United States, the United Kingdom, and France came very close to launching air strikes against the Syrian regime. On August 30, 2013, the British House of Commons rejected the government motion on Syria, with 285 votes against and 272 in favor (UK Parliament 2013a).* The punitive air strikes envisaged by the British government would have been in direct response to the Syrian regime's reported use of chemical weapons near Damascus on August 21, 2013, which is said to have caused hundreds of fatalities. At that point, over 100,000 people had died in the conflict in Syria, according to UN figures released in July 2013. Prime Minister Cameron respected the parliamentary vote and did not pursue any further military action. Despite the British Parliamentary vote on the matter and the close cross-Channel partnership sealed in November 2010 at Lancaster House in London, French President François Hollande remained intent on carrying out military strikes against the

* The motion put forward by Prime Minister Cameron included that the House of Commons "agrees that a strong humanitarian response is required from the international community and that this may, if necessary, require military action that is legal, proportionate and focused on saving lives by preventing and deterring further use of Syria's chemical weapons" (UK Parliament 2013b).

regime in Syria.* However, France's ambitions were tamed by the United States, which eventually decided against striking the Syrian regime. On September 10, 2013, U.S. President Obama announced that he would postpone a vote in Congress on the use of force in Syria, arguing that he had "resisted calls for military action because we cannot resolve someone else's civil war through force" (White House 2013a).

Less than a year later, the United States launched aerial strikes not against the Syrian regime, but against one of the groups fighting it. The Islamic State has indeed carried out atrocities in Iraq and poses grave security concerns in Syria, where it, for instance, seized the air base of Tabqa in August 2014. There was far less hesitation around the decision to conduct military strikes against the Islamic State than there was a summer earlier regarding the Syrian regime, which had killed tens of thousands of protesters and opponents as part of the violent repression of the popular demonstrations that started in 2011. As Jane Kinninmont of Chatham House pointed out, the strikes indicated "the continuing primacy of counterterrorism in the U.S. approach to the Middle East" (Kinninmont 2014). The terrorist threat posed by the Islamic State eventually proved more convincing than the violent repression carried out by a former ally in the war on terror on its own people.

The war on terror has also had significant impact in other countries. Its narrative allowed for massive human rights violations in Sri Lanka. The Sri Lankan conflict is one of the longest civil wars in history, lasting from 1983 to 2009, and one of the most brutal too—with up to 130,000 dead, including approximately 40,000 in the final few months of the conflict, in addition to abductions, rapes, numerous cases of torture, and child soldiers (*The Economist* 2012). Although the civil war began in 1983, the conflict has much more deep-rooted grievances, including ethnic tensions between the Tamil and the Sinhalese, largely exacerbated during British colonial rule, as the Sinhalese resented what they perceived as British favoritism toward the Tamils. Between 1948, when the country gained independence, and 1972, a corrupt political system marked by "elitism, political dynasties and extreme ethno-religious ideology" was established (Sri Lanka Campaign for Peace and Justice [SLC] 2014). The Sinhalese government put in place discriminatory laws against the Tamil and Muslim minorities.

* It is worth noting that there is a more direct chain of command between the president and the military in France than there is between the prime minister and the UK military, partly reflecting the differences between a semi-presidential system and a parliamentary system, which also explains the differences in attitudes between the two countries.

Gradually, the Tamil formed militia groups, and in 1976, the Liberation Tigers of Tamil Eelam (also known as Tamil Tigers or LTTE) was created (SLC 2014). Following an LTTE ambush on an army convoy during which 13 soldiers were killed, riots erupted leading to 2500 fatalities. For the next 26 years, a civil war raged on, with systemic repression, violence and human rights violations on both sides primarily through bombings and suicide bombings from the LTTE and military repression from the government (*BBC News* 2014e). The war on terror played a key role in creating imbalances between the two sides, placing disproportionate blame on the *terrorist* group LTTE instead of the equally-at-fault government and creating a permissive environment for the civil war to end the way it did.

In 1997, the U.S. State Department placed LTTE on its Foreign Terrorist Organizations list (U.S. State Department 1997). From 9/11 onward, the Sri Lankan government skillfully adopted the discourse of the war on terror, aligning their actions with the global strategy led by the United States and capturing the language of humanitarian military intervention to justify their actions in the northeast part of the country toward the end of the civil war (Carver and Gowing 2014). The government used international mechanisms against terrorist financing, money laundering, and arms smuggling to fight the LTTE—with the United States, for instance, freezing the assets of Tamil charities (Montlake 2009). More broadly, the government played on the sympathies of the international community against the LTTE, whose terrorist tactics became more unpopular than the military repression carried out by the government.

The LTTE surrendered on May 17, 2009, only 5 months after President Barack Obama assumed office (International Crisis Group [ICG] 2012). Subsequently, the United States became a leading advocate for the respect of human rights in Sri Lanka. However, the victory over the LTTE in 2009 has emboldened the government to continue oppressing the Tamil population and political dissent at home and export the so-called Sri Lanka model abroad (Carver 2014; Mortimer 2014). As Fred Carver, the director of the Sri Lanka Campaign, notes, Sri Lanka has held "a series of 'defeating terrorism' seminars, and a 'Galle Dialogue Naval Seminar' in which they lectured up to 250 delegates from around the world" (Carver 2012). Burma, Bangladesh, Thailand, Turkey, Indonesia, and the Philippines are among the countries to have *compared notes* with Sri Lanka (Carver 2012). Most recently, the Nigerian military has discussed with the Sri Lankan army ways to employ the Sri Lankan method against Boko Haram

(Reuters 2014). Andrew Stroehlein of Human Rights Watch was quick to respond: "It's hard to imagine a worse idea" (Stroehlein 2014).

As V.K. Shashikumar argues in the *Indian Defence Review,* the Sri Lanka model, or "Rajapaksa model of fighting terror," as he puts it, is based on eight central characteristics: unwavering political will, telling the international community to *go to hell,* no negotiations with the LTTE, unidirectional flow of conflict information, no cease-fire, complete operational freedom, accent on young commanders, and keep your neighbors in the loop—referring to the unsigned strategic partnership with India (Shashikumar 2009, pp. 111–112). Combined, these steps highlight the brutality of the Sri Lankan strategy, disregard for the consequences of the complete disproportionate use of force, blurring of the line between civilians and insurgents, and last but not least, the illusion that complex political problems can be solved by merely eliminating an enemy militarily.

As Sri Lankan opposition lawmaker R. Sampanthan points out, "I don't think a people can be beaten down by force. What has been happening in the latest military operation has left deep wounds and scars in the minds of young Tamils" (Montlake 2009). The scars, wounds, and enduring grievances of the Tamils make a return to violence inevitable in the current political configuration, which is partly due to the *us vs. them* approach advocated by the war on terror. As Holt has argued, the international community's "condemnation of increasing levels of violence was muted, and criticism of human rights abuses appeared hypocritical given the U.S. and UK involvement in extraordinary rendition, torture and detention of terror suspects" (Holt 2011, p. 158).

In short, and in addition to the concepts of *narco-terrorism* and *cyber terrorism* explored in Chapter 3, there is extensive evidence that the war on terror has often led to oversimplifications of challenges that were in fact much more complex and multifaceted. This flawed analysis has repeatedly given way to inadequate, disproportionate, and ineffective policies, often supporting dictatorial and repressive regimes in the name of countering international terrorism.

COUNTERTERRORISM POLICIES HAVE CONTRIBUTED TO A DISPROPORTIONATE LEVEL OF FEAR ACROSS SOCIETY

The third main negative consequence of counterterrorism policies is that they have often contributed to a widespread sense of fear within Western societies that is not on par with the actual threat posed by terrorism.

The annual Chatham House–YouGov Survey has shed light on the persistent belief among the British public that international terrorism remains the greatest threat to the British way of life and that countering it should be the main priority in UK foreign policy. Both views consistently rank first in their respective categories over the first 4 years of the survey (2011–2014). However, three interesting subtleties have emerged from the results. First, age is an important factor: younger people surveyed indicated less concern than those within older age categories. In 2012, only 33% of the 18–24-year-olds considered international terrorism to be the greatest threat to the British way of life, compared to 59% for those aged 60 and over—despite the fact that there is no evidence that terrorists target older people more specifically. Second, people living in London are relatively less concerned by terrorism (45% selected it as the greatest threat in 2012) than people living in the rest of the south (53%), the Midlands/Wales (47%), and the north (54%). This is somewhat surprising given London's historical prominence as the main target of terrorist attacks in the United Kingdom, along with Northern Ireland. Third, there are clear differences between opinion formers and the general public. Among opinion formers, a group of 735 influential adults with leading roles in business, media, academia, and politics, terrorism ranks only fourth as a threat to the British way of life, in contrast with the general public, which ranks it first. Seventy-one percent of opinion formers consider the failure of the international financial system to be the predominant concern for the United Kingdom (only 39% in the general public), while 50% of the general public regard international terrorism as the greatest threat to the British way of life (39% among opinion formers) (Chatham House–YouGov 2012).

By definition, terrorist attacks are designed to cause fear and panic through violence in order to bring about political change. The 2014 survey results confirm the same trends in public perceptions among the British public, who rank international terrorism ahead of nuclear proliferation, organized crime, cyber security, and energy security as the top threat to the United Kingdom (Niblett 2014). Understandably, the public fears risks over which they have little control. But as previous sections have explored, the statistical likelihood of being killed by a terrorist attack in the United Kingdom ranks significantly below cancer—more than 150,000 deaths in 2012 (Cancer Research UK 2014); smoking—almost 100,000 people died from smoking-related diseases in 2011 (Action on Smoking and Health [ASH] 2013); alcohol—more than 15,000 people per year die from alcohol poisoning and related diseases (Institute of Alcohol Studies [IAS] 2013); HIV—which accounted for around 490 deaths in 2012 (Public Health

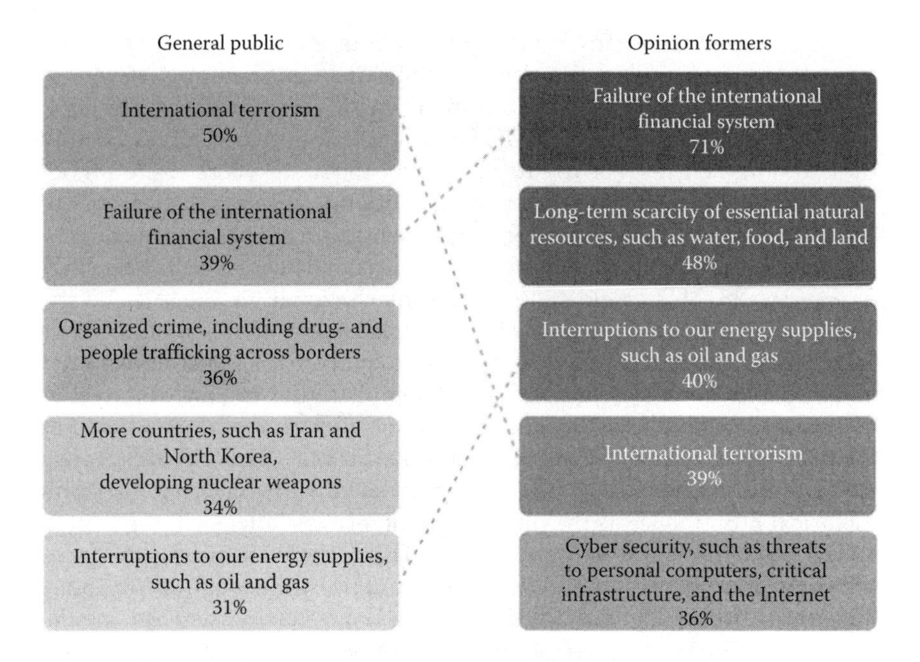

Figure 5.6 Answers to the question "What are the five greatest threats to the British way of life?" among the general public and opinion-former respondents in the United Kingdom. *Note*: Only the top five results in each sample have been included in this figure. (From Chatham House–YouGov Survey 2012, British attitudes towards the UK's international priorities, Survey Results, July 2012.)

England 2013); car accidents (almost five people die on UK roads every day—UK Department for Transport 2014); or traffic pollution (almost 5,000 deaths per year—Yim and Barrette 2012). In contrast, a total of 57 people have died as a result of terrorist attacks in the United Kingdom between 2002 and 2012 (GTD 2014) (Figure 5.6).

Notwithstanding these figures, an overriding sense of fear of terrorism remains. The reality is that no government in the world can prevent every single terrorist attack, and terrorism should therefore be seen not as a threat to the British way of life but as a risk to be managed and contained. And although CONTEST has rightfully aimed to focus on the goals of risk management and mitigation, the government should place a higher priority on addressing the pervasive sense of fear that the potential for future attacks appears to induce. Instead, some of the media and political discourses, focusing on the worst-case scenarios and a *better safe than sorry* mentality, have actually contributed to this pervasive fear. This situation has arisen through repeated reminders of how serious the threat is—intelligence reports very rarely conclude that the threat has substantially diminished—and enhanced measures, new legislations, and investment to counter the threat. The combination of these developments has helped to maintain high levels of fear among the general public, almost regardless of the actual threat.

Terror-phobia, as commentators including John Mueller, Mark Stewart, and Tom Engelhart have dubbed it, is of course not exclusive to the United Kingdom, which is in fact quite a resilient society, used to dealing with terrorist attacks or the threat thereof. In the United States, immediately following the attacks of September 11, 2001, more than half of respondents expressed concerns about "being victimized by another act of terrorism" (May et al. 2011). More tellingly, a 1999 Gallup Poll showed that "individuals with higher incomes were less likely than those with lower incomes to report a fear of terrorist attacks" (Moore 1999). This disconnect remained constant after 9/11, illustrating similar patterns to the ones highlighted by the Chatham House–YouGov surveys in the United Kingdom. In 2003, almost half of New Yorkers said they were *very concerned* about another major attack, more than half about biological attacks, and over 40% about a nuclear attack. Although fear levels regarding terrorism declined in the years following 9/11, they often remained higher than pre-9/11 levels (Gallup 2014). Most recently, a study by the START Consortium at the University of Maryland found that Americans are more likely to think about the possibility of a terrorist attack than hospitalization or violent crime victimization, although statistics point to a much smaller likelihood (START 2013). With the emergence of the Islamic State in Iraq and Syria, an NBC News/*Wall Street Journal* Poll carried out in September 2014 showed that almost half of Americans reported they "believe the country is less safe now than before the Sept. 11, 2001 terrorist attacks," compared to 20% in September 2002 and 28% in 2013 (NBC News 2014).

It is often said that it is in fact in governments' interest to maintain high levels of fear, especially as it relates to terrorism. As Zbigniew Brzezinski, former national security adviser to President Jimmy Carter, argues in an article on how the war on terror has created a culture of fear: "Fear obscures reason, intensifies emotions and makes it easier for demagogic politicians to mobilize the public on behalf of the policies they want to pursue." According to Brzezinski, "The war of choice in Iraq could never have gained the congressional support it got without the psychological linkage between the shock of 9/11 and the postulated existence of Iraqi weapons of mass destruction" (Brzezinski 2007). Beyond policy goals, politicians have also been criticized for using fear of terrorism for electoral and political goals: "Even democracies... use it to exert control over the populace and serve the government's principle aim: consolidating power... by leaning not just on the danger of a terrorist attack, but on the fact that the possible perpetrator are frightening individuals who are not like us" (Ludlow 2014).

A strong correlation has been established between social phobia and politically conservative attitudes (Hatemi et al. 2013). This may comfort some incumbent politicians' impression that a more fearful society is beneficial, as it would lead to more support for the status quo or a reinforcement of current policies. Fear can serve as a catalyst for positive change, when accompanied by accurate information about the dangers of a phenomenon, for instance, smoking (Caplin 2003, p. 3). However, fear often leads to increased risk aversion, which is detrimental to the economy. Kahneman has shown that human beings generally fear loss much more than we value gains, a natural tendency which would be further reinforced by a politics of fear (Kahneman 2012, pp. 283–286). Fear also leads to more reclusive and xenophobic attitudes (Bornewasser 1993) that can create resentment, anger, tension, and ultimately conflict within our societies and, overall, support for policies that are not primarily based on evidence and therefore fail to match the reality of the situations they aim to address.

COUNTERTERRORISM HAS AT TIMES BEEN COUNTERPRODUCTIVE

Some of the counterterrorism policies put in place since 9/11 have proved counterproductive, either leading to an increase in terrorist attacks in the short term or creating further alienation and resentment in the long term. This section will explore four key dimensions of these counterproductive effects, namely, (1) the copycat effect, (2) discriminatory practices in immigration and law enforcement after 9/11, (3) the more recent responses to the challenges posed by foreign fighters returning from Syria and Iraq, and (4) the effects of the so-called enhanced interrogation techniques carried out by the CIA between late 2001 and early 2009.

Copycat Effect

There is growing recognition that terrorist attacks are highly concentrated in time and space, following a *burstiness* pattern, as Gary LaFree, the director of the START Consortium at the University of Maryland, demonstrates. Based on the Global Terrorism Database, which includes data dating back to 1970, LaFree and his colleagues have shown that terrorist incidents are rarely isolated and tend to be highly concentrated in time (in clusters or *bursts*) and localized. For example, more than 50% of all terrorist attacks, fatalities, and injuries in 2013 occurred in only three countries, Iraq, Afghanistan, and Pakistan; over the last four decades, approximately 5% of the world's countries have accounted for about 50% of terrorist attacks worldwide, while 10% of them have witnessed more 75% of the world's attacks (GTD 2014). In the United States, almost a third of all terrorist attacks between 1970 and 2008 occurred in just five metropolitan U.S. counties (START 2012). As LaFree simply puts it, "when [terrorism] starts to happen there is a tendency for it to occur in the same place a lot" (LaFree 2013).

There are two main ways to explain this *burstiness* finding. The first, perhaps most widely accepted theory, is that terrorist attacks are largely part of broader, longer campaigns of terrorism—in other words, one attack is simply part of a series of attacks. However, the second one is less frequently reported upon: the copycat effect in terrorism. This refers to a situation where "violence-prone individuals and groups imitate forms of (political) violence attractive to them, based on examples usually popularized by mass media" (Nacos 2009)—in other words, individuals, not necessarily part of the same terrorist organization or connected in any direct way, decide to commit a similar attack, inspired by the one that just occurred. An important distinction is worth noting here, between contagion and imitation: "criminal *contagion* contributes to the emergence of a criminal personality," while "criminal *imitation* presumes an already developed criminal personality that draws from other examples of ideas for concrete ways and means of committing criminal acts" (Geerds 1981). Terrorist attacks may lead either to the emergence of other terrorists or to attacks carried out in similar ways by people that could already be defined as terrorists.

There is extensive literature on copycat and contagion psychology, "ranging from infectious yawning and laughter, through consumer fads, fashions, and crazes, to the more serious contagions of eating disorders, suicide, hysteria, violence and even murder" (Marsden 2000a). As Loren Coleman points out, the repetitive, embellishing, and intensive mass media coverage of the murders committed by Jack the Ripper perhaps led to the first occurrence of copycat crime (Coleman 2004, pp. 135–136). The reporting led to what researcher Jean-Gabriel de Tarde called a "suggestion effect," causing "the imitation cycle [to feed on] itself from one celebrity copycat to the next" (Coleman 2004, pp. 136–137). Similarly, suicide also begets suicide (Marsden 2000). This emulation effect in suicides has been referred to as suicide contagion, suicide cluster, or the Werther effect—based on Goethe's novel *The Sorrows of Young Werther,* whose tragic fate was replicated by a number of young men.

A similar effect occurs in terrorism. As Marsden points out, it makes sense from a psychological standpoint: "A phenomenon of 'disinhibition' can occur when suicidal or murderous thoughts—inhibited by conscience, uncertainty or fear—are exposed to what is perceived as the positive consequences of suicide or murder" (Marsden 2001). In other words, the more terrorist attacks occur, the more they may be seen by other individuals as a plausible course of action: "The suicide bombers of Hamas serve as models of acceptable behavior among their peers, which is via the copycat effect" (Coleman 2004, p. 143). The success of terrorists and criminal groups is often dependent on the size of their membership and the level of support they enjoy within their community (Felbab-Brown 2011). Therefore, terrorist organizations are likely to consider that it is in their interest to encourage this copycat effect and inspire other individuals to carry out attacks. In addition, previous cases show that some terrorists, perhaps *lone wolves* even more so than others, are desperate for publicity and fame. Thus, it seems that the massive media coverage of Timothy McVeigh, who set off a bomb that destroyed the Alfred P. Murrah Federal Building in downtown Oklahoma City (OKC) on April 19, 1995, killing 168 people and injuring almost 700 other, frustrated Ted Kaczynski (also known as the Unabomber). Displeased that his mail bombs had received such little media attention in comparison to the bombing, he may have intensified his campaign as a result (Nacos 2009, pp. 3–4).

Regarding the copycat effect in terrorism, much of the academic focus has been on the role of the media. As Brigitte L. Nacos points out (Nacos 2009, p. 5), Alex P. Schmid and Janny de Graaf have shown that "the media can provide the potential terrorist with all the ingredients that are necessary to engage in this type of violence. They can reduce inhibitions against the use of violence, they can offer models and know-how to potential terrorists and they can motivate them in various ways" (Schmid and de Graaf 1982, p. 142). Gabriel Weimann and Conrad Winn have demonstrated that their data constituted "considerable evidence of a contagion effect wrought by coverage" (Weimann and Winn 1994, p. 277). Paul Marsden notes that "with a perverse irony, the global attention and blanket media coverage accorded [to] the U.S. terrorist attacks may actually help make up some desperate minds and legitimise future murder-suicides" (Marsden 2000).

The May 2013 attack in Woolwich, a neighborhood in southeast London, certainly shows how powerful mass media can be for terrorists. Following the violent murder of British soldier Lee Rigby outside the Royal Artillery Barracks in Woolwich, the front pages of most national British newspapers were filled with pictures of one of the two perpetrators, holding a machete covered in blood, along with sensationalist titles—for example, "You Will Never Be Safe, We Will Never Stop Fighting," "Beheaded on a British Street," "Blood on His Hands, Hatred in His Eyes," and "Terror Returns to Britain." Indeed the attack seems to have been carried out in a way expressly designed to gain such coverage, as a means of creating a sense of outrage and fear in British society, disproportionate to the real risk of physical injury. This disconnect between perception and reality owes a great deal to the way the media covers terrorist attacks and other violent crimes. This not only allows the killers to gain publicity for their actions, but also stimulates the fantasies of certain people and increases the likelihood of copycat attacks. Studies on media coverage have shown that widely publicized stories of dangerous and deviant behavior influence copycat incidents (e.g., Phillips 1974; O'Carroll 1994; Lindberg et al. 2012). Media overreaction risks giving an opportunity for groups with their own agendas to gain publicity, as seen with the English Defence League's counterrally that was organized following the Woolwich killing. The dangers of instant reaction on social media are much debated—and rightfully so—as they have altered the way news is reported and information spread across the world. Nonetheless, traditional media have also reported such events in a way that is likely to have propagated further fears rather than reassuring the public with measured analysis and putting these incidents in context (Gomis 2013a).

A number of useful guidelines already exist as to how the media should cover suicide and school shootings, and could be applied to terrorism as well. In 1994, the U.S. Centers for Disease Control and Prevention recommended that, in order to mitigate the risk of suicide contagion, the media should avoid: "presenting the event as an accomplishment, repetitious or excessive reporting of the event, sensationalizing the event, 'how-to' descriptions of the event, portraying the event as painless for those responsible, presenting simplistic explanations for the event, glorifying the event or those responsible for it and giving a positive rationale for those responsible for the event" (CDC 1994). Forensic psychiatrist Park Dietz has also repeatedly urged the media to alter the way they report on mass murders: "Don't start the story with sirens blaring. Don't have photographs of the killer. Don't make this 24/7 coverage. Do everything you can not to make the body count the lead story, not to make the killer some kind of anti-hero. Do localize the story to the affected community and make it as boring as possible in every other market. Because every time we have intense saturation coverage of a mass murder, we expect to see one or two more within a week" (Park Dietz & Associates 2014). These two sets of simple, practical, and realistic recommendations of what not to do are certainly valid for the media coverage of terrorist incidents as well.

Evidently, some media outlets often fail to follow guidelines on responsible reporting. Spectacular, dramatic stories often tend to sell more newspapers and generate more website hits than more measured analyses. As the Pew Research Center found, the top four categories of news that attracted *above-average attention* between 1986 and 2006 were *war and terrorism, bad weather, man-made disasters,* and *natural disasters* (Robinson 2007, p. 13) (Figure 5.7).

As Daniel Kahneman's research has emphasized, this is normal human behavior. Human beings tend to be biased toward what is happening at the moment, especially spectacular events. The human brain is also designed to focus on bad news, which attracts greater attention than happy events (Kahneman 2012, pp. 300–309). This explains why media reports on bad news outweigh those on good news by as much as 17 to 1 (Williams 2014).

Attempts to alter media reporting toward more positive coverage have not had much success to date. Continuous censorship is obviously not a desirable option, as it is likely to breed more ignorance and lead to counterproductive effects. Other kinds of substantial reform are also hard to put in place, as the 2012 Leveson Inquiry illustrated in the United Kingdom. The process led by Lord Justice Leveson looked into the "culture, practices and ethics of the press," in particular the relationships between the press on the one hand and the public, the police, and politicians on the other. Its recommendations "for a more effective policy and regulation that supports the integrity and freedom of the press while encouraging the highest ethical standards" have proved interesting, yet were hotly debated, and it remains to be seen how many will be implemented (*BBC News* 2012; The Leveson Inquiry 2014).

Ultimately, the main responsibility for leading the response to terrorism, and mitigating the possibility of copycat attacks, lies with elected politicians. Thomas Jensen concluded from his 2007 quantitative analysis that "spending more on anti-terrorism may increase the probability

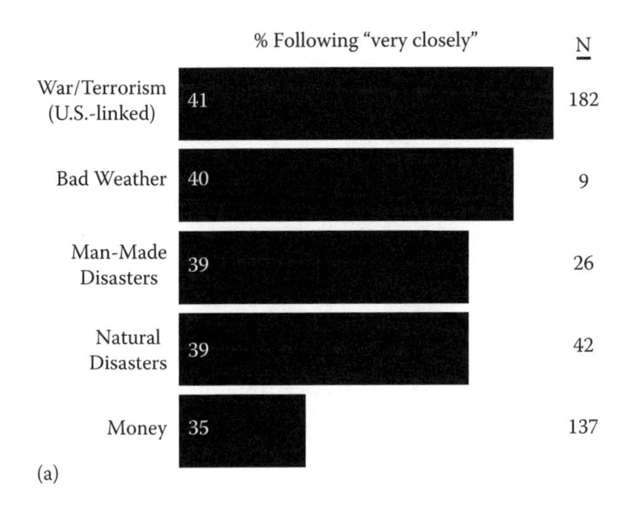

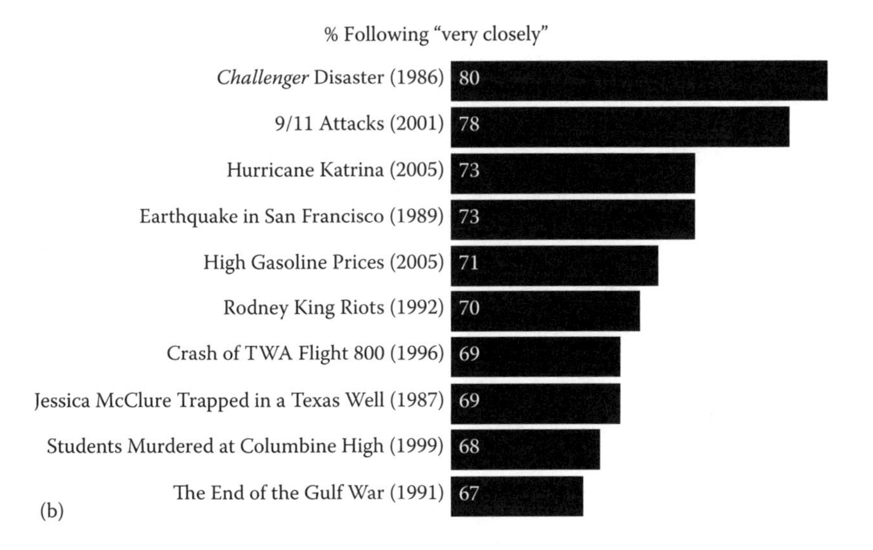

Figure 5.7 (a) Five categories of news that attracted above-average attention (1986–2006). (b) Top 10 news stories (1986–2006). (From Robinson, M.J. 2007, *The News Interest Index, 1986–2007*. Pew Research Center for the People and The Press, pp. 1–36.)

of a terrorist attack. Suppose that there has just been a terrorist attack and that the authorities increase the level of anti-terrorism only to try to calm down the public. This effort can have the effect that another terrorist attack becomes more likely" (Jensen 2007, p. 78). Governments of course do not actively encourage copycat attacks. However, giving too much attention to terrorist attacks—through speeches, press conferences, repeated interventions in the media, public debates in parliament, etc.—may lead to the same kind of contagion spurred by intense media saturation. Too much political attention may indeed grant terrorists some kind of legitimacy and credibility, thereby creating the conditions for further attacks. The aim of most terrorists is to spread fear among the public and cause overreaction from government to further their own political agenda. There is therefore a great need for governments to react to terrorism in a measured way, addressing the challenges posed by terrorism and responding to attacks without overpublicizing the tactics and objectives of the perpetrators.

Discriminations

Counterterrorism policies have also discriminated against specific communities, especially Muslim communities, primarily via tightened immigration policies and reinforced security and law enforcement measures. Understandably, the United States and its allies resorted to a range of policy tools to counter the terrorist threat in their efforts to ensure that another terrorist attack on the scale of 9/11 would not occur again. However, by putting in place such a wide-ranging arsenal, policies have also created further marginalization, alienation, anger, and resentment—sentiments that are often key drivers behind terrorism in the first place.

From an immigration policy standpoint, a number of discriminatory policies and practices emerged shortly after 9/11. Internationally, immigration policy quickly became a key tool in response to the terrorist threat. The UN Security Council Resolution 1373, adopted unanimously on September 28, 2001, included a number of provisions on immigration, including the following:

- "Prevent the movement of terrorists or terrorist groups by effective border controls and controls on issuance of identity papers and travel documents, and through measures for preventing counterfeiting, forgery or fraudulent use of identity papers and travel documents."

- "Find ways of intensifying and accelerating the exchange of operational information, especially regarding actions or movements of terrorist persons or networks; forged or falsified travel documents."
- "Take appropriate measures in conformity with the relevant provisions of national and international law, including international standards of human rights, before granting refugee status, for the purpose of ensuring that the asylum seeker has not planned, facilitated or participated in the commission of terrorist acts."
- "Ensure, in conformity with international law, that refugee status is not abused by the perpetrators, organizers or facilitators of terrorist acts, and that claims of political motivation are not recognized as grounds for refusing requests for the extradition of alleged terrorists" (UNSC 2001).

These measures may seem understandable and legitimate in many ways. However, their implementation has often proved problematic, tilting the balance toward countering terrorism at all costs and at the expense of respecting the rule of law and human rights. Daniel Moeckli has noted that, at the request of the Counterterrorism Committee, states began to introduce new legislations and systems, including in customs, immigration, and border control (Moeckli 2008, p. 168). Beyond the opportunity costs previously explored—some UN states that are not facing a significant terrorist threat have been asked to conform with international standards, despite more urgent investments needed in other policy areas, for example, education and health—some of the measures put in place led to violations of basic human rights for immigrants and refugees.

In the United States, authorities have been granted the right to indefinitely detain immigrants suspected of endangering national security (*New York Times* 2006). A number of other programs have proved highly controversial. As Moeckli and others have pointed out, these include the following:

- The so-called Voluntary Interview Program, as part of which the Immigration and Naturalization Service (INS) "compiled a list of aliens whose characteristics (including type of visa, gender, age, date of entry into the United States, and country that issued the passport) were similar to those of the hijackers," according to the U.S. General Accounting Office (GAO 2003, pp. 1–2). Between November 2001 and March 2003, law enforcement officers conducted interviews with 3216 individuals. While the Department of Justice (DOJ) claimed that those interviews were voluntary, attorneys noted that "although aliens were not coerced to participate in the interviews, they worried about repercussions, such as future INS denials for visa extensions or permanent residency, if they refused to be interviewed" (GAO 2003, p. 2). In other words, individuals were specifically targeted by a branch of the U.S. government on the basis of the mere similarity of their profile to those of the perpetrators of the 9/11 attacks. Beyond the blatant violation of the presumption of innocence, among other human rights, research has shown that there is not just one path to terrorism, but rather a multitude of different terrorist backgrounds and profiles—hence the pointless nature of this exercise.

- The "National Security Entry–Exit Registration System," created in June 2002, imposed "fingerprinting, photographing, and registration requirements for all males who are citizens of, or were born in, certain designated countries." By 2003, 24 out of the 25 states considered to pose an "elevated national security risk" had predominant Arab and/or Muslim populations—the exception being North Korea. Once again, this meant that some individuals, just because they happened to come from countries that were considered to pose a heightened terrorist threat, would face reinforced security measures.
- Last but not least, *Operation Liberty Shield* was a DHS-led, interagency program launched in March 2003 to "increase security and readiness" and "help protect our citizens, our infrastructure and… help deter those who plan further terrorist attacks" (DHS 2003). Among other things, the operation requested the automatic *temporary detention* of all asylum seekers from a list of 34 countries, including Iraq—Operation Liberty Shield was launched in the eve of the U.S. military intervention. As Human Rights Watch noted, "Many of these countries have well-documented records of human rights abuse that prompt men, women and children to seek refuge in the United States" (HRW 2003).

While the scale of immigration measures put into place in the United States was generally not replicated in other countries, the United Kingdom put in place substantial legislative changes to enhance the use of deportations. The Immigration, Asylum and Nationality Act 2006 authorized the home secretary to remove British citizenship if the home secretary was "satisfied that deprivation is conducive to the public good" (Moeckli 2008, p. 168).

In the aftermath of the July 7, 2005, bombings in London, the then British prime minister Tony Blair warned: "The rules of the game have changed. If you come to this country from abroad, don't meddle with extremism, because if you do, or get engaged with it, you are going to go back out again" (Moeckli 2008, p. 169). France has resorted to deportations, confiscations of passports, and removals of citizenship even more than the United Kingdom—as noted earlier.

Immigration has traditionally been a controversial and highly politicized issue. At times of crises, related to terrorism or not, politicians have often used immigrants and foreigners as scapegoats for broader societal problems. While there is significant evidence of the clear positive effects that immigration has for a country—both economically and culturally—conservative, inward-looking ideas continue to appeal to sizable segments of the population. It is worth insisting that these political opinions are rarely based on empirical data. In France, rural areas, where there are proportionally fewer foreigners and immigrants than urban areas, often hold more Front National voters. In the United Kingdom, a member of the European Parliament for Euroskeptic and anti-immigration party UKIP warned that 1.5 million Bulgarians and Romanians would move to the United Kingdom as soon as the border restrictions were lifted in January 2014—7 years after Bulgaria and Romania officially joined the EU (Duevell 2013; *Independent* 2014a). Migration Watch predicted that only 50,000 would migrate to the United Kingdom on an annual basis (Migration Watch 2013). The number of Bulgarians and Romanians moving to the United Kingdom has in fact remained stable, similar to those in the months preceding the lifting of the restrictions—one study even estimated that the number of people born in Romania and Bulgaria now working in Britain in fact fell between December 2013 and March 2014, from 144,000 to 140,000 (*Economist* 2014b).

Beyond these ethical and legal issues, tackling measures against illegal immigration to counter the terrorist threat is not likely to be very effective. In a 2006 study, Robert S. Leiken and Steven Brooke found that 87% of the 373 charged, convicted, and/or killed terrorists in Western Europe and North America they studied were immigrants. However, "only 6% entered their host country illegally." In addition, the authors noted that the list of terrorists they explored included "twice as many Frenchmen as Saudis and more Britons than Sudanese, Yemenis, Emiratis, Lebanese, or Libyans," despite much tougher checks for Saudis, Sudanese, Yemenis, Emiratis, Lebanese, and Libyans at the port of entry to the United States. This disparity once again denotes that some of the counterterrorism and immigration checks put in place after 9/11 have been based on misperceptions rather than evidence and blatant racial discrimination (Leiken and Brooke 2006, pp. 503–504). As Gabriela Rodríguez Pizarro, the then UN Special Rapporteur on the human rights of migrants, pointed out, "[t]he concept that immigration is a security issue has continued to gain ground since 11 September 2001 and has taken precedence over all other issues, including human rights" (Moeckli 2008, p. 174).

From a more specific law enforcement standpoint, ethnic minorities have been disproportionately affected by the measures put in place as part of the war on terror. In the United Kingdom, ethnicity data (no data were available based on religion) show that *Asian, black,* and *other* ethnic groups are more often stopped and searched than *white* people (Choudhury 2012, p. 39). Of the 1,221 people arrested for terrorism and the 256 charged for terrorism-related offenses between April 2005 and March 2011, 41% of those arrested and 44% of those charged defined themselves as Asian, 26% and 22% as white, and 12% and 21% as black, showing a lopsided focus on ethnic minorities compared to the more universal profiles of terrorists (Anderson 2012, pp. 72–73). Although ethnic profiling was not born in 2001, it certainly increased in the aftermath of the terrorist attacks. In the United Kingdom, stops and searches of individuals of Asian origin carried out under counterterrorism powers increased threefold after 9/11 and fivefold after the attempted attacks in London and Glasgow in 2007 (Open Society Institute [OSI] 2009, p. 9). Between 2001 and 2003, Germany conducted a wide-ranging data mining operation (*Rasterfahndung*) that collected and analyzed sensitive personal data from 8.3 million people based on characteristics similar to those of the *Hamburg cell,* which included some of the perpetrators of 9/11. The traits included "being 18–40 years old, being male, being a current or former student, being Muslim, and being from one of 26 countries with a predominantly Muslim population." The massive operation did not find any terrorist suspects (OSI 2009, p. 68). Once again, ethnic profiling proved to be not only ethically wrong, but also unhelpful.

Rasterfahndung, just like the U.S. Voluntary Interview Program and other similar undertakings, diverted law enforcement officials from serious investigations based on individual behaviors, focusing instead on misleading ethnic, religious, and other personal traits. This approach was problematic in many ways, removing crucial partners in policing efforts within local communities, fostering resentment and distrust toward the government from targeted populations, hampering economic and social prospects, and creating tensions and unfounded suspicions within society.

There have been numerous examples of biased treatment of Arab and Muslim majorities as a result of counterterrorism measures. The way the British government responded to the murder of Lee Rigby in Woolwich in May 2013—with Prime Minister David Cameron rushing back from a meeting with French President François Hollande in Paris, convening a crisis response Cabinet Office Briefing Room A meeting, and government members making numerous public remarks on the issue—when compared to the relatively tame way it handled the fatal stabbing of Mohammed Saleem, an 82-year-old living in Birmingham in April 2013, or the explosions at mosques in Walsall, Tipton, and Wolverhampton following the Woolwich murder, led to allegations of double standards (*Independent* 2013). More recently, the response of Western governments to the challenges posed by foreign fighters is worth exploring.

Foreign Fighters

In recent years, a number of young individuals, often Muslim men between the ages of 18–29, primarily from North Africa, the Middle East, Western Europe, and North America, have left their home countries to *join the jihad* and fight against the Assad regime in Syria, and more recently in Iraq. Bearing in mind the discriminatory, harmful, and largely ineffective programs the previous section of this book explored, it is worth emphasizing that hundreds of millions of people fit this profile (i.e., male, Muslim, 18–29 years old, from North Africa, the Middle East, and North America), but a tiny proportion (i.e., thousands out of hundreds of millions) have become *foreign fighters*—also creatively referred to as *extremism travelers, high-risk travelers,* or *terror tourists.* The issue is far from new: the conflicts in Bosnia, Chechnya, Afghanistan, and Libya, among many others, had already seen young individuals from abroad join the combat. However, it has become increasingly visible with regard to Syria, partly because many foreign fighters now boast about their activities on social media, including Twitter and Facebook. In the first 3 years of the conflict, over 12,000 have fought in Syria, notably 300–700 French nationals, 200–250 Belgians, 100–120 Dutchmen, 300–400 Britons, approximately 300 Germans, over 800 from Russia, and many others from more than 70 countries (Gomis 2014b). The number of European individuals who have traveled to fight in Syria increased fourfold between April 2013 and April 2014 and is still growing at the time of writing (Bakker et al. 2013, p. 2; ICSR 2013; *Economist* 2014c). Turkey is a key country in this foreign fighters' issue, a place of origin for approximately 400 jihadi fighters (as of the spring of 2014), as well as a stopping point for those on their way from other European countries. As of Spring 2014, at least 30 Frenchmen, 28 Britons, 13 Dutchmen, 15 Spaniards, and 100 Turks have perished in the Syrian conflict (Gomis 2014b). However, most foreign fighters in Syria and Iraq originate from Tunisia, Saudi Arabia, Jordan, Lebanon, Morocco, and other countries in the Middle East and North Africa (Radio Free Europe 2014) (Figures 5.8 and 5.9).

Intelligence services across the Western world are watching the issue closely, especially given the possibility that some foreign fighters might attempt to carry out terrorist attacks in their own country upon their return. However, it is worth stressing that these individuals do not constitute a homogeneous body with the same motivations and goals. Some of them were active, socialized members of their society, outraged by the ongoing humanitarian crisis in Syria and the bloody repression that the Assad regime has carried out on innocent people across the country. Others, disguised under religious claims, are

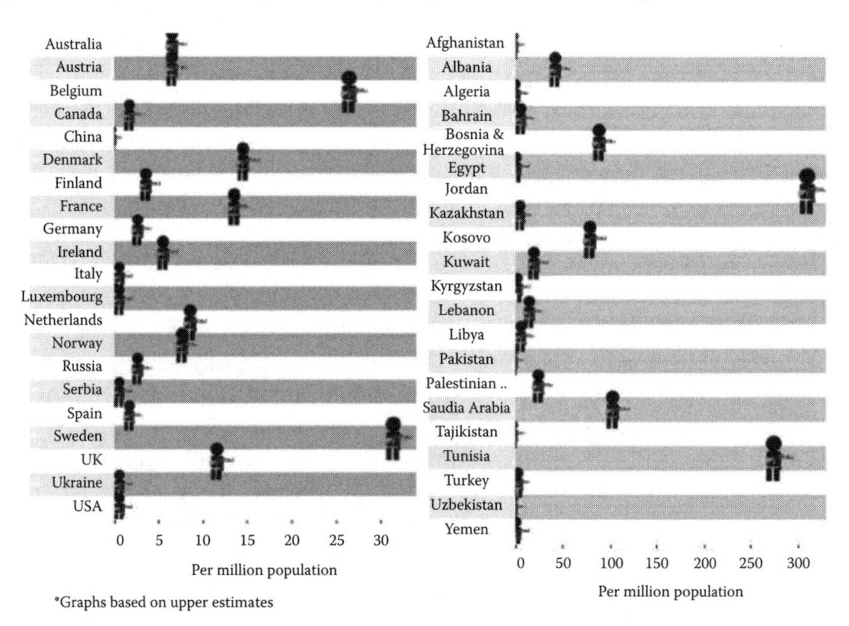

Figure 5.8 Proportion of foreign fighters by country (adjusted for population size). (From Radio Free Europe, Foreign fighters in Iraq and Syria: Where do they come from? December 9, 2014.)

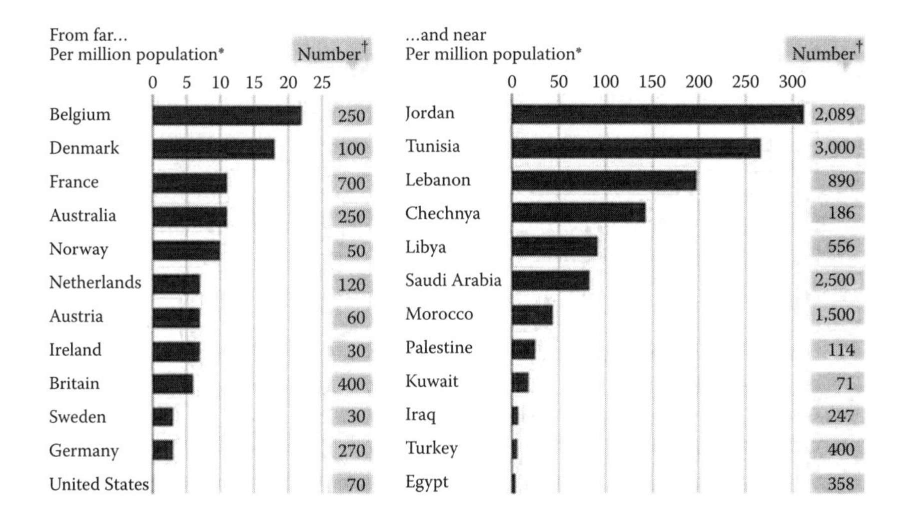

Figure 5.9 Foreign fighters in Syria. (From the *Economist*, It ain't half hot here, mum, August 30, 2014.)

motivated by the social experience, adventure, fun, and status associated with it—as evident by their posts on social media (*Vice News* 2013).

The challenges foreign fighters pose when they return are therefore mixed. They may include physical and psychological trauma, marginalization, heightened distrust of government, criminal, and violent behavior, and political activism. The most widely discussed threat—that some of these individuals would launch terrorist attacks in their home countries—is not only the most alarming one but also the least likely. As Sir Richard Dearlove points out, the mere fact that these individuals are traveling to Syria and Iraq shows that the West is not the primary target (Dearlove 2014). Nonetheless, research has shown that individuals with training and direct combat experience tend to carry out deadlier attacks (Hegghammer 2013).

National responses in the West to the challenges posed by foreign fighters can be broken down into six main categories, namely prevention, deterrence, management, monitoring, prosecution, and reintegration measures (Bakker et al. 2013; Gomis 2014b). The issue has caused much concern in France. In March 2012, Mohammed Merah carried out deadly shootings in Montauban and Toulouse after traveling to Afghanistan and Pakistan (L'Express 2012). In May 2014, Franco–Algerian Mehdi Nemmouche killed four people at the Brussels Jewish Museum. Nemmouche had spent several years incarcerated in the south of France and had taken part in combat operations in Syria, according to Paris prosecutor François Molins (*Le Monde* 2014). Since the May 2012 attacks, France has expanded its antiterrorism laws. In April 2014, the government announced a package of 20 measures designed to address the issue, such as a hotline for families to signal suspicious behavior and the requirement for minors (individuals under 18) to obtain permission to leave the territory—thereby reinstating a measure that had previously been abolished (Ministère de l'intérieur 2014).

In Germany, the *Bundesamt für Verfassungsschutz*, like many others, is closely monitoring a few individuals, and the federal government has confiscated a number of passports. In Belgium, the police arrested Fouad Belkacem, the leader of the dismantled *Sharia4Belgium*, which was found to be helping young Belgians travel to Syria. However, some of the repressive measures recommended by a new Task Force led by Interior Minister Joëlle Milquet were rejected. In the Netherlands, "participating in armed jihad or jihadist training abroad" is a criminal offense under the country's Criminal Code, while other terrorism and immigration laws provide additional legal tools to address the problem (Bakker et al. 2013, p. 4). Canada created the High Risk Travel Case Management Group to assess specific cases of extremist travelers. In 2013, the government created four new offenses with a view to dissuading these individuals from traveling abroad "for terrorism-related purposes," added six new organizations to the list of those associated with terrorism as per the country's criminal code, and took part in research and NGO programs including "Cross-Cultural Roundtable on Security's dialogue on security-related matters, Canada's Multiculturalism Program… and the Kanishka Project's support for academic research" (Public Safety Canada 2014). In the United Kingdom, around half of MI5's ongoing counterterrorism investigations are said to involve Britons who have traveled to fight in Syria (FT 2014a).

UK Home Secretary Theresa May has also led discussions with other European countries on how to best counter the threat of Europeans traveling to and returning from Syria. The measures being considered include banning travel, shutting down organizations, freezing bank accounts, extraditing Muslim preachers, revoking passports, and removing social benefits (Gomis 2014b). In September 2014, a new law was put forward in Australia, under which traveling to certain regions would be considered a crime in itself, even in the absence of any proof that the travel was intended for terrorist activities (FT 2014b).

There is a risk that these initiatives could prove ineffective or even counterproductive. First, research has shown that removing online content very often has the unintended consequence of publicizing the information far more widely—what some refer to as the *Streisand effect*, named after the singer and actress Barbara Streisand, who in 2003 sued the California Coastal Records Project because it had included a picture of her mansion in California as part of their photographic archive of a large part of the state's coastline, only for the picture to be shared much more extensively as a result (*Economist* 2013).

Second, revoking passports and social services or threatening foreign fighters with automatic prison sentences upon their return may very well create more resentment, anger, and marginalization within communities. The International Centre for the Study of Radicalisation and Political Violence (ICSR) reported that some of these individuals contacted the center to share their desire to come home to the United Kingdom. Disillusioned with the situation in Syria—they were forced to fight against other militant groups instead of the regime of Bachar al Assad—they reportedly feared that they will be put in jail upon their return if they came back to their home country (*Independent* 2014b). As ICSR's Shiraz Maher and Peter Neumann point out, "Treating all foreign fighters as terrorists… risks becoming a self-fulfilling prophecy. It may sound tough, but it isn't likely to be effective. Arrests and prosecutions will be needed, but they are just one part of the government's armoury. It must also offer a way out. This is not about being soft: it's about being smart" (Maher and Neumann 2014). A program set up in the city of Aarhus in Demark—which we will explore at greater length in Chapter 7—is a relevant example of how foreign fighters may be successfully rehabilitated and reintegrated upon their return without the threat of incarceration. In addition, on a practical note, a national ID card allows citizens to travel across the Schengen area, in search of countries with more porous borders, making confiscation of passports of little help.

Third, deporting individuals who pose a threat in their home country, or preventing them from returning, merely displaces the problem—often to countries that lack the institutional capacity to deal with such issues in an effective and proportionate way, and that have systematically violated human rights. David Anderson QC, commenting on the proposed legislation in the United Kingdom, warned that revoking citizenship presents a number of legal difficulties (the right of citizenship entails the right of abode and the right to return to one's home country) and practical questions (i.e., When should the person be stopped? Where should they go?).

Importantly, putting in place this type of measure would imply that other countries could very well do the same, thereby leading to a "game of pass the parcel" instead of actually addressing the issues at hand within each country (BBC 2014).

Last but not least, blanket policies dealing with all returning foreign fighters uniformly are inappropriate, given the vast differences among them with regard to personal motivation and actual action on the ground. Crucially, many of these *high-risk travelers* may indeed be fighting against the Assad regime—and thereby share a *common enemy* with their home countries, therefore not warranting the same kind of treatment as the most active members of the Islamic State.

Enhanced Interrogation Techniques

In December 2014, the U.S. Senate Select Committee on Intelligence released its study on the CIA's *Detention and Interrogation Program*, which was put in place in the aftermath of 9/11. It focuses on "the abuses and countless mistakes made between late 2001 and early 2009," before President Obama's Executive Order 13491 put an end to the program.

The findings are unequivocal. The study found that the CIA's use of *enhanced interrogation techniques* was ineffective (it did not prevent any terrorist attack and produced a significant amount of fabricated information), brutal, and far worse than the CIA reported. The agency repeatedly lied about its practices and the program's results, and obstructed oversight, including from the White House, Congress, and the DOJ. The program damaged relationships with foreign countries and "caused immeasurable damage to the United States' public standing, as well as to the United States' longstanding global leadership on human rights in general and the prevention of torture in particular" (U.S. Senate 2014b, pp. 1–19).

In the foreword to the report, Committee Chair Dianne Feinstein wrote: "it is my personal conclusion that, under any common meaning of the term, CIA detainees were tortured. I also believe that the conditions of confinement and the use of authorized and unauthorized interrogation and conditioning techniques were cruel, inhuman, and degrading," noting that the evidence was *overwhelming and incontrovertible* (U.S. Senate 2014a, p. 4).

The report revealed details on some of the gruesome interrogation techniques. These included involuntary rectal feeding and rectal hydration (regardless of medical needs), facial and abdominal slaps and punches, facial grab, stress positions, standing sleep deprivation (e.g., one detainee was held with "his hands affixed over his head for approximately two and a half days"), nudity, water dousing (including until a detainee would turn blue), threats to harm the children of a detainee, threats to sexually abuse the mother of a detainee, threat to *cut [a detainee's] mother's throat, insult slap,* confinement in a coffin-shaped box, walling, placing a pistol and a power drill near a detainee, and playing Russian roulette with a detainee (U.S. Senate 2014c; Wing 2014).

Despite these shocking revelations, several commentators argued that the program did not represent torture. Former Vice President Dick Cheney went as far as saying that *rectal feeding* was not torture and that it was done for *medical reasons.* Refusing to define the term, he noted that torture, to him, "is an American citizen on a cell phone making a last call to his four young daughters shortly before he burns to death in the upper levels of the Trade Center in New York City on 9/11" (Real Clear Politics 2014). More worryingly, an opinion poll conducted in the United States days after the release of the Senate report found that 56% believed that *enhanced interrogation techniques* helped prevent terrorist attacks, even though the Senate report demonstrated otherwise. Of the respondents, 51% also thought that the CIA's interrogation methods were justified, including 76% among Republicans (Pew Research 2014a). When interviewed in previous years on specific torture techniques, including electric shock, water boarding, sexual humiliation, punching/kicking, exposure to extreme heat and cold, and forced nudity, a strong majority of the population (between 58% and 89%) opposed them (Gronke et al. 2010). This suggests that more information and education on what *enhanced interrogation techniques* entail can help shape public opinion on CIA activities and counterterrorism in general (Table 5.1).

Understandably, 9/11 had an extreme psychological impact on many people in the United States and across the world. Thousands of innocent lives were taken, and more attacks were expected to hit the country. And yet, as Dianne Feinstein puts it, "such pressure, fear, and expectation of further terrorist plots do not justify, temper, or excuse improper actions taken by individuals or organizations in the name of national security. The major lesson of this report is that regardless of the pressures and the need to act, the Intelligence Community's actions must always reflect who we are as a nation, and adhere to our laws and standards" (U.S. Senate 2014a, p. 3). Republican Senator John McCain concurred, strongly condemning the CIA program: "It's about who we were, who we are, and who we aspire to be... We need not risk our national honor to prevail in this or any war" (Business Insider 2014).

Table 5.1 American Attitudes on Specific Torture Techniques

Method	Year	Polling Organization	Oppose	Favor
Electric Shock	2004	PIPA/Knowledge Networks	81	19
		ABC News/Washington Post	82	17
Waterboarding*	2004	PIPA/Knowledge Networks	81	17
		ABC News/Washington Post	78	21
	2007	CNN/Opinion Research Corp.	58	40
Sexual Humiliation*	2004	PIPA/Knowledge Networks	89	10
		ABC News/Washington Post	84	16
Forced Naked*	2004	PIPA/Knowledge Networks	75	25
		ABC News/Washington Post	74	35
Exposure to Extreme Heat/Cold†	2004	PIPA/Knowledge Networks	65	34
		ABC News/Washington Post	58	40
Punching/Kicking†	2004	PIPA/Knowledge Networks	81	18
		ABC News/Washington Post	69	29
Stress Positions*	2004	PIPA/Knowledge Networks	47	52
Deny Food/Water†	2004	PIPA/Knowledge Networks	54	44
		ABC News/Washington Post	61	38
Noise Bomb†	2004	PIPA/Knowledge Networks	43	56
		ABC News/Washington Post	45	54
Sleep Deprivation*	2004	PIPA/Knowledge Networks	35	65
		ABC News/Washington Post	33	66
Harsh Interrogation	2009	Gallup	36	55

* Indicates the technique approved by Bybee or Bradbury memoranda.
† Indicates a technique similar to the techniques approved by the Bybee or Bradbury memoranda.
Source: Gronke, P. et al., 2010, PS: *Pol. Sci. Pol.* 43(03): 441.

Torture is ineffective and breeds more terrorism. Alastair Horne perhaps put it best, in reference to torture carried out by French authorities during the Algerian war (1954–1962): "From a purely intelligence point of view, experience teaches that more often than not the collating services are overwhelmed by a mountain of false information extorted from victims desperate to save themselves further agony. Also, it is bound to drive into the enemy camp the innocents who have wrongly been submitted to torture" (Horne 1977). He goes on to quote Albert Camus: "torture has perhaps saved some at the expense of honour, by uncovering thirty bombs, but at the same time it has created fifty new terrorists who, operating in some other way and in another place, would cause the death of even more innocent people" (Horne 1977).

The CIA's *Detention and Interrogation Program* is one of the prime examples of overreaction in post-9/11 counterterrorism: an ineffective, harmful, and counterproductive approach. In January 2009, President Obama restricted CIA detention to a "short-term, transitory basis" and limited "interrogation techniques, approaches and principles" to those listed in the Army Field Manual 2-22.3 (Obama 2009). Nonetheless, more transparency and stronger oversight and accountability measures are needed to ensure that these limitations are respected. The Guantanamo Bay detention camp is another well-known illustration that in the name of the war on terror, exceptions to basic human rights were made, with great harm and little counterterrorism success. Politicians, military officials, experts, and other commentators should continue to make the case against torture and strive to uphold the rule of law. Otherwise, future leaders may indeed return to post-9/11 practices, despite overwhelming evidence of its counterproductive and ineffective effects.

TERRORISM HAS OFTEN BEEN USED BY POLICY OFFICIALS AS A POLITICAL VEIL OR TOOL FOR OTHER PURPOSES

As we have explored previously in this book, terrorism is a powerful label, which draws a great deal of attention in many circles including the media, academia, industry, government, and the general population. Because of the widespread—and often misguided—perception that terrorism is indeed the biggest threat that the world faces, government officials in many different countries have relied on the concept to disguise other intentions or raise popular support for causes only indirectly related.

The governments of Syria, Egypt, Russia, China, and Sri Lanka—to name just a few—have repeatedly used the terrorism label to delegitimize political opponents and ethnic minorities. In addition to the examples already cited in this book, Uighurs have been targeted in western China: as discussions were under way at the UN regarding measures to address the challenges posed by foreign fighters, Chinese officials pushed for tougher measures against separatists, notably sentencing the Uighur academic Ilham Tohti to life in prison for promoting separatism in Xinjiang, his main crime being the creation of a website aimed at increasing understanding between the Chinese-speaking Han majority and Xinjiang's Turkish-speaking Uighur minority, which included opinion essays and investigative reports (Lynch and Groll 2014). In addition, Russian indigenous communities have continuously been harassed, for example, when they tried to travel to New York for the World Conference on indigenous peoples in September 2014 (Scheinin 2014). In Western Europe, France and the United Kingdom have seemingly played up the threat posed by terrorism on some occasions, with a view to gaining popular support for domestic and foreign policies.

In the lead-up to the French military intervention in Mali, for example, Francois Hollande and his government insisted on the direct threat that Al Qaeda in the Islamic Maghreb (AQIM) posed to France. A week after the beginning of *Opération Serval*, the French president noted that troops would remain on the ground "as long as necessary for terrorism to be defeated" (Elysée 2013). French interests have been targeted in the region, including through the kidnapping of four French nationals in 2012 (Le Figaro 2012). However, AQIM poses only a very limited direct threat to the French territory as such. As Jason Burke pointed out, "it has 1,000 or so active members at most, limited resources and almost no reach into Europe beyond a few scattered sympathizers. Its operations have been largely local and, though some of their antecedent groups in the region launched attacks in Europe, it has yet to do so." He continues: "It's not often that someone based in northern Mali, one of the most remote, poorest and desolate parts of the world, is described as an increased threat to anyone, let alone the UK or Europe" (Burke 2011). Similarly, Steve Coll, a reporter for the *New Yorker* on issues of intelligence and national security, commented on the organization's limited reach: "AQIM and its splinters enforced a brutal Islamist ideology when they captured territory in Mali last year, and a breakaway unit attacked a remote gas field in eastern Algeria in January. These groups, however, lack a demonstrated capacity to strike in Europe or across the Atlantic" (Coll 2013). The actual objectives of French military operations in Mali are salutary: to stabilize the country and the broader region. Nonetheless, the French government's overreliance on a counterterrorism narrative as justification for military interventions is problematic, in the sense that it diverts attention away from the more important issues of weak governance, corruption, underdevelopment, and regional insecurity and toward the overhyped, oversimplified, and all-encompassing threat of terrorism. There is strong support in France for an interventionist foreign policy posture: in 2013, 80% of the French population had a positive opinion of the armed forces and 90% of the French population think that it is important or essential for France to remain a global military power if it wants to retain influence in the world (De Durand and Pertusot 2013; Gomis 2014c). Despite this, drawing popular support to spend public funds to defend a faraway government in a poor and complex region of the world is still considered an easier task when a terrorist threat has been established. This has been perhaps even more evident in the case of Western attitudes toward military operations in Syria.

In August 2013, the British Parliament rejected military action against the Syrian regime, despite a widespread military crackdown against civilians, multiple killings, torture, and the use of chemical weapons by the government of Bachar al-Assad. Just over a year later, the British Parliament overwhelmingly approved strikes in neighboring Iraq, against one of the terrorist organizations fighting against the regime—the Islamic State (by 524 votes to 43) (UK Parliament 2014). While other factors (including the legacy of previous military interventions in Iraq and Afghanistan, time pressure, and coalition politics) came into consideration, the difference in the outcome of these two parliamentary debates demonstrated once again that terrorism is a very powerful catalyst for political and popular support, even though Parliament only created the legal framework for UK strikes against Islamic State targets in Iraq, not Syria (BBC World Service 2014). Striking a faraway dictator crushing his own population has certainly proved harder to justify and draw popular support for than going after a terrorist organization.

Our societies are generally more inclined to support counterterrorism policies than other types of foreign policies, including foreign aid. The 2012 Chatham House–YouGov survey found that the British public "greatly overestimates the amount Britain spends on aid," with a median estimate of £20 billion and a mean estimate of £79 billion, far from the actual expenditure of £8.5 billion (Chatham House–YouGov 2012, p. 21). In addition, there is a general belief among the population (56%) that "the UK should give 'not very much' or none at all." When respondents were informed of the actual, and much smaller spending on development in real terms, "61% still felt that this was too high" (Chatham House–YouGov 2012, p. vii). One of the main reasons for this disconnect may be that human beings tend to pay much closer connection to things they can personally and emotionally relate to (Kahneman 2012, p. 323).

The UNSC Resolution 2178 may further reinforce the use of counterterrorism tools for other political, non-terrorism purposes. Adopted unanimously on September 24, 2014, the resolution pertains to the "threats to international peace and security caused by terrorist attacks" (UNSC 2014). It is legally binding, as it was adopted under Chapter VII of the UN Charter. It has been accused of being "so sweeping and vague that it effectively leaves it to each country to decide who to target, and how" (Lynch and Groll 2014). This is not a new problem: as we found in the first chapter of this book, there is no universally agreed-upon definition of terrorism. The resolution reaffirms that "terrorism *in all forms and manifestations* [emphasis mine] constitutes one of the most serious threats to international peace and security and that any acts of terrorism are criminal and unjustifiable *regardless of their motivations, whenever and by whomsoever committed*" [emphasis mine] (UNSC 2014)—thereby reinforcing the lack of clarity as to what should and should not be included within the term. Martin Scheinin, former UN Special Rapporteur on Human Rights and Counterterrorism (2005–2011), warns: "It imposes upon all Member States far-reaching new legal obligations without any effort to define or limit the categories of persons who may be identified as 'terrorists' by an individual state. This approach carries a huge risk of abuse, as various states apply notoriously wide, vague or abusive definitions of terrorism, often with a clear political or oppressive motivation" (Scheinin 2014). Scheinin notes that the resolution—its sixth provision in particular on the prosecution of "any person who participates in the financing, planning, preparation or perpetration of terrorist acts or in supporting terrorist acts"—provides a "handy tool for oppressive regimes that choose to stigmatize as 'terrorism' whatever they do not like, for instance political opposition, trade unions, religious movements, minority or indigenous groups, etc." (Scheinin 2014).

An excellent book entitled *Playing Politics with Terrorism*, edited by George Kassimeris, makes an inventory of cases of political instrumentalization of terrorism, noting that "governments in many countries… have manipulated the threat and fear of terrorism for their own political advantage," including Putin's Russia, Fujimori's Peru, Italy in the 1970s, and Spain in 2004—when Prime Minister Aznar quickly blamed ETA for the terrorist attacks in Madrid, "to avoid the charge that it had attracted the bombers by taking Spain into the Iraq war against the wishes of 90% of the Spanish population" (Kassimeris 2007, pp. 2–4). What's even more striking is perhaps that government narratives and policies that overplay the terrorist threat and denounce political opponents as terrorists may lead to self-fulfilling prophecies. Military crackdowns against political opponents labeled as terrorists may foster extremism and drive some to resort to terrorist tactics in order to further their cause and have their voices heard. Egypt's Muslim Brotherhood and initial peaceful political opposition turned violent in Syria are some of the most pertinent examples of that possible phenomenon (Byman and Wittes 2014).

COUNTERTERRORISM POLICIES HAVE INFRINGED ON PRIVACY: THE SNOWDEN REVELATIONS

In 2013, Edward Snowden, an American computer analyst working as an NSA contractor for Booz Allen Hamilton, released thousands of classified documents to journalists Glenn Greenwald and Laura Poitras. After review, the first documents were published in the *Guardian* and other newspapers around the world in June 2013, exposing large-scale intelligence programs run by the NSA, GCHQ, and other agencies across the world, especially within the so-called *Five Eyes*—an intelligence partnership between Australia, Canada, New Zealand, the United Kingdom, and the United States.

Some of Snowden's revelations were not new. For example, in 2010, the *Washington Post* released the findings of an investigation into *Top Secret America*, which reported on the tremendous growth of the country's intelligence apparatus since 9/11, as we explored earlier on. Over 1,200 government agencies and almost 2,000 private companies were found to be working on counterterrorism, homeland security, and intelligence programs. Over 850,000 people held Top Secret clearances. Thirty-three building complexes for Top Secret intelligence work were built or were being built between 9/11 and October 2010 in Washington and its surrounding area, together occupying approximately 17 million square feet of space—or, as the study points out, the "equivalent of almost three Pentagons or 22 U.S. Capitol buildings." Fifty-one federal organizations and military commands, located in 15 different cities across the United States, track flows of money used by terrorist organizations. It was estimated that intelligence analysts publish around 50,000 intelligence reports every year (*Washington Post* 2010). Strikingly, it was found that "collectively, this apparatus launched far more covert operations in the aftermath of 9/11 than it had during the entire 45 years of the Cold War" (Priest and Arkin 2011, p. 86). However, the intelligence disclosures revealed by Edward Snowden also provided details of far-ranging programs previously unknown to the general public.

The 702 and 215 programs—referring to the sections of the Foreign Intelligence Surveillance Act (FISA) under which they were authorized—were among the key measures that came under public scrutiny. Section 702 of FISA was added by amendment to the 1978 FISA in 2008 and provides the legal basis for *PRISM* as well as the *upstream* collection (Brennan Center for Justice 2013, Privacy and Civil Liberties Oversight Board [PCLOB] 2014). It allows the NSA to gather electronic communication information, including content from e-mail and phone conversations. Conditions include a judicial approval as prerequisite, that the target is outside the United States and is not a U.S. citizen,* that the information flows through U.S. networks, and that there is an appropriate and documented foreign intelligence purpose for the collection (Rollins and Liu 2013, p. ii; Mueller and Stewart 2014, p. 3). Section 215 of the U.S. Patriot Act, which amended FISA, is less targeted and allows for bulk collection of "phone records—including the number that was dialed from, the number that was dialed to, and the date and duration of the call—of customers of Verizon and possibly other U.S. telephone service providers. It does not collect the content of the calls or the identity of callers" (Rollins and Liu 2013, p. ii). In other words, it refers to *metadata*—"that is, the Who, When, How, and Where—but perhaps not the What" (Livingstone 2013).

Following the first leaks, the director of National Intelligence (DNI) released a series of statements and fact sheets with the view to clarifying some details of intelligence-gathering programs that had suddenly come under media and public scrutiny. One fact sheet noted that "PRISM is not an undisclosed collection or data mining program" but an "internal government computer system used to facilitate the government's statutorily authorized collection of foreign intelligence information from electronic communication service providers under court supervision, as authorized by Section 702 of the Foreign Intelligence Surveillance Act (FISA) (50 U.S.C. § 1881a)." In other words, James R. Clapper wanted to clarify that the program was not new, had been approved by Congress in 2008, even adding that it had "been widely known and publicly discussed since its inception" (DNI 2013).

The U.S. government was not the only one exposed by the revelations. Confidential GCHQ and NSA memos revealed details on operation

* As Rollins and Liu note, "the [Obama] Administration has acknowledged that technical limitations in the 'upstream' collection result in the collection of some communications that are unrelated to the target or that may take place between persons in the United States." However, they add that the Foreign Intelligence Surveillance Court (FISC) has not questioned the legality of the program (Rollins and Liu 2013, p. ii).

Tempora and its two sister programs entitled "Mastering the Internet (MTI)" and "Global Telecoms Exploitation," which allows analysts at GCHQ and the NSA to analyze a vast amount of data drawn from more than 200 fiber-optic cables, including 600 million *telephone events* a day. Data gathered through MTI do include not only metadata but also content of e-mails, Facebook entries, and browsing history of Internet users (*Guardian* 2013b). Just like in the United States, this program was technically agreed upon by Parliament, through the 2000 Regulation of Investigatory Powers Act—however, likely with little understanding at that time of the size and scope of interception and collection that future technology would allow. An internal document quoted the then director of the National Security Agency Lieutenant General Keith Alexander posing the following question in 2008: "Why can't we collect all the signals all the time? Sounds like a good summer project for Menwith," referring to the NSA's intercept station in Menwith Hill, North Yorkshire, in the United Kingdom (*Guardian* 2013b). Other intelligence programs the United States and the United Kingdom have cooperated on to include MUSCULAR, Dishfire, Stateroom, Edgehill, and the so-called Echelon program, the latter which Patrick Radden Keefe explored at length in a 2005 book entitled *Chatter: Dispatches from the Secret World of Global Eavesdropping* (Radden Keefe 2005).

The classified documents leaked by Edward Snowden also exposed specific instances of the United States spying on allies, including Germany, Brazil, and Mexico. This and the other aforementioned revelations caused major political and popular backlash across the world. In particular, the wide-ranging efforts to monitor European diplomatic offices and communications networks have led a number of officials to voice their discontent publicly. German Justice Minister Sabine Leutheusser-Schnarrenberger said that U.S. behavior "was reminiscent of the actions of enemies during the Cold War," while French Foreign Minister Laurent Fabius warned: "These acts, if confirmed, would be completely unacceptable" (Gomis 2013b). At the UN General Assembly, Brazilian President Dilma Rousseff declared "tampering in such a manner in the affairs of other countries is a breach of international law and is an affront to the principles that must guide the relations among them, especially among friendly nations," adding "Brazil... knows how to protect itself. We reject, fight and do not harbor terrorist groups" (Rousseff 2013). Even in the United States, Secretary of State John Kerry acknowledged that U.S. electronic surveillance performed "on an automatic pilot because the technology is there," adding that "in some cases, it has reached too far inappropriately," while Jay Carney, the then White House spokesperson, admitted the need for "additional constraints on how we gather and use intelligence" (Zenko 2013a). In January 2014, the European Parliament's Committee on Civil Liberties, Justice and Home Affairs condemned the NSA's surveillance program and similar activities conducted by EU member states. It focused specifically on the NSA's "direct access to the central servers of leading U.S. internet companies (PRISM programme), the circumvention of online encryption (BULLRUN), access to computer and telephone networks and access to location data, as well as to systems of the UK intelligence agency GCHQ such as its upstream surveillance activity (Tempora programme) and decryption programme (Edgehill)." The report noted that similar programs, "even if on a more limited scale," likely exist in other countries such as France, Germany, and Sweden. The 52-page draft report lists a number of impacts of the surveillance programs, including decrease in political trust, an infringement on "the established paradigm of criminal law in democratic societies" and "effects on the freedom of the press, thought and speech." It criticized in particular the detention of David Miranda (partner of journalist Glenn Greenwald) and the seizure of the material in his possession under Schedule 7 of the UK's Terrorism Act 2000, as well as the request to the *Guardian* to destroy and hand over the Snowden files (European Parliament 2014, p. 16, 17, 26).

The release of classified documents on intelligence and surveillance programs has led to numerous discussions on their legality, morality, efficacy, necessity, and proportionality. The following sections will highlight and challenge 10 arguments often raised in defense of these programs.

"If You Have Nothing to Hide, You Have Nothing to Fear"

In an interview with the BBC a few days after the first leaks, the then UK Foreign Secretary William Hague aimed to reassure the British public: "If you are a law-abiding citizen of this country... you have nothing to fear about the British state or intelligence agencies listening to the content of your phone calls or anything like that. Indeed you'll never be aware of all the things these agencies are doing to stop your identity being stolen and to stop a terrorist blowing you up tomorrow" (*Guardian* 2013). This statement, similar to many others made by government officials, intelligence officials, and experts since June 2013, is problematic on three main counts. First, Hague's argument that "you'll never be aware of all the things these agencies are doing" is far from reassuring. In itself, secrecy does not and should not lead to automatic support. On the contrary, without any information on what is being done, how can one reasonably assess that measures put in place have been appropriate? Intelligence agencies obviously need some secrecy and cannot share many operational details with the public. However, without the appropriate levels of monitoring, scrutiny, and overall checks and balances, citizens have no guarantee that intelligence agencies will stay within the expected legal and ethical boundaries.

Second, the right to privacy is a fundamental right, guaranteed by the Universal Declaration of Human Rights, whose Article 12 stipulates that "no one shall be subjected to arbitrary interference with his privacy, home, family or correspondence" (UN 1948). The presumption of innocence is another basic legal right in liberal democratic societies, based on the principle that one should be considered innocent until proven guilty. Intelligence programs led by the NSA and other agencies now seem to be weakening this overarching principle. Data collection is indeed based on the assumption that some individuals may indeed be carrying out or linked to terrorist and other criminal activities.

Third, triangulating information does not necessarily lead to an accurate depiction of reality. As Dan Geer put it, "the more inane the questions are, the more inane the picture painted becomes." Using a role-play to demonstrate his point, he adds: "if you get to pick the questions and the subject is sufficiently willing to keep answering them, then you can pretty much box in your subject however you like" (Geer 2013). Similarly, as computer security expert Mikko Hypponen pointed out in a TED Talk in Brussels in November 2013, "whoever tells you that they have nothing to hide simply hasn't thought about this long enough" (Hypponen 2013). Michael Humphrey, an instructor in entrepreneurial journalism at Colorado State University and a writer, told the story of a student claiming she had nothing to hide from intelligence agencies. Humphrey thus asked the student "about a scenario in which she had an informant whose identity needed to be protected and mentioned that in many places communication can be a matter of life and death." The student replied that this case was different, as "they were talking about the government spying on 'regular citizens'" (Humphrey 2014). This particular instance shows how we may misjudge how targeted intelligence programs have been since 9/11. I have had similar conversations with colleagues and students who had not thought of specific scenarios under which they could be wrongfully considered suspicious of terrorist activities by the NSA or other intelligence agencies, neglecting to consider travels to specific countries, online discussions on sensitive topics, or exchanges with

NGOs operating in areas affected by terrorism. However, given the scale of intelligence programs in place around the world, these programs affect us all, not only practically but also morally, from a societal standpoint. Governments should be held accountable for breaches of basic rights. In the name of the war on terrorism, the United States and other Western governments have permitted significant infringements on privacy and civil liberties in order to tackle a threat that has been in fact vastly overblown and oversimplified.

"This Is Not Surprising. We All Knew This Was Happening"

Many researchers and commentators have claimed that the Snowden revelations did not add anything new. This is simply not true. While there had been reports of large-scale data collection, vast increases in intelligence gathering, and evidence of privacy breaches, the classified documents released in the *Guardian* and other newspapers presented a lot of new information and important details on the programs, and therefore tangible evidence to study. As Hypponen reminds us, "We didn't know about PRISM. We didn't know about XKeyscore. We didn't know about Cybertrans. We didn't know about DoubleArrow. We did not know about Skywriter—all these different programs run by U.S. intelligence agencies—but now we do" (Hypponen 2013). In addition to the inaccuracy of the claim that the Snowden leaks did not contain anything surprising, the implication is that no further discussion is therefore needed, given that "we already knew this was happening."

"Snowden Had Other Courses of Action"

NSA Deputy Director Richard Ledgett, among others, made this argument at the TED annual conference in Vancouver in March 2014: "There are a variety of venues to address if folks have a concern. First up, you can go to your supervisor through the supervising chain in the organization. If you're not comfortable with that, there are inspectors general. In the case of Mr. Snowden, he had the option of the NSA Inspector General, the Navy Inspector General, the Pacific Fleet Inspector General, the Intelligence Committee Inspector General. Any of whom would have kept concerns in classified channels and addressed them. There are also Congressional committees and mechanisms in place. He didn't do any of that" (TED 2014).

It may be true that Snowden did not exhaust all possible courses of action within Booz Allen Hamilton, Dell (where he previously worked), or the NSA. In 2012, President Obama signed the Whistleblower Protection Enhancement Act, which revised the Whistleblower Protection Act of 1989. In addition, he issued the Presidential Policy Directive 19, specifically aimed to protect whistleblowers with access to classified information. Among other things, the directive prohibits retaliation against whistleblowers who release classified information to an inspector general or a member of a relevant congressional committee. However, it is unclear what reality would have looked like. There is uncertainty around some of the elements of the directive, particularly on the differences in protection between employees and contractors (*Washington Post* 2012).

Additionally, Snowden's objections to the NSA's work did not only pertain to one or two specific aspects or measures, but rather to extensive programs that had been put in place after 9/11 and approved by the three branches of government—a whole system, in other words. Addressing those concerns with supervisors and managers at the NSA or even the legislative or judicial branches could thus have been difficult, to say the least. Crucially, such a course of action would most likely have resulted in the programs never coming under public scrutiny with regard to their appropriateness or indeed legality.

A fairer argument in opposition to the leaks carried out by Snowden refers to the number of classified documents he released (thousands) and the way he did it (by passing them on to journalists). While this strategy was perhaps not the most effective, there were a high number of relevant documents related to the programs Snowden wished to challenge and therefore impracticalities related to that. In addition, he purposely reached out to journalists for them to meticulously go through all documents, identify those that would be most relevant to release, and remove all information that would compromise any individual in the security services.

"I Disagree with Snowden But Welcome the Debate"

NSA's Ledgett has admitted that despite his disagreement with the way Snowden has challenged current programs, he welcomes the debate: "I think the discussion is an important one to have. I do not like the way he did it; there were a number of other ways to do it that would not have endangered our people and people of other nations by losing visibility into what our adversaries are doing. But I do think it's an important conversation" (TED 2014). Even DNI James Clapper conceded: "I think it's clear that some of the conversations this has generated, some of the debate, actually needed to happen" (*Los Angeles Times* 2013). Similarly, President Obama noted that "in the absence of institutional requirements for regular debate—and oversight that is public, as well as private or classified—the danger of government overreach becomes more acute." He has launched a review process into the activities of intelligence agencies as a result of the revelations by Snowden (White House 2014). Nevertheless, neither Ledgett, nor Clapper, nor President Obama, had taken any steps to initiate the debate on these issues prior to Snowden's revelations. The discussion on the role of intelligence agencies in democratic societies, practicalities of oversight mechanisms, the balance between secrecy and public accountability, and whether the terrorist threat warrants the scope of these intelligence programs—among other relevant questions—is indeed an essential one to have. However, there was only very limited discussion both within Western governments and among the general public before the Snowden revelations, which in itself demonstrates a possible justification for his actions.

"Countries around the World Have Always Spied on Each Other. Everybody Does It, So It's Fine"

It is true that intelligence-gathering programs aimed at other states are nothing new. However, spying on allies for political and economic reasons under the cover of fighting terrorism is bound to be politically damaging and further reinforces the perception that terrorism is more pervasive and serious than it actually is. Additionally, most of the revelations of Edward Snowden focused on indiscriminate data collection of ordinary citizens, not government officials.

"What Private Companies Do Is Much Worse"

Private companies indeed collect and analyze significant amounts of personal data, including web-browsing history, content of e-mails, location, contacts, and other types of Internet activity. For instance, as per the company's terms of services, Google analyzes "content (including e-mails) to provide you personally relevant product features, such as customized search results, tailored advertising, and spam and malware detection" (Gillmor 2014). However, there is a crucial difference between companies and intelligence agencies: the former do so for marketing purposes—with a view to increasing revenue—while data collection by the latter may have much more serious practical and legal implications, including intimidation, arrests, and prosecution. In other words, although checks and balances are needed to manage the challenges posed by the increasing commercial monitoring of personal data, the difference between the two fields comes down to being considered a suspected customer or a suspected terrorist.

"It's Only Metadata"

Another widely used argument points to the *benign* nature of metadata. In other words, intelligence gathering is not as damaging as it may sound—the argument goes, since the content of e-mails, messages, texts, and phone calls is not actually collected. But as Geer argues: "the soothing mendacity of proxies for the President saying 'It's only metadata' relies on the ignorance of the listener" (Geer 2014).

Two objections must indeed be raised here. First, a number of revealed programs do indeed collect some actual content. While the 215 program reportedly accumulates only metadata, PRISM also gathers content from e-mail and phone conversations (Rollins and Liu 2013, p. ii; Mueller and Stewart 2014, p. 3).

Second, collecting metadata from a large number of innocent individuals is not benign. As Jesselyn Radack, national security and human rights lawyer and former whistleblower, puts it: "If I call an abortion clinic, suicide prevention line or Alcoholics Anonymous, you have an idea of what I'm calling about" (Crikey 2014). During a congressional hearing with officials from the NSA, former Deputy Director John C. Inglis noted that NSA analysts, provided the court gives them permission, can "do not just first hop analysis, meaning what numbers are in contact with that selector, but to then from those numbers go out two or three hops" (U.S. Congress 2013, p. 36). This means that the NSA can look at data not only from a suspected terrorist but also from everyone that particular suspect has communicated with (first hop), everyone those people communicated with (second hop), and everyone those people communicated with as well (third hop) (*Guardian* 2013). In his testimony, Inglis declared: "During 2012, we only initiated searches for information in this dataset using fewer than 300 unique identifiers" (Congress 2013, p. 10). However, as Jameel Jaffer, the deputy legal director of the American Civil Liberties Union Foundation, pointed out later on the same day: "I don't think anybody should be misled by this 300 number, which makes it sound like this is a very targeted program. But if you think about the 300 number in relation to what was said on the previous panel about three hops, the first hop takes you to, say, 100 people whose communications are pulled up. The second one takes you to 10,000, and the third one takes you to 1 million. And you do that 300 times. I think it is safe to say that every American's communications have been pulled up at least once" (U.S. Congress 2013, p. 124). U.S. District Judge Richard Leon went even further in a trial that ended with an important ruling in December 2013 when he ordered the federal government to stop collecting data on two Verizon customers and destroy the data collected in the 5 years prior: "Suppose, for instance, that there is a person living in New York City ... (who) is approved as a 'seed.' And suppose this person who may or may not be actually associated with any terrorist organization, calls or receives calls from 100 unique numbers. But now suppose that one of the numbers he calls is his neighborhood Domino's Pizza shop. The court won't hazard a guess as to how many different phone numbers might dial a given Domino's Pizza outlet in New York City in a five-year period, but to take a page from the Government's book of understatement, it's 'substantially larger' than the 100 in the second hop of my example" (Gigaom 2013).

This gives a better sense of the massive scale of intelligence gathering carried out by the NSA. It is also worth pointing out that the FISA court has reportedly "rejected only 11 of the more than 33,900 surveillance applications made by the federal government between 1979 and June 2013" (Zenko 2013b), which illustrates the superficial judicial oversight under which the NSA has operated.

"It's Better to Be Safe Than Sorry. I'd Rather Give Up Some of My Privacy for Increased Security"

The balance between privacy and security is an often-quoted concept. According to this argument, there are trade-offs between those two elements: more security means less privacy and vice versa. The NSA, among others, has insisted on this point. In October 2013, the NSA approved the release of a series of memos following a Freedom of Information Act request by Al Jazeera. The memos contained NSA talking points for the media, Congress, and the Obama Administration surrounding the intelligence leaks. The category *Sound Bites That Resonate* include the following statement, playing up the trade-offs between privacy and security: "I much prefer to be here today explaining these programs, than explaining another 9/11 event that we were not able to prevent" (NSA 2013, p. 4). It is fair to argue that the NSA and its defenders have overplayed the automatic relationship between privacy and security. More security does not necessarily have to entail less privacy. As Bruce Schneier contends, it is a false dilemma: "I've never liked the idea of security vs. privacy, because no one feels more secure in a surveillance state... There's plenty of examples of security that doesn't infringe on privacy. They are all around. Door locks. Fences... Firewalls. People are forgetting that quite a lot of security doesn't affect privacy." In other words, he adds: "The real dichotomy is liberty vs. control" (Kelley 2013).

On June 7, 2013, President Barack Obama said: "You can't have 100% security, and also then have 100% privacy and zero inconvenience" (Kelley 2013). However, no one should—and very few do—expect 100% security, an unrealistic scenario evoking the naive wishes of a *drug-free world*. Terrorism is not a threat that can be fully eradicated, but a risk that can be mitigated and managed. Hypponen's rhetorical question perhaps puts it best: "Do we really think terrorism is such an existential threat that we are ready to do anything at all?" (Hypponen 2013).

"Intelligence Programs Only Target Foreigners"

U.S. intelligence agencies—excluding the FBI—indeed have the legal right to monitor only foreigners. However, given the technology available, and given that checks and balances have been kept to a minimum, it is fair to assume that U.S. nationals have been affected as well—especially in light of the *three-hop* query previously explained. The Obama Administration has even acknowledged that "technical limitations in the 'upstream' collection result in the collection of some communications that are unrelated to the target or that may take place between persons in the United States"—the so-called incidental collection (Rollins and Liu 2013, p. ii). Crucially, the rest of the world is largely dependent on U.S. and Western technology providers. This gives the United States and other *Five Eyes* countries the opportunity to collect data as it passes through their respective countries. Ultimately, the U.S. population accounts for approximately 4.4% of the world population, which means that the NSA can technically monitor the remaining 95.6%.

"We Are Less Safe Now Because of the Snowden Revelations: Terrorists Know What We're Up To and Will Change the Way They Operate as a Result"

NSA Deputy Director Rick Ledgett, for instance, indicated that the actions Edward Snowden took "were inappropriate because of the fact that he put people's lives at risks in the long run," later adding that "the unconstrained disclosure of those capabilities mean the targets see it and recognize it and move away from our ability to have insight into what they're doing" (TED 2014). In a Congressional hearing, Lt. General Michael Flynn, director of the Defense Intelligence Agency, warned: "I think that the greatest cost that is unknown today, but we will likely face, is the cost in human lives on tomorrow's battlefield or in someplace where we will put our military forces, when we ask them to go into harm's way" (*Washington Post* 2014b). In the unclassified NSA *talking points* memo, some of the key items indeed relate to this argument: "Disclosures have done irreversible and significant damage to security; every time there are disclosures, it makes out job harder; our adversaries are paying attention and we already see signs they are making adjustments" (NSA 2013, p. 3).

This argument has crossed borders as well, to other countries of the *Five Eyes*: "Disclosure of highly sensitive information can be damaging. It can certainly undermine our security, certainly it can put lives at risk," noted UK Security Minister James Brokenshire (Reuters 2013). But the exchange between Australia's attorney general George Brandis and the Greens senator Scott Ludlam was perhaps most revealing. Ludlam asked Brandis if he could identify a single case of a life having been put at risk as a result of the intelligence leaks, to which Brandis replied: "You ask me if I'm aware of particular cases; the answer to your question is yes, on the basis of intelligence briefings I receive." Ludlam sarcastically retorted: "We'll just have to take your word for it" (*Guardian* 2014). Intelligence officials have indeed overwhelmingly refused to provide specific examples of any practical implications of the Snowden leaks, under the cover of *national security*. While there are of course numerous particular cases and intelligence operations that should not be revealed, our societies have allowed such high levels of secrecy and such little oversight that it is almost impossible to know for sure whether lives—and if, so under what circumstances—have indeed been put at risk as a result of the revelations by Edward Snowden.

Importantly, terrorists and members of organized crime groups were already aware that intelligence agencies and the police had the capacity to monitor their electronic conversations. Therefore, the Snowden revelations offer little new information in this regard from their perspective: face-to-face interactions remain the most effective and safest way to operate. As John Mueller comically points out, "Conceivably, as some maintain, there still exist some exceptionally dim-witted terrorists or would-be terrorists who are oblivious to the fact that their communications are rather less than fully secure. But such supreme knuckle-heads are surely likely to make so many mistakes—like advertising on Facebook or searching there or in chatrooms for co-conspirators—that sophisticated and costly communications data banks are scarcely needed to track them down" (Mueller and Stewart 2014, p. 5). In addition, the extremists and criminals that do openly document their illegal activities on social media for bragging, social status, prestige, and adventure are unlikely to alter their behavior because of the Snowden revelations (Mohar and Gomis 2014).

In conclusion, it is worth noting that there have been unsubstantiated claims, exaggerated reports, misinformation, and confusion in the media as to what the Snowden leaks revealed and on the specificities of the intelligence programs run by the NSA and others. The complexity—along with the opacity—of these programs is such that it is extremely difficult to fully understand what is being carried out. During a conversation with Keith Alexander, President Obama reportedly lost his patience after an extremely technical explanation on a surveillance program, asking whether the NSA director could do it again, "but this time in English" (Klaidman 2013).

However, what is perhaps most striking about the intelligence-gathering programs the United States and others have developed since 9/11 is that they have not resulted in any significant increase in law enforcement effectiveness, despite the tremendous amounts of money, time, personnel, and energy expended. Prior to September 2001, U.S. counterterrorism agencies had not suffered from a lack of data. The failure to disrupt the 9/11 plot was not in itself an information collection problem, but instead reflected flaws in information sharing between the CIA and the FBI in particular, and an overall incapacity to act upon relevant intelligence that had in fact been received. Similarly, in November 2009, Umar Farouk Abdulmutallab's father, concerned with his son's extremist views, reported him to the U.S. Embassy in Abuja, Nigeria. While Umar's name was reportedly added to the U.S. Terrorist Identities Datamart Environment (TIDE), a database run by the U.S. National Counterterrorism Center, neither it was added to the FBI's Terrorist Screening Database, which feeds the Secondary Screening Selectee list and the U.S. no-fly list, nor was his U.S. visa revoked. Additionally, his name was included in a diplomatic cable sent by intelligence officials, indicating that *Umar Farouk* had spoken to American-Yemeni preacher Anwar al-Awlaki in Yemen. However, his last name was not specified. This chain of events failed to prevent Abdulmutallab from boarding Northwest Airlines Flight 253 from Amsterdam to Detroit on December 25, 2009, and attempting to detonate a bomb, hidden in his underwear, in midair (U.S. Senate 2010).

If anything, overloading a system with too much irrelevant information is likely to make it more ineffectual. While there was a concededly too-low 16 people on the U.S. no-fly list before 9/11, by August 2013, there were approximately 48,000 (AP 2014; Bergen 2014). The U.S. DHS lists as many as 18 sectors as *critical infrastructure*, namely, "agriculture and food; banking and finance; chemical; commercial facilities; communications; critical manufacturing; dams; defense industrial base; emergency services; energy; government facilities; healthcare and public health; information technology; national monuments and icons; postal and shipping; transportation systems; water; and nuclear reactors, materials and waste" (Clemente 2013b, p. 14). The National Asset Database grew from 160 in 2003, to 28,000 in 2004, and 77,069 in 2006, and over 300,000 today, including terrorist targets such as the Indiana Apple and Pork Festival and the annual Mule Day Parade in Columbia, Tennessee (Brzezinski 2007; Clemente 2013b, p. 19; Jones and Silberzahn 2013). As of 2009, the TIDE database contained approximately 640,000 names of suspected terrorists (500,000 separate *identities*) while the FBI's Terrorist Screening Data Base (TSDB) held roughly 1,000,000 names (400,000 separate *identities*) (FBI 2008; Pincus 2009). Between March 2008 and March 2009, on average, 1600 new names were suggested *daily* for the TSDB (Pincus 2009).

Bruce Schneier has offered a useful metaphor for how gathering more intelligence may prove counterproductive: "Piling more data onto the mix makes it harder, not easier. The best way to think of it is a needle-in-a-haystack problem; the last thing you want to do is increase the amount of hay you have to search through" (Schneier 2014b). While it might sound counterintuitive, collecting more data to keep us safe might have the unintended—yet, once again, foreseeable—opposite effect.

Although there was significant political and public opposition to NSA activities in the immediate aftermath of the initial revelations by Edward Snowden, it has diminished since then, for three main reasons. First, European officials have been facing much more pressing issues, including a persistent economic crisis, high levels of unemployment, the future of the Eurozone, and budget deficits—and all that in spite of the dramatic measures implemented so far, either in the form of bailouts, public investments, or austerity programs. Much attention and many resources have therefore been devoted to addressing these challenges as a priority.

Second, several governments in Western Europe that have publicly expressed their discontent regarding the recently revealed U.S. intelligence programs have inconsistencies and contradictions in their own policies, specifically their attitudes toward civil liberties. In particular, France has implemented very harsh counterterrorism policies over the past three decades, for example, through widespread intelligence and surveillance measures, apparently indiscriminate raids on Muslim communities and numerous deportations. Meanwhile, the early version of the UK counterradicalization program known as prevent, stop and search measures and some of the schemes of GCHQ (e.g., Tempora, Edgehill) have caused controversy. As the European Parliament's Committee on Civil Liberties, Justice and Home Affairs noted, other EU member states such as Sweden and the Netherlands may also be running similar intelligence-gathering programs (European Parliament 2014, p. 19). In 2004, a report by the German Max Planck Institute for Foreign and International Criminal Law revealed that Italy and the Netherlands topped the Western world ranking of wiretaps per capita, with respectively 76 and 62 per 100,000 inhabitants—by way of comparison, the United States then reportedly conducted only 0.5 wiretaps per 100,000 (European Digital Rights 2004). All of this sheds light on some of the hypocrisy of political reactions to U.S. intelligence programs in Europe (Gomis 2013b).

Third, the rising threat of the Islamic State and foreign fighters—tangible yet often exaggerated—has made far-ranging intelligence programs appealing again, not only in Europe but also in the United States, despite early signs of a reform process, for instance with the enactment of the USA Freedom Act. The Pew Research Center for the People and the Press found that "In a reversal from last year after Edward Snowden's NSA leaks, 50% today say they are more concerned that government antiterrorism policies have not gone far enough to protect the country, while 35% are more concerned that the policies have gone too far in restricting civil liberties" (Pew Research 2014b). American University Professor Stephen Vladeck noticed that "there was a lot of movement on surveillance reform in Congress... but it has been totally overtaken by ISIS" (Lynch 2014).

This is a worrying development, yet one which once again demonstrates the urgency of comprehensive reform of counterterrorism policies. Challenges to current policies are often dismissed as irresponsible or complacent, but as President Obama put it in a speech at the National Defense University in 2013, "America is at a crossroads. We must define the nature and scope of this struggle, or else it will define us" (White House 2013b). The same is true in Europe. The time has come to turn rhetoric into practice and reform counterterrorism policies substantially across the West (Gomis 2013b).

REFERENCES

Abrahms, M. 2006. Why terrorism does not work. *International Security* 21(2): 42–78.

Amnesty International. 2014. U.S. Policy in Colombia. URL: http://www.amnestyusa.org/our-work/countries/americas/colombia/us-policy-in-colombia. Accessed on August 21, 2014.

Anderson, D. 2012. The Terrorism Acts in 2011. Report of the Independent Reviewer on the Operation of the Terrorism Act 2000 and Part 1 of the Terrorism Act 2006, June 2012.

AP. 2014. AP Exclusive: U.S. changing no-fly list rules. URL: http://news.yahoo.com/ap-exclusive-us-changing-no-fly-list-rules-223919022–politics.html. Accessed on August 19, 2014.

Arbour, L. 2014. From Syria to Crimea: Is global governance at a loss? Event organized by the School of International Studies, Simon Fraser University. Vancouver, September 25, 2014.

ASH. 2013. Smoking statistics: Illness and death. ASH fact sheet, April 2013.

Australian Financial Review. 2013. McAfee regrets 'flawed' trillion dollar cybercrime claims, URL : http://www.afr.com/technology/enterprise-it/mcafee-regrets-flawed-trillion-dollar-cybercrime-claims-20130819-jha8k. Accessed on August 19, 2013.

Bakker, E., Paulussen, C., and Entenmann, E. 2013. Dealing with European foreign fighters in Syria: Governance challenges and legal implications. ICCT Research Paper, December 2013.

BBC News. 2012. Press "need to act" after Leveson, November 30, 2012.

BBC News. 2014a. Military spending: Balance tipping towards China, February 5, 2014.

BBC News. 2014b. Ukraine crisis timeline, May 8, 2014.

BBC News. 2014c. Tony Blair: "West should focus on radical Islam," April 23, 2014.

BBC News. 2014d. Million Syria refugees registered in Lebanon—UN, April 3, 2014.

BBC News. 2014e. Sri Lanka profile. URL: http://www.bbc.com/news/world-south-asia-11999611. Accessed on September 17, 2014.

BBC Radio 4. 2014. "Safeguards needed" over anti-terror powers. Today Programme, September 2, 2014.

BBC World Service. 2014. The Syria vote. The Documentary, November 12, 2014.

Beittel, J. 2013. Mexico's drug trafficking organizations: Source and scope of the violence. Congressional Research Service, April 15, 2013.

Bergen, P. 2014. Forecasts of terrorist apocalypse? Never mind. CNN, February 26, 2014.

Bloomberg. 2014. China's Treasury holdings climb to record in government data, January 15, 2014.

Bornewasser, M. 1993. Social psychological reactions to social change and instability: Fear of status loss, social discrimination and foreigner hostility. *Civilisations* 42(2): 91–103.

Brennan Center for Justice. 2013. Are they allowed to do that? A breakdown of selected government surveillance programs. New York University School of Law, New York, July 15, 2013.

Brito, J. and Watkins, T. 2011. Loving the cyber bomb? The dangers of threat inflation in cybersecurity policy. *Harvard National Security Journal* 3: 39–84.

Brzezinski, Z. 2007. Terrorized by "war on terror." Opinions, *Washington Post*. URL: http://www.washingtonpost.com/wp-dyn/content/article/2007/03/23/AR2007032301613.html. Accessed on March 25, 2007.

Burke, J. 2011. Stop looking for the next al-Qaida. *The Guardian*. URL: http://www.theguardian.com/commentisfree/2011/dec/25/stop-looking-next-al-qaida. Accessed on December 25, 2011.

Business Insider. 2014. John McCain: The brutal CIA interrogations "stained our national honor," December 9, 2014.

Byman, D.L. and Wittes, C.T. 2014. Now that the Muslim Brotherhood is declared a terrorist group, it might become one. Brookings Institution, January 10, 2014.

Cancer Research UK. 2014. Cancer mortality for common cancers. URL: http://www.cancerresearchuk.org/cancer-info/cancerstats/mortality/cancerdeaths/uk-cancer-mortality-statistics-for-common-cancers. Accessed on September 17, 2014.

Caplin, A. 2003. Fear as a policy instrument: Economic and psychological perspectives on intertemporal choice. In Loewenstein, G., Read D., and Baumeister, R. (eds), *Time and Decision*. New York: Russell Sage Foundation, pp. 441–458.

Carver, F. 2012. Where did Assad go to school? Sri Lanka Campaign blog, March 11, 2012.

Carver, F. 2014. Losing battles but winning wars: How Sri Lanka is crushing dissent. *International Policy Digest*. URL: http://www.internationalpolicydigest.org/wp-content/uploads/2015/02/1577553350389.pdf. Accessed on August 9, 2014.

Carver, F. and Gowing, R. 2014. Interview with the author, June 2014.

CDC. 1994. Centers for Disease Control and Prevention. Suicide contagion and the reporting of suicide: Recommendations from a National Workshop. *Morbidity and Mortality Weekly Review* 43-6: 9–18.

Chatham House–YouGov. 2012. The Chatham House–YouGov Survey 2012. British attitudes towards the UK's international priorities. Survey Results, July 2012.

Choudhury, T. 2012. Impact of Counter-terrorism on Communities: UK Background Report. Institute for Strategic Dialogue and Open Society Foundations, September 2012.

Clemente, D. 2013a. The Internet in 2020: Tranquil or turbulent? Series: Governing the Internet: Chaos, Control or Consensus? Centre for International Governance Innovation, January 22, 2013.

Clemente, D. 2013b. Cyber security and global interdependence: What is critical? Programme Report, Chatham House, February 2013.

Clinton, H. 2011. America's Pacific Century. *Foreign Policy*. URL: http://foreign-policy.com/2011/10/11/americas-pacific-century/. Accessed on October 11, 2011.

CNN. 2001. Transcript of President Bush's address, September 21, 2001.

CNS News. 2011. Syrian President Assad regarded as a "Reformer," Clinton says, March 28, 2011.

Coleman, L. 2004. *The Copycat Effect: How the Media and Popular Culture Trigger the Mayhem in Tomorrow's Headlines*. New York: Pocket Books, September 14, 2004.

Coll, S. 2013. Name calling. *The New Yorker*. URL: http://www.newyorker.com/magazine/2013/03/04/name-calling-2. Accessed on March 4, 2013.

Congress. 2013. Hearing before the Committee on the Judiciary House of Representatives. Serial No. 113-45, July 17, 2013.

Congressional Budget Office. 2014. Estimated impact of the American Recovery and Reinvestment Act on Employment and Economic Output in 2013. Report, February 21, 2014.

Cornish, P. et al. 2010. On cyber warfare. Chatham House Report, November 2010.

Crikey. 2014. "Nothing to hide, nothing to fear": Whistleblowers warn of threats to privacy, August 5, 2014.

Dearlove, R. 2014. Terrorism and national security: Proportion or distortion? Event, RUSI, July 7, 2013.

De Durand, E. and Pertusot, V. 2013. Defense matters: IFRI contribution on France, September 2013.

Deputy Secretary of Defense Memorandum. 2008. The definition of cyberspace, May 12, 2008.

DHS. 2003. Operation Liberty Shield: Press briefing by Secretary Ridge, March 18, 2003.

DNI. 2013. Facts on the collection of intelligence pursuant to Section 702 of the Foreign Intelligence Surveillance Act, June 8, 2013.

Duevell, F. 2013. Romanian and Bulgarian migration to Britain: Facts behind the fear, March 28, 2013.

Ebinger, C.K. and Zambetakis, E. 2009. The geopolitics of Arctic melt. *International Affairs* 85(6), 1215–1232.

Economist. 2012. Shattered lives, November 19, 2012.

Economist. 2013. What is the Streisand effect? *The Economist* explains, April 15, 2013.

Economist. 2014a. Crowning the dragon. Daily Chart, April 30, 2014.

Economist. 2014b. Immigration: No flood, after all, May 17, 2014.

Economist. 2014c. Daily chart: Stranger in a strange land, September 2, 2014.
Economist. 2014d. It ain't half hot here, mum, August 30, 2014.
Elysée. 2013. Extrait du discours des voeux du Président de la République à Tulle sur la situation international, January 19, 2013.
Emmerson, C. and Lahn, G. 2012. Arctic opening: Opportunity and risk in the high north. Chatham House—Lloyd's Risk Insight Report, April 2012.
European Digital Rights. 2004. Italy and the Netherlands top Wiretap Chart. EDRI-gram. URL: https://edri.org/edrigramnumber2-14wiretap/. Accessed on July 15, 2004.
European Parliament. 2014. Draft Report on the U.S. NSA surveillance programme, surveillance bodies in various Member States and their impact on EU citizens' fundamental rights and on transatlantic cooperation in Justice and Home Affairs. European Parliament, Committee on Civil Liberties, Justice and Home Affairs. 2013/2188 (INI), January 8, 2014.
FBI. 2008. Statement before the House of Representatives Committee on Homeland Security, Subcommittee on Transportation Security and Infrastructure Protection. Rick Kopel, Principal Deputy Director, Terrorist Screening Center. Washington, DC, September 9, 2008.
Felbab-Brown, V. 2011. Narcoterrorism and the long reach of U.S. law enforcement. Testimony before the U.S. House of Representatives Subcommittee on Terrorism, Nonproliferation and Trade. Brookings Institution, October 12, 2011.
FT. 2014a. MI5 focuses on British jihadists returning from Syria. March 14, 2014.
FT. 2014b. Australia set to ban travel to terrorist hotspots, August 5, 2014.
Gallup. 2014. Terrorism in the United States. URL: http://www.gallup.com/poll/4909/terrorism-united-states.aspx. Accessed on September 17, 2014.
GAO. 2003. Homeland Security: Justice Department's Project to Interview Aliens after September 11, 2011. GAO-03-459, April 11, 2003.
Geer, D. 2013. Tradeoffs in cyber security. Presentation at University of North Carolina Charlotte, Charlotte, NC, October 9, 2013.
Geer, D. 2014. We are all intelligence officers now. Presentation at RSA, San Francisco, February 28, 2014.
Geerds, F. 1981. Criminal Contagion and Criminal Imitation. *Archiv fuer Kriminologie* 168(1–2): 1–16. July/August 1981.
Gigaom. 2013. How feds use one "seed" and 3 "hops" to spy on nearly everyone, December 17, 2013.
Giles, K. 2014. Russia will take whatever it can. Expert Comment. Chatham House, March 3, 2014.
Gillmor, D. 2014. As we sweat government surveillance, companies like Google collect our data. *Guardian.* URL: http://www.theguardian.com/commentisfree/2014/apr/18/corporations-google-should-not-sell-customer-data. Accessed on April 18, 2014.
Gold, D. 2005. The costs of terrorism and the costs of countering terrorism. International Affairs Working Paper 2005-03, The New School, March 2005.
Gomis, B. 2013a. Woolwich attack: Managing fear. Expert Comment, Chatham House, May 24, 2013.

Gomis, B. 2013b. U.S. intelligence leaks offer chance for European counterterrorism reform. *World Politics Review*, July 8, 2013.
Gomis, B. 2014a. Illicit drugs and international security: Towards UNGASS 2016. Briefing Paper. Chatham House, February 2014.
Gomis, B. 2014b. Growing threat of European fighters in Syria highlights need for EU cooperation. Briefing. World Politics Review, July 10, 2014.
Gomis, B. 2014c. Global Gendarme: The future of French security policy. *IHS Jane's Intelligence Review*, 30–35.
Google Books Ngram Viewer, accessed on April 10, 2014.
Gronke, P. et al. July 2010. U.S. Public opinion on torture, 2001–2009. *PS: Political Science & Politics* 43(03): 437–444.
GTD 2014. Global terrorism database. START. University of Maryland. URL: http://www.start.umd.edu/gtd/. Accessed on September 17, 2014.
Guardian. 2013a. Data snooping: Law abiding citizens have "nothing to fear," says Hague—Video, June 9, 2013.
Guardian. 2013b. GCHQ taps fibre-optic cables for secret access to world's communications, June 21, 2013.
Guardian. 2013c. NSA warned to rein in surveillance as agency reveals even greater scope, July 17, 2013.
Guardian. 2014. George Brandis refuses to back up claim that Snowden put lives at risk, February 24, 2014.
Hammersley, B. 2011. My speech to the IAAC (Information Assurance Advisory Council). Benhammersley.com, September 6, 2011.
Hatemi, P.K. et al. 2013. Fear as a disposition and an emotional state: A genetic and environmental approach to out-group political preferences. *American Journal of Political Science* 57(2): 279–293.
The Heartbleed Bug. 2014. heartbleed.com. URL: http://heartbleed.com. Accessed on September 2, 2014.
Hegghammer, T. 2013. Should I stay or should I go? Explaining variation in Western Jihadists' choice between domestic and foreign fighting. *American Political Science Review* 107(1): 1–15.
Holt, S. 2011. *Aid, Peacebuilding and the Resurgence of War: Buying Time in Sri Lanka*. Basingstoke: Palgrave Macmillan.
Horne, A. 1977. *A Savage War of Peace: Algeria 1954–1962*. London, UK: Macmillan; Torture in a savage war of peace: Revisiting the battle of Algiers. Reproduced in War on the Rocks, 2014, December 17, 2014.
HRW. 2003. U.S. "Operation Liberty Shield" Undermines Asylum Seekers' Rights. March 26, 2003.
Human Rights Watch. 2003. U.S. "Operation Liberty Shield" undermines Asylum Seeker's rights, March 26, 2003.
Humphrey, M. 2014. 9/11 vs Snowden: My students' surprising debate about privacy and government. *Forbes*. URL: http://www.forbes.com/sites/michaelhumphrey/2014/09/11/911-vs-snowden-my-students-surprising-debate-about-privacy-and-government/. Accessed on September 11, 2014.

Hypponen, M. 2013. How the NSA betrayed the world's trust—Time to act. Transcript. TED. November 2013.
IAS. 2013. Health impacts of alcohol. Factsheet. September 2013.
ICG. 2012. Sri Lanka after the war: A timeline. In Pursuit of peace blog, May 31, 2012.
ICSR. 2013. ICSR Insight: Up to 11,000 foreign fighters in Syria; steep rise among Western Europeans. December 2013.
IISS. 2014. The military balance 2014. February 2014.
Independent. 2013. Government accused of "double standards" in aftermath of Woolwich murder of Drummer Lee Rigby, July 28, 2013.
Independent. 2014a. Are Romanians and Bulgarians really stealing all our jobs? The latest figures suggest otherwise, May 14, 2014.
Independent. 2014b. Syria crisis: British jihadists becoming disillusioned with fighting rival rebels and want to come home, September 5, 2014.
Institute for Economics and Peace. 2014. Global Terrorism Index 2014.
IPCC. 2013. Climate change 2013: The physical science basis. Fifth assessment report of the Intergovernmental Panel on Climate Change. September 2013.
ITU. 2014. Cybersecurity—Facts and figures. URL: http://www.itu.int/en/ITU-D/Partners/Pages/Call4Partners/CYBLDCStats.aspx. Accessed on December 24, 2014.
Jacques, M. 2010. Understanding the rise of China. TED Salon, London. October 2010.
Jensen, T. 2007. Terrorism, anti-terrorism, and the copycat effect. Research Paper. Department of Economics, University of Copenhagen, København.
Jones, M. and Silberzahn, P. 2013. Snowden and the challenge of intelligence: The practical case against the NSA's big data. *Forbes*. URL: http://www.forbes.com/sites/silberzahnjones/2013/07/11/snowden-and-the-challenge-of-intelligence-the-practical-case-against-nsa-big-data/. Accessed on July 11, 2013.
Kahneman, D. 2012. *Thinking, Fast and Slow*. London: Penguin Books.
Kassimeris, G. (ed.). 2007. *Playing Politics with Terrorism: A User's Guide*. London: C. Hurst & Co. Publishers.
Kelley, M. 2013. Experts destroy Obama's argument that Americans must sacrifice privacy for security. Business Insider, July 8, 2013.
King, C. 2008. The five-day war: Managing Moscow after the Georgia crisis. *Foreign Affairs*, November/December. URL: http://www.foreignaffairs.com/articles/64602/charles-king/the-five-day-war
Kinninmont, J. 2014. Airstrikes in Iraq expose failure to rebuild. Expert Comment. Chatham House, August 11, 2014.
Klaidman, D. 2013. Obama's defining fight: How he will take on the NSA's surveillance state in 2014. *Daily Beast*, December 12, 2013.
LaFree, G. 2013. Public Policy and (Myths About) Terrorism. ISN, May 22, 2013.
Le Figaro. 2012. Aqmi menace de tuer les otages français au Mali, January 29, 2012.
Leiken, R.S. and Brooke, S. 2006. The quantitative analysis of terrorism and immigration: An initial exploration. *Terrorism and Political Violence* 18(4), 503–521.

Le Monde. 2011. Tunisie: Les propos "effrayants" d'Alliot-Marie suscitent la polémique, January 13, 2011.

Le Monde. 2014. Tuerie de Bruxelles: Mehdi Nemmouche a été livré à la Belgique, July 29, 2014.

The Leveson Inquiry. 2014. Leveson inquiry: Culture, practice and ethics of the press. About the inquiry. URL: http://www.levesoninquiry.org.uk. Accessed on September 18, 2014.

Lindberg, N., Sailas, E., and Kaltiala-Heno, R. 2012. The copycat phenomenon after two Finnish school shootings: An adolescent psychiatric perspective. *BMC Psychiatry* 12(91): 91–106.

Livingstone, D. 2013. Prism: Between security and civil liberties. Expert Comment. Chatham House, June 9, 2013.

Lomborg, B. 2004. *Global Crises, Global Solutions*. Cambridge: Cambridge University Press.

Los Angeles Times. 2004. Georgian President's bloc appears headed for landslide, March 29, 2004.

Los Angeles Times. 2013. Clapper: Snowden case brings healthy debate, more disclosures to come, September 12, 2013.

Ludlow, P. 2014. Fifty states of fear. *New York Times*, January 19, 2014, opinion pages.

Lynch, C. 2014. The Islamic State makes electronic surveillance respectable again. *Foreign Policy*. URL: http://foreignpolicy.com/2014/09/24/the-islamic-state-makes-electronic-surveillance-respectable-again/. Accessed on September 24, 2014.

Lynch, C. and Groll, E. 2014. Obama's foreign fighters campaign is a gift to the World's police states. *Foreign Policy*. URL : http://foreignpolicy.com/2014/09/30/obamas-foreign-fighters-campaign-is-a-gift-to-the-worlds-police-states/. Accessed on September 30, 2014.

L'Express. 2012. Mohamed Merah, un petit délinquant devenu djihadiste, March 23, 2012.

Maher, S. and Neumann, P. 2014. ICSR insight—Offering foreign fighters in Syria and Iraq a way out, August 26, 2014.

Marsden, P. 2000a. Mental epidemics. *New Scientist* 2237: 46–47.

Marsden, P. 2000b. The Werther effect: Suicide contagion—A critical evaluation, theoretical reconceptualisation and empirical. Investigation doctoral thesis, University of Sussex, Brighton.

Marsden, P. 2001. Letter: Copycat terrorism: Fanning the fire. *Journal of Memetics – Evolutionary Models of Information Transmission*, 5. URL: http://cfpm.org/jom-emit/2001/vol5/marsden_p_let.html.

May, D.C. et al. 2011. Predictors of fear and risk of terrorism in a rural state. *International Journal of Rural Criminology* 1(1): 1–22.

McAfee. 2013. The economic impact of cyber crime and cyber espionage. With the Center for Strategic and International Studies (CSIS). Report, July 2013.

Mchedlishvili, G. 2013. Russia-Georgia war: Moscow's loss? Expert Comment. Chatham House, August 9, 2013.

Migration Policy Institute. 2003. America's challenge: Domestic security, civil liberties, and national unity after September 2011, 42–45.

Migration Watch. 2013. Incentives for Romanian and Bulgarian migration to the UK.

Ministère de l'intérieur. 2014. Lancement d'une plateforme d'assistance aux familles et de prévention de la radicalisation violente, April 25, 2014.

Moeckli, D. 2008. *Human Rights and Non-Discrimination in the "War on Terror."* Oxford: Oxford University Press.

Mohar, J. and Gomis, B. 2014. Bragging rights: Mexican criminals turn to social media. *IHS Jane's Intelligence Review*, 46–49.

Montlake, S. 2009. How U.S. "war on terror" emboldened Sri Lanka's. Christian Science Monitor, March 6, 2009.

Moore, D.E. 1999. Fear of terrorism affects many American's plans for new year celebration. Gallup, December 28, 1999.

Mortimer, E. 2014. Hidden from view, Sri Lanka is trampling over the human rights of its Tamil population. *Independent*, August 11, 2014.

Mueller, J. and Stewart, M. 2014. Secret without reason and costly without accomplishment: Questioning the National Security Agency's Metadata Program. *Symposium on the NSA controversy. I/S: A Journal of Law and Policy for the Information Society*, January 2, 2014.

Mueller, J. and Stewart, M.G. 2011. Balancing the risks, benefits, and costs of homeland security. *Homeland Security Affairs* 7. URL: https://www.hsaj.org/articles/43

Nacos, B.L. September 2009. Revisiting the contagion hypothesis: Terrorism, news coverage, and copycat attacks. *Perspectives on Terrorism* 3(3): 3–13.

NASA. 2014. Climate change: How do we know? URL: http://climate.nasa.gov/evidence/. Accessed on May 8, 2014.

NATO. 2011. NATO–Russia Council action plan on terrorism, April 15, 2011.

NATO PA. 2009. Climate change and global security. 184 STC E REV 1, November 2009.

NATO PA. 2010. Security at the top of the world: Is there a role for NATO in the High North? 213 DSCTC 10 #, April 2010.

NBC News. 2014. ISIS threat: Fear of terror attack soars to 9/11 high, NBC News/WSJ Poll Finds, September 9, 2014.

New York Times. 2006. Held in 9/11 net, Muslims return to accuse U.S., January 23, 2006.

New York Times. 2011. Qaddafi's grip on the capital tightens as revolt grows, February 22, 2011.

Niblett, R. 2014. In Britain, NATO has popular support to reverse decline. Expert Comment. Chatham House, September 4, 2014.

Nixey, J. 2014. Responding to Putin's latest ruse. Expert Comment. Chatham House, May 9, 2014.

Nordhaus, W. 2012. Why the global warming skeptics are wrong. *The New York Review of Books*. URL: http://www.nybooks.com/articles/archives/2012/mar/22/why-global-warming-skeptics-are-wrong/ . Accessed on March 22, 2012.

NSA. 2013. Letter to Mr. Leopold, Al Jazeera. Central Security Service. FOIA Case: 711184B, October 17, 2013.

Obama, B. 2009. Ensuring lawful interrogations. Executive Order. 13491. White House, January 22, 2009.

OSI. 2009. Ethnic profiling in the European Union: Pervasive, ineffective and discriminatory. Open Society Justice Initiative.

O'Carroll, P.W. 1994. Suicide contagion and the reporting of suicide: Recommendations from a National Workshop. Centers for Disease Control and Prevention.

Park Dietz & Associates. 2014. Inspiring Copycat Crimes.

PCLOB. 2014. Report on the Surveillance Program operated pursuant to Section 702 of the Foreign Intelligence Surveillance Act, July 2, 2014.

Pew Research. 2014a. About half see CIA interrogation methods as justified. Pew Research Center for the People and the Press, December 15, 2014.

Pew Research. 2014b. Growing concern about rise of Islamic extremism at home and abroad, September 10, 2014.

Phillips, C. 2010. Syria and the West: Another wasted decade. Comment is free. *Guardian*. URL: http://www.theguardian.com/commentisfree/2010/jul/25/syria-and-the-west-wasted-decade. Accessed on July 25, 2010.

Phillips, D. June 1974. The influence of suggestion on suicide: Substantive and theoretical implications of the Werther effect. *American Sociological Review* 39: 340–354.

Pincus, W. 2009. 1,600 are suggested daily for FBI's list. *Washington Post*. URL: http:\\www.washingtonpost.com/wp-dyn/content/article/2009/10/31/AR2009103102141.html. Accessed on November 1, 2009.

Priest, D. and Arkin, W.M. 2011. *Top Secret America: The Rise of the New American Security State*. New York: Little, Brown.

Public Health England. 2013. HIV in the United Kingdom: 2013 Report, November 2013.

Public Safety Canada. 2014. Public report on the terrorist threat to Canada. September 23, 2014.

Radden Keefe, P. 2005. *Chatter: Dispatches from the Secret World of Global Eavesdropping*. New York: Random House.

Radio Free Europe. 2014. Foreign fighters in Iraq and Syria: Where do they come from? December 9, 2014.

Real Clear Politics. 2014. Dick Cheney: Torture, to me, is what terrorists did on 9/11. December 14, 2014.

Reuters. 2011. France okayed tear gas as Tunisia revolt peaked, February 1, 2011.

Reuters. 2013. Leaks like Snowden's put lives at risk: UK minister, July 3, 2013.

Reuters. 2014. Nigeria military studies Sri Lankan tactics for use against Boko Haram, June 13, 2014.

Reveron, D.S. 2008. Counterterrorism and intelligence cooperation. *Journal of Global Change and Governance*. 1(3): 1–13.

Rid, T. 2013. Cyberwar and peace: Hacking can reduce real-world violence. *Foreign Affairs*, November/December. URL: http://www.foreignaffairs.com/articles/140160/thomas-rid/cyberwar-and-peace
Roberts, R. 2007. Getting the most out of life: The concept of opportunity cost. Library of Economics and Liberty, February 5, 2007.
Robinson, M.J. 2007. Two decades of American News Preferences. Part 1: Analyzing What News the Public Follows—and Doesn't Follow. *The News Interest Index, 1986–2007*. Pew Research Center for the People & The Press, 1–36." (http://www.pewresearch.org/files/old-assets/pdf/NewsInterest1986–2007.pdf).
Rollins, J.W. and Liu, E.C. 2013. NSA surveillance leaks: Background and issues for Congress. Congressional Research Service, September 4, 2013.
Rousseff, D. 2013. Statement by H.E. Dilma Rousseff, President of the Federative Republic of Brazil, at *The Opening of the General Debate of the 68th Session of the United Nations General Assembly*, September 24, 2013, New York.
RUSI. 2008. Georgia-Russia conflict timeline (includes South Ossetia and Abkhazia). RUSI Analysis, August 11, 2008.
San Jose Mercury News 2007. Part III: U.S. targets terrorists as online thieves run amok. URL: http://www.mercurynews.com/ci_7442979?nclick_check=1. Accessed on November 13, 2007.
Scheinin, M. 2014. Back to post-9/11 panic? Security Council resolution on foreign terrorist fighters. Just Security, September 23, 2014.
Schmid, A.P. and de Graaf, J. 1982. *Violence and Communication: Insurgent Terrorism and the Western News Media*. London: Sage.
Schneier, B. 2014a. Heartbleed. Schneier on security, April 9, 2014.
Schneier, B. 2014b. *Carry On: Sound Advice from Schneier on Security*. Indianapolis, IN: Wiley.
Shashikumar, V.K. 2009. Lessons from the war in Sri Lanka. *Indian Defence Review* 25(2). URL: http://www.indiandefencereview.com/spotlights/lessons-from-the-war-in-sri-lanka/0/.
Silke, A. 2008. Research on terrorism: A review of the impact of 9/11 and the global war on terrorism. In Chen, H., Reid, E., Sinai, J., Silke, A., and Ganor, B. (eds), *Terrorism Informatics: Knowledge Management and Data Mining for Homeland Security*, Integrated Series in Information Systems, Vol. 18. Berlin: Springer.
Singer, P.W. and Friedman, A. 2013. *Cybersecurity and Cyberwar: What Everyone Needs to Know*. New York: Oxford University Press.
SLC. 2014. History of the conflict. Accessed on September 17, 2014.
START. 2011. Background Report: 9/11, Ten Years Later, September 2011.
START. 2012. Urban U.S. counties hot spots of terror, but rural areas are not exempt, January 31, 2012.
START. 2013. U.S. attitudes toward terrorism and counterterrorism. Report to the Resilient Systems Division, Science and Technology Directorate, U.S. Department of Homeland Security, March 2013.

Stroehlein, A. 2014. Dispatches: 40,000 reasons why Sri Lanka is no model for Nigeria. Human Rights Watch, June 16, 2014.

Suskind, R. 2007. *The One Percent Doctrine: Deep Inside America's Pursuit of Its Enemies Since 9/11*. New York: Simon & Schuster.

Syrian Refugees. 2014. A snapshot of the crisis—In the Middle East and Europe. A project by European University Institute, Robert Schuman Centre for Advanced Studies, and the Migration Policy Centre. As updated in October 2014. URL: http://syrianrefugees.eu. Accessed on December 17, 2014.

TED. 2014. The NSA responds to Edward Snowden's interview at TED. TED Blog. March 20, 2014.

TU. 2014. Cybersecurity—Facts and figures. URL: http://www.itu.int/en/ITU-D/Partners/Pages/Call4Partners/CYBLDCStats.aspx. Accessed on December 24, 2014.

UK Department for Transport. 2014. Reported road casualties in Great Britain: Main results 2013. Statistical Release, June 26, 2014.

UK Parliament. 2008. Russia: A new confrontation? Defence Committee—Tenth Report. June 30, 2009.

UK Parliament. 2013a. House of Commons debate on Syria, August 30, 2013.

UK Parliament. 2013b. Business of the day: Chamber for Thursday August 30, 2013. House of Commons Business Papers.

UK Parliament. 2014. Commons recalled to debate Iraq: Coalition against ISIL, September 26, 2014.

UN. 1948. The Universal Declaration of Human Rights. Adopted by the UN General Assembly on December 10, 1948.

UN. 2011a. Resolution 1973. Adopted by the Security Council at its 6498th meeting, March 17, 2011.

UN. 2011b. Resolution 1970. Adopted by the Security Council at its 6491st meeting, February 26, 2011.

UNDP. 2013. Citizen security with a human face: Evidence and proposals for Latin America. Executive Summary. Regional Human Development Report 2013–2014, November 2013.

UN News Centre. 2014. More than 191,000 people killed in Syria with "no end in sight"—UN, August 22, 2014.

UNODC. 2005. World Drug Report.

UNODC. 2011. Estimating Illicit Financial Flows Resulting from Drug Trafficking and Other Transnational Organized Crimes. Research Report, October 2011.

UNODC. 2013a. Comprehensive study on cybercrime. Draft, February 2013.

UNODC. 2013b. UNODC homicide statistics.

UNODC. 2014. World Drug Report 2014, June 2014.

UNRWA. 2014. Socioeconomic and damage assessment report: UNRWA microfinance clients in Syria. Report of the situation in June 2013, March 2014.

UNSC. 2001. Resolution 1973 (2001). Adopted by the Security Council at its 4385th meeting, September 28, 2001.

UNSC. 2014. Resolution 2178 (2014). Adopted by the Security Council at its 7272nd meeting, September 24, 2014.
U.S. DOD. 2006. Bush Issues Progress Report in Terror War. News—American Forces Press Service, September 7, 2006.
U.S. State Department. 1997. Foreign terrorist organizations. URL: http://www.state.gov/j/ct/rls/other/des/123085.htm. Accessed on September 17, 2014.
U.S. Senate. 2010. Unclassified Executive Summary of the Committee Report on the Attempted Terrorist Attack on Northwest Airlines Flight 253. U.S. Senate Select Committee on Intelligence, May 18, 2010.
U.S. Senate. 2014a. Foreword by U.S. Senate Select Committee on Intelligence Chairman Dianne Feinstein. Committee Study of the Central Intelligence Agency's Detention and Interrogation Program, December 9, 2014.
U.S. Senate. 2014b. Findings and Conclusions. Committee Study of the Central Intelligence Agency's Detention and Interrogation Program, December 9, 2014.
U.S. Senate. 2014c. Executive Summary. Committee Study of the Central Intelligence Agency's Detention and Interrogation Program, December 9, 2014.
Vice News. 2013. Jihad selfies: These British extremists in Syria love social media, December 5, 2013.
Washington Post. 2010. A hidden world, growing beyond control. Part of Top Secret America: A *Washington Post* investigation, July 19, 2010.
Washington Post. 2012. Edward Snowden's claim that he had "no proper channels" for protection as a whistleblower. *Fact Checker*, March 12, 2012.
Washington Post. 2014a. Cybersecurity and cyberwar: A Q&A with Peter Singer, January 14, 2014.
Washington Post. 2014b. Transcript: Senate intelligence hearing on national security threats, January 29, 2014.
Weimann, G. and Winn, C. 1994. *The Theater of Terror: Mass Media and International Terrorism*. New York: Longman.
White House. 2013a. Remarks by the President in Address to the Nation on Syria. Office of the Press Secretary, September 10, 2013.
White House. 2013b. Remarks by the President at the National Defense University. Office of the Press Secretary. Office of the Press Secretary, May 23, 2013.
White House. 2014. Remarks by the President on review of signals intelligence. DOJ, Washington, DC, January 17, 2014.
Williams, R. B. 2014. Why we love bad news more than good news. *Psychology Today*. URL: https://www.psychologytoday.com/blog/wired-success/201411/why-we-love-bad-news-more-good-news. Accessed on November 1, 2014.
Wing, N. 2014. Here are the most horrific details from The Senate Torture Report. Huffington Post. URL: (http://www.huffingtonpost.com/2014/12/09/senate-torture-report-details_n_6295396.html . Accessed on December 9, 2014.
World Bank. 2014. China overview. Accessed on May 8, 2014.
Yim, S.H.L. and Barrette, S.R.H. 2012. Public health impacts of combustion emissions in the United Kingdom. *Environmental Science & Technology* 46(8): 4291–4296.

ZDNet. 2014. Worldwide spam rate falls 2.5 percent but new tactics emerge, January 23, 2014.

Zenko, M. 2013a. Shouting "9/11" in a Crowded Internet. *Foreign Policy*. URL: http://foreignpolicy.com/2013/11/05/shouting-911-in-a-crowded-internet/. Accessed on November 5, 2013.

Zenko, M. 2013b. To protect and defend... *Foreign Policy*. URL: http://foreignpolicy.com/2013/06/11/to-protect-and-defend/. Accessed on June 11, 2013.

Section III

How to Break the Cycle? Rethinking the Policy Response

Thus far, this book has explored the current state of terrorism and counterterrorism, highlighting, in particular, the risks associated with overestimating and overreacting to the threat. While terrorism is an important problem in today's world, it is not the existential threat it is often made out to be. Terrorism is an all-encompassing and simplistic label, which often blurs the lines between a wide range of actors and circumstances and undermines legitimate grievances, especially in countries ruled by authoritarian regimes. However, terrorism continues to sell and scare, hence the repetition of a similar cycle, with an immediate overreaction to an exaggerated threat, leading to a number of unintended yet foreseeable and negative consequences, fueling further alienation and resentment. This final section of the book suggests alternative options for the way forward. Chapter 6 focuses on the need to allow for more challenges to current policies in the first place, and Chapter 7 explores some of the key tenants of a more measured and comprehensive response.

6

Challenging Counterterrorism Policies

> Criticism may not be agreeable, but it is necessary. It fulfills the same function as pain in the human body. It calls attention to an unhealthy state of things.
>
> **Winston Churchill**

Counterterrorism policies in the Western world are in dire need of reform. Of course, policies differ greatly from one country to another. As we have explored in previous chapters, some of the key underlying assumptions and characteristics are shared across borders. These include the lack of challenge to policy, as some of the systems put in place have not allowed enough room for constructive criticism, oversight, or suggestions for reform and alternative policy options. In the United States in particular, successive administrations have contributed to building such a considerable counterterrorism apparatus that almost any suggestion that the terrorist threat is exaggerated faces cries of complacency and pushbacks driven by career and budgetary motivations. Any substantial reform would thus take significant time to agree upon and implement.

The United States continues to spend more on its military than the next 10 countries combined (IISS 2014), a large portion of which is designed to tackle terrorist threats against allies, U.S. interests abroad, or U.S. territories. Numerous governmental organizations have been created to primarily focus on terrorism since 9/11, bringing the total number of government agencies working on counterterrorism, homeland security, and intelligence programs to 1,200 as of 2010 (*Washington Post* 2010). In addition, 2,000 private companies are working on these same topics—from intelligence contractors to defense companies and private military companies, the counterterrorism industry now extends far beyond the public sector (*Washington Post* 2010). Albeit at a much smaller scale, similar challenges exist in other countries. While the creation of large bureaucracies was initially intended to tackle the full range of dimensions associated with terrorism, their mere existence and evident cumbersomeness constitute clear obstacles to meaningful reform. In other words, there are numerous domestic obstacles to break the current cycle, steer away from the status quo or a mere reinforcement of existing infrastructures, or even openly and constructively discuss some alternative policy options.

CASE STUDY: CHALLENGES TO DRUG POLICIES

Current developments in international drug policy demonstrate that it is possible to challenge policy constructively and that these contributions may lead to meaningful policy reform, despite the controversial and politically sensitive nature of the issues at hand.

The international drug control system is based on a number of UN conventions and documents, including the 1961 Single Convention on Narcotics Drugs, the 1971 Convention on Psychotropic Substances, and the 1988 Convention against Illicit Traffic in Narcotic Drugs and Psychotropic Substances. As Mike Trace, chair of the International Drug Policy Consortium (IDPC), points out, the system was built upon a "belief that that there was a simple linear relationship between the scale of the drug market and the level of harm to human health and welfare (i.e., the smaller the market, the fewer the harms)." Thus "the singular focus of the system has been on reducing the scale of the illegal drug market, with the eventual aim of a 'drug-free world,'" as claimed by the United Nations in its last UN General Assembly Special Session (UNGASS) in 1998 (Trace 2011).

Since the early 1970s, when then U.S. President Richard Nixon announced the launch of a *War on Drugs*, policies have been marked by a lack of convincing results—attempts at reducing the overall size of the drug market have failed, often pushing drug users toward other substances, moving production to nearby areas, or shifting drug trafficking routes and thereby creating further instability along the way. In addition, it has created a myriad of damaging impacts, including the imposition of the death penalties for drug offenses (33 countries retain capital punishment for drug offenses, including 13 where the sentence is mandatory [IDPC 2014]), widespread incarceration (the United States alone holds less than 5% of the world's population but over 25% of the world's prison population, with approximately half-a-million people currently incarcerated for drug-related offenses, which constitutes a 10-fold increase from 1980 [U.S. Bureau of Justice 2014]), discrimination in law enforcement (black and Asian people are, respectively, 6.3 and 2.5 times more likely to be stopped and searched for drugs than white people in the United Kingdom, despite lower levels of drug use among black and Asian people than white people [Release and LSE 2013]), human rights violations in drug treatment centers (numerous cases of forced *treatment*, illegal detention, forced labor, and physical and sexual violence in state-run drug treatment centers have been reported in countries such as Vietnam, China, Cambodia, and the Lao PDR [Human Rights Watch 2013]), and opportunity costs (with the majority of drug policy budgets relating to law enforcement measures instead of health and socioeconomic measures [UNODC 2008]) (Gomis 2014).

However, in the words of experts and officials that have been involved in the field for a long time, the drug policy debate has progressed more in the last 3 years than in the previous three decades (Gomis 2014). Following the surge in drug-related killings in Mexico from 2007 onward, an increasing number of former world leaders and NGOs have urged governments and international organizations such as the UNODC and the International Narcotics Control Board to review their strategies for tackling the challenges posed by illicit drugs, insisting on the severity of the global drug problem and the inadequacy of drug control policies. In particular, calls for reform have come from the Global Commission on Drug Policy, which includes former presidents such as Ernesto Zedillo of Mexico, César Gaviria of Colombia, Fernando Henrique Cardoso of Brazil, and Ruth Dreifuss of Switzerland, former international organization officials such as ex-UN Secretary General Kofi Annan and ex-UN High Commissioner for Human Rights Louise Arbour, former senior government officials—for example, former U.S. Secretary of State George Schultz—and business leaders including founder of the Virgin Group Richard Branson. Other NGOs have been pressing international organizations and national governments to review their misguided policies. These include IDPC, Transform, Release, the Drug Policy Alliance, as well as think tanks such as the International Institute for Strategic Studies (IISS) and Chatham House.

Crucially, a number of *current* political leaders have also joined the call for reform, including Otto Pérez Molina of Guatemala and Juan Manuel Santos of Colombia. President Santos played a key role in convincing President Barack Obama of the urgent need to reassess regional drug policies at the Sixth Summit of the Americas, which he hosted in Cartagena, Colombia, in April 2012. Colombia, a close—albeit, at times, difficult—partner to the United States in the war on drugs, has often been held as a success story for traditional counter-narcotics policies largely focused on supply eradication measures and harsh police actions and sanctions against all drug-related offenses. However, from 2011 onward, President Santos and other senior Colombian officials began to argue that despite decreased levels of drug-related violence and cocaine production in the country, policies had shifted problems to neighboring countries (especially to Peru and Bolivia in terms of coca cultivation, and Mexico with regard to trafficking-related violence), thereby not deserving the label of *success* (*World Today* 2012). The Colombian government's reversal, as well as diplomatic efforts by the Mexican and Guatemalan leaderships, led to a comprehensive review process under the auspices of the Organization of American States (OAS). The final report, published a year later in May 2013, marked the first time that an intergovernmental organization would openly challenge the drug policy status quo, explore alternative options, and call for substantive reform. In particular, the OAS highlighted the need to decriminalize drug use and other low-level offenses and to center policies on public health at the expense of law enforcement and the military (Chatham House 2013; OAS 2013). Following a joint official call by the presidents of Colombia, Guatemala, and Mexico in September 2012, the United Nations will conduct a review of international drugs policies, as part of an UNGASS specifically dedicated to the global drug problem in 2014, a first since 1998.

In parallel, actual reform has been taking place. In the United States, the states of Washington and Colorado voted to legalize and regulate the whole supply chain of cannabis in November 2012. A year later, Uruguay became the first country to fully regulate cannabis, from cultivation to sales and consumption. In 2013, Bolivia successfully re-acceded to the 1961 UN drug convention with a special exemption for coca chewing—an inherent part of the culture there, recognizing it as legal in the country. Meanwhile, Colombia is currently negotiating peace talks with the Revolutionary Armed Forces of Colombia and the National Liberation Army, as part of which the drug trade is being discussed, and the presidential advisory commission on drug policy, headed by economist

Daniel Mejia, is carrying out a separate review of domestic drug policies. Even the U.S. federal government has progressively changed its discourse on drug policy, steering away from the *War on Drugs* label and from a narrative placing responsibility on consumers and low-level drug dealers (InSight Crime 2014).* Tellingly, under the leadership of the then Attorney General Eric Holder, the Obama Administration announced that the federal government would not challenge the new cannabis regulation laws of Colorado and Washington—President Obama noted that they had *bigger fish to fry* (*Washington Post* 2012) and would call on prosecutors to remove federal mandatory minimum sentencing for some low-level drug offenses, with a view to reducing the country's prison population (DOJ 2014).

In other words, there is currently a great push for reform in international drug policy, which is much less present in counterterrorism policy. Although the challenges posed by terrorism differ in many ways from those posed by the drug trade, a series of lessons can be drawn from a comparative analysis between the two fields.

First, as Louise Arbour points out, there is far more data publicly available for researchers and activists analyzing the drug trade. Drug trafficking and organized crime are by nature difficult to estimate and study, and there is still an important amount of unreported information. However, UNODC, the WHO, the World Bank, the EMCDDA, the U.S. Bureau of Justice, Mexico's INEGI, and many other sources frequently produce relevant quantitative and qualitative data (e.g., seizures, arrests, estimates of drug flow, maps of drug routes, levels of drug production and drug consumption, number of drug consumption-related diseases, number of individuals incarcerated for drug-related offenses, drug policy budget breakdowns, details of specific drug trafficking, and organized crime cases). These provide a reliable basis for policy reviews and therefore open, practical, and frank discussions on the matter.

In contrast, much of the evidence related to counterterrorism policies remains confidential, classified by intelligence agencies on national security grounds. This is not to say there is nothing to base terrorism analysis on—otherwise this book, for instance, would look very different. The START Consortium at the University of Maryland and other databases

* The U.S. Assistant Secretary of State for the Bureau of International Narcotics and Law Enforcement Affairs William Brownfield argued that every country should "combat and resist the criminal organizations—not those who buy, consume, but those who market and traffic the product for economic gain," which illustrated a clear departure from more indiscriminate *zero tolerance* approaches (InSight Crime 2014).

of terrorism incidents such as the Chicago Project on Security and Terrorism (Suicide Attack Database run by the University of Chicago) and the RAND Database of Worldwide Terrorism Incidents are very useful sources of information on terrorist attacks; Europol's TE-SAT annual situation report on terrorism in Europe provides informative figures on the number of people charged, arrested, and incarcerated on terrorism charges, for instance; the UNODC website holds an instructive compilation of "Electronic Legal Resources on International Terrorism"; and the FBI, NCTC, the Home Office, and other agencies across the world have also made available some helpful information, including on terrorist tactics and trends.

Despite these resources, the counterterrorism field remains overall very opaque. Specific details of investigations, budgets, and law enforcement operations often remain hidden, reportedly for national security reasons. Former Central Intelligence Agency (CIA) and state department analyst Melvin A. Goodman points out that "far too much information is classified" and that "a great deal of information is classified to cover up government embarrassments and CIA misdeeds" (Goodman 2013, p. 69). Overclassification—a claim that the CIA continues to reject*—hampers further potentially useful research on how policy could be improved. Counterterrorism policy concerns us all. It should be held accountable because it is using public funds and, perhaps more importantly, because intelligence laws and practices have become so pervasive that all citizens are indirectly or directly affected. Releasing more quantitative and qualitative information to independent *watchdogs*, strengthened parliamentary or judicial committees, or independent and objective researchers would go a long way in addressing some of the current shortfalls.

Second, the participation of well-respected former heads of state and government in calls for drug policy reform has proved influential. The counterterrorism field has not seen the same type of involvement from previous national and international policy makers calling from substantive change, even though it arguably faces similarly severe shortcomings and an urgent need for reform.

Third, many world leaders have recently actively attempted to shape public opinion toward more progressive and liberal drug policies, despite polls indicating that this path would be unpopular. Across Latin America,

* In a report released in September 2014, the Office of Inspector General of the CIA indicated: "we found no instances of over-classification in the sample of [REDACTED] finished intelligence reports that we received" (CIA 2013, p. 2).

populations remain largely opposed to a liberalization of drug policies. In Mexico, for instance, only 32% of the population claimed they were in favor of any liberalization of marijuana policies, compared with 13% in Colombia and 11% in Peru, while there is a growing consensus at the highest political level than more conservative policies have proved ineffective and damaging (Gomis 2013). Uruguay is a particularly interesting case study. Shortly before the marijuana regulation bill was approved by the country's house of representatives in late 2013, an opinion poll indicated that only 26% of the people were in favor of the reform, while 64% were against it (10% said they had no opinion) (Trobo 2013). When the question was phrased differently, 80% of respondents said they would rather buy marijuana from the state than from an illegal dealer—which is effectively what the state regulation model put in place in Uruguay consists of (*Globe and Mail* 2014). This contradiction shows that raising awareness, informing and educating the population, and providing scientific evidence are tasks that may very well convince the population of the need for reform—these efforts are greatly needed, as human beings tend to prove reluctant to change (Kahneman, for instance, points out that we generally fear loss much more than we value gains, leading to a conservative default mind-set—Kahneman 2012, pp. 283–286). Additionally, people have been largely conditioned into thinking that more progressive policies would be harmful. Politicians' role is not only to represent the views of their citizens, but also to lead public opinion and make the case for change where necessary and appropriate. In 1974, French Health Minister Simone Veil successfully fought for the legalization of abortion in the face of popular opposition. Seven years later, French Justice Minister Robert Badinter pushed for and obtained the abolition of the death penalty against the wishes of the majority of the French population. These two instances demonstrate that political leadership may prove unpopular and yet manage to achieve significant societal progress.

The debate on terrorism has become more measured in recent years, with experts like Micah Zenko, Stephen Walt, John Mueller, Richard Jackson, and Edwin Bakker pointing to the marginal risk that it poses and the need for more proportionate responses. The Global Counterterrorism Forum, launched in September 2011, has proved to be a useful venue for discussions notably focusing on the rule of law, human rights, rehabilitation, and community engagement. Former Chief of the British Secret Intelligence Service Sir Richard Dearlove has advocated for a more proportionate approach to counterterrorism and to move away from a 9/11 mind-set, which "has cast a very dark, long and enduring shadow" (Dearlove 2014).

However, when a large terrorist attack occurs or a new terrorist organization emerges (e.g., the Islamic State), immediate reactions from governments, the media, and other commentators tend to contribute to the sense of fear terrorists want to instill, instead of opting for a more restrained reaction, addressing the issues at hand without overreacting to them, and thereby creating a new set of *unintended consequences*. The drug landscape is obviously different in the sense that it is often associated with consumption-related challenges that are not as spectacular as terrorist incidents, regardless of how damaging they may be. Nonetheless, drug trafficking and organized crime cause more fatalities than terrorism worldwide and are more widespread and economically disruptive than terrorism.

Change is happening in the drug policy field, and substantial reform is possible in counterterrorism too, in order to challenge the current status quo and its underlying misguided assumptions regarding the nature of the threat—chiefly that it is the most serious threat that the Western world faces, requiring high levels of secrecy and public spending, and that aggressive responses focusing on the military and far-ranging intelligence gathering make our countries safer. As we have explored in this section, allowing for more transparency, scrutiny, dissension, criticism, and input into policy—through strengthened oversight, a stronger role for independent reviewers at the national and international levels, and the inclusion of more civil society organizations—would be a first step in the right direction.

REFERENCES

Chatham House. 2013. The OAS report and the drug problem in the Americas: The way forward. *Meeting Summary*, July 31, 2013.

CIA. 2013. Report of evaluation. Evaluation required by the reducing overclassification act. Office of Inspector General, September 28, 2013.

Dearlove, R. 2014. Terrorism and national security: Proportion or distortion? *Event. RUSI*, July 7, 2013.

DOJ. 2014. Attorney general holder urges changes in federal sentencing guidelines to reserve harshest penalties for the most serious drug traffickers. Press Release, March 13, 2014.

Globe and Mail. 2014. Inside Uruguay's experiment in legalized marijuana. URL: http://www.theglobeandmail.com/news/world/the-uncharted-territory-of-how-uruguay-legalized-marijuana/article20781037/. Accessed on September 24, 2014.

Gomis, B. 2013. Regional security and counter-narcotics policies. *Presentation at the Plenary Session VI: Drug Policy Changes. Drug Policy Reform Parliamentary Seminar*. British Group Inter-Parliamentary Union, London, October 28, 2013.

Gomis, B. 2014. Illicit drugs and international security: Towards UNGASS 2016. Briefing Paper, Chatham House, February 2014.

Goodman, M.A. 2013. 9/11: The failure in strategic intelligence, Chapter 4. In Wark, K.W. (ed), *Twenty-First Century Intelligence*. London: Routledge.

Human Rights Watch. 2013. UN report highlights abuse as "Drug Treatment," March 3, 2013. URL: http://www.hrw.org/news/2013/03/03/un-report-highlights-abuse-drug-treatment.

IDPC. 2014. Too many deaths: It's high time to end the use of the death penalty for drug offences, October 10, 2014. URL: http://idpc.net/blog/2014/10/too-many-deaths-high-time-to-end-the-use-of-the-death-penalty-for-drug-offences.

IISS. 2014. The military balance 2014. The annual assessment of global military capabilities and defence economics. URL: https://www.iiss.org/en/publications/military-s-balance. Accessed on February 2014.

InSight Crime. 2014. U.S. signals shift in international drug policy. URL: http://www.insightcrime.org/news-briefs/us-drug-czar-shift-international-drug-policy. Accessed on October 13, 2014.

Kahneman, D. 2012. *Thinking, Fast and Slow*. London: Penguin Books.

OAS. 2013. The drug problem in the Americas: Analytical report; and scenarios for the drug problem in the Americas: 2013–2025. URL: http://www.oas.org/documents/eng/press/Introduction_and_Analytical_Report.pdf. Accessed on May 17, 2013.

Release and LSE. 2013. The numbers in black and white: Ethnic disparities in the policing and prosecution of drug offences in England and Wales. *Release and The Mannheim Centre for Criminology at LSE*. URL: http://www.release.org.uk/publications/numbers-black-and-white-ethnic-disparities-policing-and-prosecution-drug-offences. Accessed on August 2013.

Trace, M. 2011. Drug policy—Lessons learnt, and options for the future. *Background paper*. Global Commission on Drug Policy. Rio de Janeiro.

Trobo, J.M. 2013. Case studies (Uruguay). Presentation. Plenary Session VI: Drug Policy Changes. *Drug Policy Reform Parliamentary Seminar*. British Group Inter-Parliamentary Union, October 28, 2013, London.

UNODC. 2008. World Drug Report. URL: http://www.unodc.org/unodc/data-and-analysis/WDR-2008.html. Accessed on June 26, 2008.

U.S. Bureau of Justice. 2014. Drugs and crime facts—Drug law violations: Enforcement. Accessed on October 15, 2014.

Washington Post. 2010. A hidden world, growing beyond control. *Part of Top Secret America: A Washington Post Investigation*. URL: http://projects.washingtonpost.com/top-secret-america/articles/a-hidden-world-growing-beyond-control/. Accessed on July 19, 2010.

Washington Post. 2012. Obama: I've got "bigger fish to fry" than pot smokers. URL: http://www.washingtonpost.com/blogs/post-politics/wp/2012/12/14/obama-ive-got-bigger-fish-to-fry-than-pot-smokers/. Accessed on December 14, 2012.

World Today. 2012. Interview: President Juan Manuel Santos of Colombia. *World Today* 68(5). URL: http://www.chathamhouse.org/publications/twt/archive/view/185137.

7

Toward a More Measured and Comprehensive Policy Response

> We are still shocked by what has happened, but we will never give up our values. Our response is more democracy, more openness, and more humanity... We will answer hatred with love.
>
> **Norwegian Prime Minister Jens Stoltenberg**
> *After the attacks in Oslo and the island of Utøya on July 22, 2011*

The final chapter of this book will explore some of the key tenants of a comprehensive counterterrorism strategy steering away from an overestimation of the threat and an overreaction to it. In particular, it will look at options for preventing and countering violent extremism; addressing the role of nongovernment actors; reframing the political discourse; reviewing the impacts of foreign policy, especially as it relates to the use of drones; reforming intelligence policies; and, last but not least, redefining *success*.

CASE STUDY: NORWAY AFTER THE JULY 2011 ATTACKS

By way of introduction, it is worth examining Oslo's policy response to the terrorist attacks perpetrated by Anders Behring Breivik in the summer of 2011. On July 22, 2011, Breivik detonated a bomb near the *Regjeringskvartalet*, a building complex housing Norway's Office of the Prime Minister, the Ministry of Finance, the Ministry of Justice, the Ministry of Education, the Ministry of Energy, the Ministry of Health, and other ministerial headquarters. The attack killed 8 people and injured 209, including 12 seriously. It was followed by another attack, also carried out by Breivik on the island of Utøya, where he shot and killed 69 participants of a youth labor camp, and injured at least 110, including 55 seriously. These events did not have the same physical and material impact that the coordinated terrorist attacks on 9/11 had in the United States. However, it was the deadliest attack Norway had suffered since World War II, in a peaceful and well-functioning society with low crime rates and few gun shootings. The attacks and the devastation they caused proved all the more shocking when it was confirmed that one individual acting alone carried them out.

Despite the gravity of the attack, the policy response was exemplary in many ways. A commission was tasked to investigate the factors leading up to July 22, 2011, the responsibility of various government bodies, the attack itself, and its aftermath. Its final report provided a thorough and balanced assessment. In the introduction, it notes that "no one wants a terrorist to be able to change what is unique, transparent and worthwhile about this 'little country of ours'" (22 July Commission 2012, p. 13). The report also offers a number of level-headed policy recommendations, including the "effective implementation of already adopted security measures" at the so-called Government Complex, and a reform of emergency preparedness and management strategies. It stresses the importance that all levels of government to "work systematically to strengthen… fundamental attitudes and culture in respect of the acknowledgment of risk, implementation capacity, interaction, ICT utilization, and result-oriented leadership," also noting the need to improve coordination between intelligence services and the police (22 July Commission 2012, pp. 16–17, 458). Furthermore, the report also points to processes that worked, including health and rescue services, government's communication with the public, noting that "the ministries managed to continue their work despite the devastation" (22 July Commission 2012, p. 16). The following section of the report is perhaps most telling: "With better ways of working and a broader focus, the Police Security Service could have become aware of the perpetrator prior to 22 July. Notwithstanding, *the Commission has no grounds for contending that the Police Security Service could and should have averted the attacks* [emphasis mine]" (22 July Commission 2012, p. 16). This measured and realistic statement reflects the overall approach adopted by the commission and the response of the Norwegian government and society as a whole.

The aftermath of the attacks was indeed marked by peaceful marches and commemorations, an open and fair trial, and useful discussions on the psychiatric evaluation practice. What was perhaps most salutary was what Norway did *not* do: in general, the media, police, and government did not overreact; the country did not consider the threat to be more pervasive than it was; it did not create a new set of laws infringing on civil liberties and human rights; it did not stigmatize a whole section of the Norwegian population based on the views held by Breivik himself; and overall, it did not put in place drastic measures likely to create a whole series of unintended consequences.

Of course, the Norwegian model may not be directly applicable everywhere. Every country has its own set of historic, cultural, geographic, religious, political, socioeconomic, and other structural characteristics that greatly influence how it reacts to dramatic events. The nature of terrorism in Norway is also vastly different from many other places, given the all-encompassing definition of the term itself. Therefore, governments and other key actors in Nigeria, Yemen, or Colombia might not be able to see some of the linkages and lessons to be learned from Norway at first sight. However, guidelines on key tenants of counterterrorism strategies and examples of specific programs that have proved successful in some areas may prove beneficial to others. Although each situation is unique, a number of lessons from past experience—which the following sections will explore—are worth sharing across the world.

REFRAMING THE DISCOURSE

Five key facts about terrorism are worth insisting upon. First, terrorism is a serious problem, but not the most important threat the world faces. Other challenges such as intra- and interstate conflicts, organized crime, cyber security, climate change, pandemics, financial crises, corruption, and weak governance have proved to have a much greater human, financial, institutional, and societal impact across the world. In human terms alone, while there was a 61% increase in terrorist attacks in 2013, 40 times more people were killed in homicides than terrorist attacks—just under 18,000 died as a result of terrorist attacks in 2013, while almost half a million people were killed in an intentional homicide in 2012 (Institute of Economics and Peace 2014; UNODC 2014). Fifty-six percent of all terrorist attacks since 1970 have not caused any fatality (LaFree 2013). Terrorism can be devastating—such as the events of 9/11 demonstrated. However, even the most tragic terrorist attack in modern history had a relatively limited death toll compared to the Rwandan genocide, for instance, during which over 800,000 people were killed in 3 months, or the equivalent of almost three 9/11s a day for 100 days. These two events were of course very different. It would be foolish to underestimate the psychological and symbolic impact of an attack in the heart of the United States. However, the importance of perspective, objectivity, and evidence was often lost in the response to 9/11.

Second, terrorism is a localized problem: although terrorism is an issue in many countries around the world, 82% of all fatalities from terrorist attacks occurred in only five countries in 2013, namely, Iraq, Afghanistan, Pakistan, Nigeria, and Syria, countries that face a range of political challenges that cannot be merely described as terrorism (Institute for Economics and Peace 2014).

Third, terrorism is a complex, multi-faceted challenge. There is very little in common between the Revolutionary Armed Forces of Colombia, the Comité d'Action Viticole, Al Qaeda, the National Liberation Front of Corsica, and the Liberation Tigers of Tamil Eelam, for instance, all widely considered terrorist organizations and part of the shared threat posed by *international terrorism*. The term itself—terrorism—is problematic, as it tends to obscure differences between different manifestations and activities. However, rather than reiterating lengthy academic discussions on alternative definitions or terms, it is perhaps even more crucial to increase awareness of these nuances in policy and analysis. A blanket approach treating all of these organizations with an identical strategy is indeed likely to prove inadequate.

Fourth, terrorism largely stems from political, social, and economic factors. There is of course a multitude of *motives* (i.e., grievances, causes, factors) and *motifs* (i.e., justifications, explanations) given the wide range of realities encompassed within the term terrorism (Durodié 2007). However, very often, the widespread discourse on radicalization, ideology, and religion tends to overlook more important underlying factors. In a 2008 paper for *International Security*, Max Abrahms points out that individuals largely join terrorist organizations for social reasons—to be part of something, to feel like they belong somewhere, and to be surrounded by like-minded individuals in a society where they often feel marginalized and alienated. He argues that terrorists are not "rational actors primarily motivated to achieving political ends" as the dominant paradigm in terrorism studies then suggested, but instead "rational people who use terrorism primarily to develop strong affective ties with fellow terrorists" (Abrahms 2008). In addition, most terrorist attacks occur in countries with poor governance, authoritarian regimes, few opportunities for political engagement, high levels of discrimination, a struggling economy, and social inequalities. This has important implications for policy. The reduction of social, economic, and political inequalities, through an increased focus on local services including after-school programs for the youth, policing strategies involving the local community, education opportunities, platforms for political and civic engagement, reintegration and rehabilitation strategies, and a broader reform of governance including a focus on transparency and accountability would be worthwhile investments.

Fifth, terrorism—which is by definition a nonstate activity, as we explored in Chapter 1—often distracts from the much more important and damaging role played by states themselves in many regions of the world. Corruption, weak governance, and authoritarianism are the product of states, often recognized by the international community, and yet they perpetrate crimes of greater magnitude than smaller and less potent terrorist organizations.

With this in mind, there is a need for a broad reframing of counterterrorism strategies, away from disproportionate, simplistic, and polarizing approaches and toward more measured ones focusing on the political, economic, and social factors behind terrorism. The terrorism label is a tool that has often been used by politicians, analysts, journalists, and others for their own agenda, including delegitimizing political opponents, disregarding national and international rule of law, convincing a population of the need to intervene militarily, increasing defense and security budgets, expanding intelligence measures, selling newspapers, magazines, and books, attracting funding from governments and international organizations, and for personal careers. One may consider that it is in the interest of many to overestimate the threat posed by terrorism, in order to maintain current levels of spending, funding, or readership. However, current policies have often proved inadequate, disproportionate, and harmful, hence the urgent need for a new approach.

PREVENTING AND COUNTERING VIOLENT EXTREMISM

Various terms have been used to refer to the recent push toward "noncoercive preventive engagement to address violent extremist ideas and behaviors," including "counterradicalization" and "preventing violent extremism" (Chowdhury Fink et al. 2013, p. 1).* The overall idea remains the same: CVE intends to address the ideas and factors behind terrorism, rather than simply the manifestation of violence itself. In other words, instead of merely tackling the symptoms of a problem, it aims to address the problem itself. The approach is intentionally "soft" and contrasts with "hard" military and law enforcement options to address the issue. However, most countries use CVE as part of a larger policy toolbox, which includes both hard and soft instruments.

The U.S. State Department sees three main lines of efforts in its CVE pillar, namely, "1. Provide positive alternatives to those most at-risk of radicalization and recruitment into violent extremism; 2. Counter violent extremist narratives and messaging; and 3. Increase international partner capacity (civil society and government) to address the drivers of radicalization" (U.S. State Department 2014). A number of programs have been carried out under CVE strategies, including to strengthen community engagement and civil society participation; conduct rehabilitation initiatives for extremists in prisons, engaging women more systematically; provide narratives to counter the messages put forward by terrorist and extremist individuals and organizations, especially on social media; and create more appropriate partnerships between law enforcement and the community in which they operate.

In and of itself, CVE seems to demonstrate a willingness to treat terrorism as a "normal" problem, requiring an effective yet balanced response. This marks a clear departure from the immediate period following 9/11, where the *War on Terror* overrode any attempt to take a softer, evidence-based route. A similar trajectory is taking place in international drug policy, slowly backing away from the heavy-handed, prohibitionist, zero-tolerance policies of the *War on Drugs* and toward approaches centered on public health, decriminalization, and socioeconomic policies. In other words, the moral, binary, and unrealistic dimensions of these old models seem to be receding in favor of more evidence-based, objective, and progressive models.

Nevertheless, much progress remains to be made. As mentioned earlier, CVE is only a recent phenomenon and part of a much broader strategy that may include more problematic and controversial components. There is no guarantee that CVE initiatives will prove successful. As mentioned earlier, the early iterations of the counterradicalization program

* The Center on Global Counterterrorism Cooperation (CGCC) is now called the Global Center on Cooperative Security (and often referred to as the Global Center).

Prevent in the United Kingdom received much criticism for creating confusion between social programs and surveillance operations. However, an overall redistribution of resources away from knee-jerk measures and toward more long-term comprehensive policies focused on prevention and rehabilitation is bound to be more effective and produce a more positive impact.

The recent program aimed at returning foreign fighters in Denmark is a good example of how noncoercive initiatives can provide a powerful alternative to more stringent measures. Aarhus, the country's second most populous city, saw 30 young people go to Syria in 2013. In the country as a whole, over 100 individuals did so, which constitutes the second highest proportion of foreign fighters per capita in Western Europe—after Belgium (The Murmur 2014). As discussed earlier, upon their return to their home countries in Europe, many foreign fighters face the prospect of incarceration, surveillance, deportation, confiscation of their passport, or other travel bans. However, Aarhus has put in place an innovative—and admittedly, controversial—program to reintegrate these young individuals into society. A partnership between the local police and welfare services, it provides them with medical treatment, psychological counseling, career support, and education assistance. This follows an initial screening from law enforcement to ensure that those who have committed crimes are prosecuted for them and that those who pose immediate security risks are passed on to security services (Al Jazeera 2014).

It is difficult to assess the success of the program thus far. In October 2014, Aarhus Police Commissioner Jorgen Ilum noted: "In 2013, we had 30 young people go to Syria. This year, to my knowledge, we have had only one. We believe that the main reason is our contact and dialogue with the Muslim community" (*Washington Post* 2014). Three objections can be raised here: the sample size here is too small to draw definitive conclusions; more people might have gone to Syria and Iraq or preparing to do so without the Aarhus police being aware of it; the reduction in reported numbers of foreign fighters may be explained by factors other than the rehabilitation program; and it is too early for any type of meaningful assessment.

This type of *soft-hands approach* rarely produces the same kind of politically appealing, tangible metrics that forceful law enforcement interventions do, such as numbers of people arrested, charged, prosecuted, and incarcerated, websites removed, organizations banned, passports confiscated, or individuals deported. As a result, funding is often difficult to attract and maintain in the long run. The British experience is a case in point: community-based Prevent projects have seen their funding reduced from £140 million in 2008/2009 to £17 million in 2012/2013 and a mere £1.7 million in 2013/2014 (Brandon 2014). In addition, the rehabilitation program in Aarhus, like many others tried elsewhere, struggles to reach those who do not want to be helped. It is also not designed to resolve all the broader socioeconomic factors enabling marginalization and criminal behavior, including economic prospects, inequalities, discrimination, democratic processes, and urban planning.

With all that being said, noncoercive approaches are the best way forward. There is no easy fix for the issues of extremism and terrorism. The program put in place in Aarhus is not a panacea. However, this approach is the most likely to help understand the grievances, justifications, and motivations of these individuals, tailor responses to each individual, address some of these underlying factors behind their ideas and behaviors, and prevent further violent behavior and indoctrination. As international reporter Leela Jacinto points out: "the worst would be a hardline response that compromises the principles of justice and human rights that mark a free society" (Jacinto 2014). Noncoercive approaches to CVE are bound to be not only a long-term difficult process but also by far the most promising option.

ROLE OF NONGOVERNMENT ACTORS

Governments are often thought to be the most important actors in the fight against terrorism and violent extremism. However, it would be naive to overestimate how much they can achieve on their own with regard to CVE, law enforcement, and development objectives.

Public institutions very often may lack the credibility, legitimacy, or actual capacity to play a direct role in preventing radicalization and counter extremist ideas. While they can fund organizations, act as a facilitator, or provide impetus at an early stage, primary delivery of CVE programs may very well come from NGOs. As a report by the European Policy Planners' Network on Countering Radicalisation and Polarisation (PPN), coordinated by the Institute for Strategic Dialogue (ISD), points out, civil society, in partnership with governments, can play a role in five main ways, namely, (1) helping to prevent radicalization by "tackling the underlying economic, social and political drivers of radicalization"; (2) challenging "the narratives of radicalizers and extremists and put forward positive alternatives"; (3) spotting "the signs of vulnerability and work upstream to protect individuals from radicalization, through improved parenting, neighborhood support, and community resilience"; (4) assisting the deradicalization process; and (5) playing a role in the prevention of planned attacks "by providing information or intelligence that could help the authorities" (PPN 2010, p. 5).

There are numerous civil society organizations that have conducted important work on counterradicalization, radicalization, and CVE issues. These include ISD, notably through its projects Counterextremism.org, PPN, the Radicalisation Awareness Network, and the Against Violent Extremism, a network of key stakeholders including former violent extremists focused on CVE. The role of such individuals, having gone through similar experiences, can be very effective in providing credible voices for younger individuals to relate to and look up to (ISD 2014). Other organizations in the United Kingdom include the Channel project and the Strategy to Reach, Empower and Educate Teenagers, both funded as part of Prevent. In the Netherlands, ICCT–The Hague has played a key role as well, for instance, through its work on rehabilitation and reintegration of violent extremist offenders, especially in prisons, and the Victims' Voices project, designed to "explore ways to effectively and structurally involve victims of terrorist acts in countering violent extremism" (ICCT 2014). It is led by Max Boon, a survivor of the Marriott Jakarta terrorist bomb attack in 2009.

Similarly, most effective law enforcement strategies, designed to tackle either terrorism or extremism to deal with organized crime and gangs, have involved the local community in their actions. Although extremism and gang crime are different, as we have explored in greater detail earlier in this book, some of the factors behind low-level membership in these organizations converge: an overall lack of social, economic, and political support and opportunities, and a feeling of disenfranchisement or alienation. A number of relevant examples are worth highlighting here.

The National Crime Prevention Centre in Canada stresses the positive impact of "Gang member intervention programs that are focused on reducing cohesion among youth gangs and individual gang members"; "community-based mentoring"; and "after-school recreation (premised on the belief that providing pro-social opportunities for young people in the after-school hours can reduce their involvement in delinquent behaviour in the community)" (Welsh 2007).

In Brazil, the Police Pacification Units (UPPs) were launched in 2008 in the city of Rio de Janeiro. As of October 2014, over 40 UPPs have been created in more than 260 communities representing over 1.5 million people (Barnes 2014). This law enforcement model focuses on strengthening police capacity, with a view to bolster presence and enforcement actions in order to regain control of some key territories run by gangs, creating new recruiting methods, increasing pay, and put in place better training in community policing strategies and human rights. Crucially, UPPs have collaborated with local partners to deliver social services and create new infrastructure to boost social and economic developments in these underprivileged areas. Following early successes in crime reduction, recent challenges underline the necessity of sustained efforts in the long run, along with measures focused on reducing economic and social inequalities, improving work conditions, and decreasing school dropout rates, as the World Bank recommends (World Bank 2013).

The concept of community-based deterrence has also proved effective. One of its first applications took place in the early 1990s in Boston, when Operation Ceasefire helped reduce youth homicide in the affected areas by two-thirds (Felbab-Brown 2013, pp. 5–6). It focused on prioritizing action on specific groups, reclaiming control of some areas controlled by gangs and, more importantly, including local community leaders as integral parts of the strategy. An association of religious groups organized forums to give gang members, police officers, church ministers, and social services employees an opportunity to discuss key issue. Gang members were also offered information, education, and training in exchange for leaving gangs (DOJ 2001). Following the success of Operation Ceasefire, similar initiatives were carried out in High Point, North Carolina, and Santa Tecla, El Salvador, with positive results (OAS 2013, p. 31).

The inclusion of social and economic objectives in law enforcement strategies can be seen as part of the security-development nexus. The nexus has become commonplace in development and foreign policy making and academia. It is based on the premise that there can be no development without security and vice versa. The UN and the EU have been two prominent advocates of the security-development nexus. In 2003, the European Security Strategy stated: "Security is the first condition for development" (EU 2003, p. 13). It also stressed that a lack of development may be an obstacle to peace and thereby highlights the need for the EU to bring together instruments, capabilities, and partnerships to tackle these issues in a comprehensive manner. In 2005, the then UN secretary general Kofi Annan noted: "we will not enjoy development without security, we will not enjoy security without development, and we will not enjoy either without respect for human rights" (UN 2005, p. 6).

The security-development nexus has faced criticism. For instance, Mark Duffield contends that the argument reflects the problematic predominance of the aid industry. He criticizes the related confusion between development policy—a supposedly neutral endeavor—and foreign policy—a political process guided by self-interest (Duffield 2010, p. 56). Others have argued that aid has been *securitized,* in other words undermined and directed by higher national defense and security needs (Saferworld 2011). Sasha Jesperson argues that the nexus has also led Western policy to target countries ridden by and prone to conflict at the expense of less developed countries not affected by conflict (Jesperson 2013). To David Chandler, the concept suffers from too much hype and an oversimplification of the linkages between development and security. He also argues that the nexus provides an opportunity for Western states to make "grand policy statements of mission and purpose... while simultaneously disengaging from serious policy-making in these regions and passing responsibility to other actors" (Chandler 2007).

Nevertheless, there is little opposition to the overall idea: development and security go hand in hand. A safe environment is generally more conducive to economic and social development, which in itself is likely to lead to an increase in the reality and perception of security. Even David Chandler acknowledges the links between the two when offering the following nuance: "it would be better to understand development and security as 'equally desirable and potentially mutually reinforcing goals'" (Chandler 2007).

As we have seen, terrorism is a complex issue, which takes many different forms and stems from many different factors. It would be foolish to assume that less poverty will automatically lead to less terrorism and overall less insecurity. Several academic studies have shown that the reality is much more nuanced and complex than initial instincts would suggest (see, for instance, Abadie 2004; Piazza 2007, 2010; Crowley 2011). However, as Kruger and Malecková put it, "Terrorism is more accurately viewed as a response to political conditions and long-standing feelings, either perceived or real, of indignity and frustration that have little to do with economics" (2002). In other words, addressing political issues, even more so than economic challenges, is a crucial component of an effective counterterrorism strategy.

Whether by design or by default, civil society actors, especially at the local level, are heavily involved in the delivery of programs carried out in the spirit of the development nexus. Accordingly, both governments and local actors would do well to focus on two dimensions here: first, reduction of poverty and economic inequalities should be a key objective in its own right, whether or not it may lead to a reduction in terrorism occurrences as such; second, prioritizing on the issues of governance and capacity building to ensure that political and institutional processes are fairer and more effective, and providing political and social opportunities for the most marginalized, would go a long way in addressing crucial challenges that are related not only to terrorism but also to organized crime, corruption, and conflict. Increasingly, governments are ill suited to address today's multifaceted, interconnected, fast-changing challenges, often proving too slow to respond, too hierarchical for transversal issues that require comprehensive solutions, and not innovative enough. There is a need for Western governments to reform their policy-making processes, for instance, via special teams and units to look at issues as a whole (including terrorism, drug policy, illicit trade, or corruption) across ministerial responsibilities and beyond traditional structures. In addition, there is an opportunity for actors outside government, including NGOs and private companies to leverage their flexibility to help address some of these problems.

This book has explored a number of important dimensions of the role played by the media in countering terrorism. First, the media often acts as a vehicle of the messages that terrorist organizations want to instill through their actions and threats. By giving terrorists a platform to justify their violent actions, the media may help terrorists in spreading their propaganda. Second, by overfocusing on terrorism at the expense of other key developments in society, the media may also amplify the sense of fear surrounding terrorism and create a distorted view of the actual risk. For instance, Iyengar and Kinder found that between 1981 and 1986, the three U.S. TV networks of ABS, CBS, and NBC broadcasted more news stories on terrorism than on poverty, unemployment, racial inequality, and crime combined (Iyengar and Kinder 1987). Third, some media reporting on shootings and terrorist attacks may increase the likelihood of copycat attacks, as Park Dietz and others have found.

Journalists are not the only actors playing an important role on these matters. Academics, analysts, experts, but also businesses, consultancies, and other private sector actors often contribute to magnifying the threat posed by terrorism. The mere surge in terrorism and counterterrorism studies after 9/11 can be seen as problematic in itself. While many have helped governments and law enforcement officials gain a better understanding of the nature of terrorism and of the need for a more refined counterterrorism strategy, spending too much time, money, and effort on the topic creates opportunity costs and contributes to exaggerating the threat.

REVIEWING THE IMPACTS OF FOREIGN POLICY

Since 9/11, foreign policy has been a key component of counterterrorism policies worldwide, especially from the United States, and to a lesser extent the United Kingdom, France, and others. Following the attacks of September 2001, the United States launched a series of military interventions to fight back against international terrorism, chiefly in Afghanistan and Iraq.

These two missions did not only pertain to terrorism. From a development rationale with strong educational and infrastructure components to a counternarcotic narrative, strategic objectives in Afghanistan have evolved a number of times and often differed from one stakeholder to the other. However, from the beginning, the military operations were clearly intended as a response to 9/11, or as UNSC Resolution 1378 put it, "the Taliban for allowing Afghanistan to be used as a base for the export of terrorism by the Al-Qaida network and other terrorist groups and for providing safe haven to Usama Bin Laden, Al-Qaida and others associated with them" (UNSC 2001).

Terrorism was also a significant factor in the U.S. decision to intervene militarily in Iraq in 2003. Admittedly, the regime of Saddam Hussein had been an enemy to the United States for a long period of time, and was then accused of holding and developing Weapons of Mass Destruction (WMD). And yet, it is fair to say that had 9/11 not occurred, the U.S. military intervention in Iraq likely would not have been possible. In the lead-up to March 2003, the Bush Administration repeatedly emphasized the existence of strong links between the Iraqi regime and Al Qaeda. In February 2003, then U.S. Secretary of State Colin Powell warned: "These al Qaeda affiliates, based in Baghdad, now coordinate the movement of people, money and supplies into and throughout Iraq for his network, and they've been operating freely in the capital for more than eight months" (CNN 2003). These allegations, among a few others establishing connections between Al Qaeda and Osama bin Laden, later turned out to be largely unfounded, exaggerated, and insufficient, since Al Qaeda had operated and cooperated with individuals within other countries, including Saudi Arabia, Pakistan, Yemen, and Iran. Nonetheless, the United States intervened, and the mission was seen as a cornerstone of its prolonged war on terror.

Over a decade later, results are mixed, at best. The Saddam Hussein regime was quickly overthrown in Iraq, but no WMD were ever found in Iraq. More importantly, levels of violence and instability increased

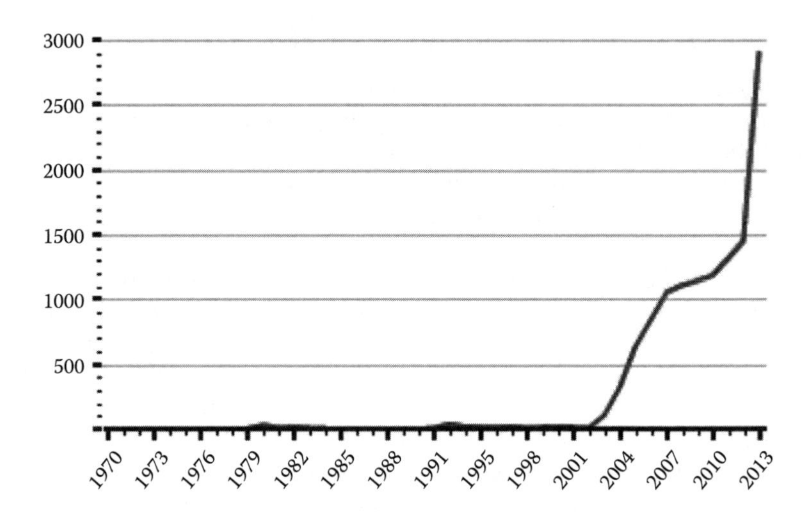

Figure 7.1 Number of terrorist attacks per year in Iraq. (From START, 2014a, GTD, accessed on December 2, 2014.)

substantially in the country. Terrorist attacks skyrocketed after 2003, as this graph from the Global Terrorism Database demonstrates (see Figure 7.1).

In 2013, Iraq accounted for approximately 25% of all terrorist attacks, 35% of deaths, and 45% of injuries worldwide (START 2014b, p. 4)—most of which occurred before the well-documented rise of ISIS. Terrorist attacks were also 40% more lethal in Iraq compared to the global average (START 2014b, p. 5). On 77 occasions in 2013, there were more than 10 incidents in 24 hours, a sign of the well-coordinated and pervasive nature of these terrorist attacks (START 2014b, p. 5). It would be unfair to solely blame the U.S.-led coalition's intervention for the instability reigning in Iraq nowadays: terrorist attacks in Iraq are obviously not perpetrated by the United States; the structural sources of the conflict have existed for centuries; and the regime of Saddam Hussein itself has killed or *disappeared* at least 250,000 people over its almost 24 years of reign, according to Human Rights Watch (Human Rights Watch 2004)—compared to the over 202,000 who have died in violent deaths in Iraq since the 2003 invasion (Iraq Body Count 2014). However, the military intervention in Iraq, led by the United States and with important contributions from the United Kingdom, largely contributed to the violence in Iraq since 2003. The original objectives of the military interventions were not to pacify the country, but to topple Saddam Hussein, destroy WMDs, and disrupt the regime's links with Al Qaeda. While the first objective was rapidly met, the second one proved unnecessary, given the absence of WMDs in the first place. With regard to the third objective, Al Qaeda and terrorist activity dramatically *increased* after 2003. In other words, it would be unwise to consider the intervention a success (see Figure 7.1).

Whether the international military operations in Afghanistan have been successful is more debatable. As previously mentioned, it is not perfectly clear what the intervention's objectives are, given numerous changes in strategy and tactics over time, and persistent disagreements between various actors. The closest there is to a consensus is perhaps what NATO has emphasized: "NATO's primary objective in Afghanistan is to enable the Afghan authorities to provide effective security across the country and ensure that the country can never again be a safe haven for terrorists" (NATO 2014). It is clear that the work conducted by the United States and NATO has helped Afghanistan in many ways: Al Qaeda has been weakened, and elections were organized in 2004, 2009, and 2014. More importantly, many social and economic indicators point toward significant progress: child, infant, maternal, and overall mortality rates have dropped since 2001; life expectancy has gone up by 6 years; the enrollment rate in primary schools has increased fivefold; and the country's GDP per capita has been multiplied by five in the decade following the military intervention (World Bank 2014). Nonetheless, it remains to be seen whether Afghan authorities will be prepared to fulfill the objectives NATO has set out for them and trained them toward once the large majority of international troops leave the country. In December 2014, NATO defense ministers agreed to launch a new training mission to support Afghan authorities the day after the complete withdrawal of combat troops by the end of 2014 (Reuters 2014). This will certainly help Afghanistan meet some of the challenges related to corruption, poor competency levels, and insider attacks—over 50 international soldiers were killed as a result of this type of attacks in 2012 alone, although numbers have decreased since then (New America Foundation 2012). Many structural issues are still to be met, and it will take time to find long-term political, institutional, and economic solutions to address the country's woes. The recent rise in casualties among the Afghan National Security Forces illustrates the fragility of the current situation: 2014 was the deadliest year for Afghan troops since 2001 (*Wall Street Journal* 2014).

Research suggests that military interventions have limited efficacy against terrorism. In an important 2008 report for RAND, Seth Jones and

Martin Libicki analyzed 648 terrorist groups that existed between 1968 and 2006, and how they ended—if they did. Their results were striking: "military force led to the end of terrorist groups in 7 percent of the cases," in stark contrast with the fact that 43% of terrorist groups ended because they joined the political process, and 40% because of policing. Another 10% of terrorist groups seized to exist because they had achieved their goals (Jones and Libicki 2008, p. xiii). This does not mean that a military response is never suited against a terrorist group. The authors note: "Militaries tended to be most effective when used against terrorist groups engaged in an insurgency in which the groups were large, well armed, and well organized," but they add: "Against most terrorist groups, however, military force is usually too blunt an instrument" (Jones and Libicki 2008, p. xiv). Even when terrorist groups become involved in an insurgency, military forces defeated them only 19% of the time (Jones and Libicki 2008, p. xv). This has significant implications for policy: military intervention should not be seen as a silver-bullet solution against terrorism, a set of complex challenges that entail political and socioeconomic issues and require a much more nuanced, comprehensive, and local response.

The most important legacy of the military interventions in Afghanistan and Iraq has perhaps been the increased reluctance of Western powers, the United States in particular, to engage in military interventions with a significant troop presence on the ground. Over 8,000 coalition soldiers have died in Afghanistan and Iraq since the beginning of military operations in 2001 and 2003, while over 50,000 have been wounded (DOD 2014; iCasualties 2014). This, added to the complexity of the situation on the ground, and the relative lack of visible progress in the fight against international terrorism, has not however led to a significant retrenchment. Instead, it led the United States to make some important changes in its military approach, including the growing use of drones, a controversial development, which we will explore in the following section.

CASE STUDY: THE USE OF DRONES

In military jargon, drones are often referred to as Unmanned Aerial Vehicles, Unmanned Combat Aerial Systems, Unmanned Combat Aerial Vehicles (UCAVs), or Remotely Piloted Aircraft (RPA). There are important distinctions between these different acronyms. *Combat* drones are armed, while the others are often used for surveillance purposes only.

As RAND points out, drones "can be fully or partially autonomous but are more often controlled remotely by a human pilot"—hence the frequent use of the RPA acronym to stress the presence, albeit remote, of a pilot (RAND 2014). Drones can also be used outside a security environment, including for environmental, agricultural, or disaster relief purposes.

The drone market is very small today, projected to grow to approximately $8.35 billion by 2018, or less than half a percent of the global defense market, estimated to reach $1.88 trillion that year (Kreps and Zenko 2014). Despite that, the use of drone strikes has become an important military instrument in the fight against terrorism for three main reasons. First, from an operational perspective, drones have been increasingly used by the United States for so-called targeted killings in recent years. While under the Bush administrations a total of 48 drone strikes were conducted, numbers rose substantially under President Obama—partly because of improvements in drone technology of course, but also because of a broader strategic rebalancing away from ground troop intervention. Between 2004 and September 2013, the United States is estimated to have launched between 330 and 374 drone strikes in Pakistan alone (Amnesty USA 2013). Although this accounts for the bulk of U.S. drone strikes worldwide, other countries have been affected. In Yemen, the United States conducted between 42 and 52 confirmed drone strikes between 2002 and 2012, according to the Bureau of Investigative Journalism (TBIJ), who estimates a possible additional 66–79 U.S. drone strikes (TBIJ 2013). In Somalia, there is even more uncertainty as to the scale of drone strikes there—between 10 and 21 according to the Columbia Law School's Human Rights Clinic and Center for Civilians in Conflict—but they appear to be on the rise (2012, p. 17). Drone strikes have also been reported in Afghanistan, Iraq, and Libya (TBIJ 2013).

Second, while drone proliferation is often exaggerated, a number of countries are investing in surveillance and combat drone capabilities. The United Kingdom and France, on the back of the Lancaster House treaties on bilateral defense and security cooperation signed in November 2010, are currently jointly developing a UCAV program referred to as the Future Combat Air System (Embassy of France in the United Kingdom 2014). Both countries increasingly see drones, including for combat purposes, as an important pillar of their future military strategy. A UK MOD spokesman noted in Spring 2013: "The expectation is that our future combat air capability will be based around a suitable mix of manned fast jets and remotely piloted air systems" (*Guardian* 2013). In other words, while drones may only account for a small part of defense arsenals today, procurement decisions are increasingly being made to rely on drones more heavily in the future.

Third, drone strikes present operational and political advantages, chiefly that they are less humanly costly than military interventions with so-called "boots on the ground." Removing soldiers from war zones naturally leads to fewer casualties. Following the difficult experiences in Afghanistan and Iraq, the United States was keen to reduce the number of ground troops in conflict zones. In addition, drone strikes are meant to be more *targeted* than other types of military air strikes and thereby cause less collateral damage. Importantly, public opinion has perhaps not been as opposed to the use of drone strikes as one might think. A poll conducted in the United Kingdom by YouGov for RUSI in February and March 2013, found that popular support was not very strong among women and younger respondents, and 47% worried that drone technology "makes it too easy for Western governments to conduct military strikes in foreign countries." However, 54% of respondents favored assassinating individual terrorists abroad, while 31% were opposed to the idea. About 55% supported British assistance to a U.S. drone attack against *known terrorists.* When respondents were told that the attack could "prevent an imminent terror attack against the UK," support increased to 74% and remained high at 64% and 60% when the scenario involved 2–3 innocent civilians and 10–15 innocent civilians, respectively (RUSI 2013). Similarly, a Gallup Poll conducted in the United States around the same time as the YouGov/RUSI survey found that 65% of respondents thought the "U.S. government should use drones to launch airstrikes in other countries against suspected terrorists." Perhaps even more significant was the finding that only 49% of Americans are following news on drones *very* or *somewhat closely,* much lower than the "61% average across more than 200 news events that Gallup has measured in this way"—an illustration of the widespread apathy on the issue (Gallup 2013).

Drones are here to stay. It would be foolish to expect their downfall, given the arguments in favor of their use, the lack of overwhelming political and public opposition against them, and current investments in 20–30 year long procurement cycles for this type of technology. However, there is an urgent need for more transparency, oversight, political and public debate, and a thorough analysis of the current use of drone strikes and the potential long-term effects they may have.

Drone strikes do indeed cause civilian casualties—up to 881 in Pakistan alone between 2004 and 2012, including 176 children (TBIJ 2013). Meanwhile, the number of *high-level* targets killed as a result of drone strikes only accounted for 2% of overall casualties (NYU and Stanford 2012), which contrasts with the often-held argument that the majority of drone casualties are leading terrorist figures. The psychological, social, and economic impact of drones hovering over communities in Pakistan and elsewhere on a daily basis is much harder to quantify, yet has significant ramifications. Drones have also been accused of radicalizing more individuals into carrying out terrorist attacks against the United States and other Western countries. While few wide-ranging quantitative studies have been able to assess to what extent that is the case, public perceptions against the United States in Pakistan have certainly been affected. While 94% of Pakistani respondents familiar with the drone campaign believed that "the attacks kill too many innocent people," 74% consider that they are not "necessary to defend Pakistan from extremist organizations" (NYU and Stanford 2012). The percentage of people in Pakistan considering the United States as an enemy has also increased from 64 in 2009 to 74 in 2012, while Pakistani support for the United States to provide financial and humanitarian aid dropped from 72% to 50% over the same period (Pew Research 2012). Terrorists have also used the U.S. drone strikes as a justification for their actions. During his trial for attempting to detonate a bomb in Times Square in New York, Faisal Shahzad mentioned the drone strikes in "Somalia and Yemen and in Pakistan" as to why he was pleading guilty "100 times forward" and why "we will be attacking U.S." (*Guardian* 2010). As James de Waal, senior consulting fellow at Chatham House, puts it, "A campaign which is based on drones is quite good at dealing with the symptoms but it does little with the causes of an insurgency. In fact, it might exacerbate them. [Drones] are an attractive tactic but they are not necessarily a good strategy" (*Financial Times* 2014).

The U.S. drone strike practices have been very opaque, allowing for barely any oversight and accountability. The DOJ memoranda providing the mere legal basis for the U.S. targeted killings in Pakistan have not been released (NYU and Stanford 2012); it remains unclear who is the leading authority behind the strikes (e.g., the CIA? the White House? the Department of Defense?); and details on the identities of those targeted and the reasons behind the strikes are rarely released. *Signature strikes* are particularly controversial: this type of strike targets unknown individuals whose behavior and characteristics appear suspicious.

Without actual information, more public debate, stronger congressional and judiciary oversight, independent investigations, and pressure from international organizations and civil society, the current system is bound to continue untouched. The European Parliament passed a resolution on the use of armed drones in February 2012 to condemn practices to date, stressing, for instance, "its grave concern over the use of armed drones outside the international legal framework," calling for EU authorities to "oppose and ban the practice of extrajudicial targeted killings," and "to promote greater transparency and accountability on the part of third countries in the use of armed drones with regard to the legal basis for their use and to operational responsibility, to allow for judicial review of drone strikes and to ensure that victims of unlawful drone strikes have effective access to remedies" (European Parliament 2014). These are critical guidelines for the way forward, and ones that the United States and others would do well to apply, in order to begin to reform an untenable system.

REFORMING INTELLIGENCE POLICIES

Intelligence policies are another important component of counterterrorism strategies, and rightfully so. Previously cited research shows that 40% of terrorist groups analyzed by Jones and Libicki have ended because of policing (Jones and Libicki 2008, p. xiii). As the authors point out, "police and intelligence services have better training and information to penetrate and disrupt terrorist organizations than do such institutions as the military." They stress the importance of traditional local police and intelligence agencies who "usually have a permanent presence in cities, towns, and villages; a better understanding of the threat environment in these areas; and better human intelligence" (Jones and Libicki 2008, p. xiv)—in other words, a strategy that is different from the mass surveillance programs revealed by Edward Snowden.

The mass gathering of metadata or data is problematic in many ways, as we have discussed in Chapter 5. First, the effectiveness of these intelligence programs is still unclear. There is very little evidence that the United States, the United Kingdom, and others are significantly safer as a result. Second, privacy rights have been infringed upon, with little knowledge of it, little congressional and public debate on the matter, and little possible recourse for action from civil society. Third, all the money, time, and effort spent on these largely indiscriminate ventures obviously have opportunity costs and seem to be preventing a more measured, targeted, and effective approach. Once again, the problem with intelligence before 9/11 was not that there was not enough information available, but rather that the information was not properly shared and acted upon. As Bruce Schneier puts it, "Piling more data onto the mix makes it harder, not easier. The best way to think of it is a needle-in-a-haystack problem; the last thing you want to do is increase the amount of hay you have to search through" (Schneier 2014).

It is easy to simply dismiss recent revelations over intelligence programs, by criticizing Edward Snowden himself, by arguing that there will always be a lot that we do not know, by suggesting we simply trust our elected government to do their job or by considering it an issue for experts only. However, the intelligence debate concerns all of society. Reform is urgently needed and would do well to include the following: consultation of a range of key institutional actors when drafting new legislation and creating new intelligence measures; continuous parliamentary and judiciary oversight on the overall strategy and the details of intelligence programs; increased transparency from government and intelligence agencies; and more political and public discussions as to where the balance should be struck in terms of spending and key components of intelligence strategies. Crucially, all of this should take into consideration the fact that the threat posed by terrorism is often overestimated and that overreacting is likely to cause a range of unintended consequences worth anticipating. Given the nature of terrorism and the fear associated with it, effective checks and balances are essential to ensure that emotional reactions do not get in the way of evidence-based, objective, and rational policy making.

REFERENCES

22 July Commission. 2012. Rapport fra 22. Juli-kommisjonen. English version of selected chapters. Preliminary, Oslo, August 13, 2012.

Abadie, A. 2004. Poverty, political freedom, and the roots of terrorism. National Bureau of Economic Research (NBER) Working Paper No. 10859, October 2004.

Abrahms, M. 2008. What Terrorists Really Want: Terrorist Motives and Counterterrorism Strategy. *International Security* 32(4), 78–105. Spring 2008.

Al Jazeera. 2014. Denmark introduces rehab for Syrian fighters, September 7, 2014.

Amnesty USA. 2013. "Will I Be Next?" U.S. Drone Strikes in Pakistan, October 22, 2013.

Barnes, N. 2014. With Brazil in spotlight, Rio's Favela Pacification Program at a crossroads. *World Politics Review*, June 9, 2014.

Brandon, J. 2014. The UK's counterradicalization strategy just failed: What now? *War on the Rocks*, September 18, 2014.

Chandler, D. 2007. The security-development nexus and the rise of "anti-foreign policy." *Journal of International Relations and Development* 10: 362–386.
Chowdhury Fink, N., Romaniuk, P., and Barakat, R. 2013. Evaluating countering violent extremism and programming: Practice and progress. Center on Global Counterterrorism Cooperation—CGCC, September 2013.
CNN. 2003. Selling an Iraq–al Qaeda connection, March 11, 2003.
Columbia Law School's Human Rights Clinic & Center for Civilians in Conflict. 2012. The civilian impact of drones: Unexamined costs, unanswered questions. *Part of the Modern Issues in Conflict Series*, September 2012.
Crowley. 2011. Terrorism and poverty: Debunking the myth. MacDonald-Laurier Institute, January 24, 2011.
DOD. 2014. U.S Military Casualties—GWOT Casualty Summary by Casualty Type. Defense Casualty Analysis System. As of December 2, 2014.
DOJ. 2001. Reducing gun violence. The Boston Gun Project's Operation Ceasefire. Research Report, September 2001.
Duffield, M. 2010. The liberal way of development and the development-security impasse: Exploring the global life-chance divide. *Security Dialogue* 41(1): 53–76.
Durodié, B. 2007. Fear and terror in a post-political age. *Government and Opposition* 42(3): 427–450.
Embassy of France in the UK. 2014. United Kingdom/UCAVs—Communiqué issued by the Defence Ministry, November 5, 2014.
EU. 2003. A secure Europe in a better world. European Security Strategy. Brussels, December 12, 2003.
European Parliament. 2014. Joint motion for a resolution on the use of armed drones (2014/2567 (RSP)), February 25, 2014.
Felbab-Brown, V. 2013. Focused deterrence, selective targeting, drug trafficking and organised crime: Concepts and practicalities. Report 2. *Modernising Drug Law Enforcement*, February 2013.
Financial Times. 2014. Drone strikes on ISIS loom large in allies' strategy, October 12, 2014.
Gallup. 2013. In U.S., 65% support drone attacks on terrorists abroad. *Politics*, March 25, 2013.
Guardian. 2013. British military has 500 drones, May 6, 2013.
Guardian. 2010. Inside the mind of the times square bomber, September 19, 2010.
Human Rights Watch. 2014. War in Iraq: Not a humanitarian intervention, January 26, 2004.
iCasualties.org (Iraq Coalition Casualty Count). 2014. Coalition military fatalities by year. Iraq coalition casualty count. Accessed on December 3, 2014.
ICCT. 2014. About. *Activities*. Accessed on November 20, 2014.
Institute for Economics and Peace. 2014. *Global Terrorism Index 2014*.
Iraq Body Count. 2014. Accessed on December 2, 2014.
ISD. 2014. Counter-extremism. *Current projects*. Accessed on November 20, 2014.
Iyengar, S. and Kinder, D.R. 1987. *News That Matters*. Chicago: University of Chicago Press.

Jacinto, L. 2014. The regretful jihadists of the Islamic State. *Foreign Policy*, October 23, 2014.

Jesperson, S. 2013. Whither post-post-conflict development? Development in the security-development Nexus. Africa at LSE blog. *LSE*, June 21, 2013.

Jones, S.G. and Libicki, M.C. 2008. How terrorist groups end: Lessons for countering al Qa'ida. RAND Corporation.

Kreps, S. and Zenko, M. 2014. The drone invasion has been greatly exaggerated. *Foreign Policy*, March 10, 2014.

Krueger, A.B. and Malecková, J. 2001. Education, poverty and terrorism: Is there a causal connection? NBER Working Paper No. 9074, July 2002.

LaFree, G. 2013. Public policy and (myths about) terrorism. *ISN*, May 22, 2013.

The Murmur. 2014. Reintegrating returning foreign fighters, October 8, 2014.

NATO. 2014. NATO and Afghanistan. Accessed on December 2, 2014.

New America Foundation. 2014. Attacks on U.S. and NATO Soldiers by Afghan Security Forces. Accessed on December 2, 2014.

NYU and Stanford. 2012. Living under drones: Death, injury and trauma to civilians from U.S. drone practices in Pakistan. Report by the International Human Rights and Conflict Resolution Clinic of Stanford Law School (Stanford Clinic) and the Global Justice Clinic at New York University School of Law (NYU Clinic), September 25, 2012. http://www.livingunderdrones.org.

OAS. 2013. Scenarios for the drug problem in the Americas: 2013–2025, May 2013.

Pew Research. 2012. Pakistani public opinion ever more critical of U.S. global attitudes project, June 27, 2012.

Piazza, J.A. 2007. Global poverty, inequality, and transnational terrorism: A research note. *Perspectives on Terrorism* 1(4): 12–20.

Piazza, J.A. 2011. Poverty, minority economic discrimination, and domestic terrorism. *Journal of Peace Research* 48(3): 339–353.

PPN. 2010. The role of civil society in counterradicalisation and de-radicalisation. A Working Paper of the European Policy Planners' Network on Countering Radicalisation and Polarisation (PPN).

RAND. 2014. Unmanned aerial vehicles. Resources Page. Accessed on December 3, 2014.

Reuters. 2014. NATO backs U.S.-led training force for Afghanistan, December 2, 2014.

RUSI. 2013. Hitting the target? How new capabilities are shaping international intervention, March 26, 2013.

Saferworld. 2011. The securitization of aid? Reclaiming security to meet poor people's needs. *Saferworld Briefing*, February 2011.

Schneier, B. 2014. *Carry On: Sound Advice from Schneier on Security*. Indianapolis, IN: Wiley.

START. 2014a. GTD. Accessed on December 2, 2014.

START. 2014b. Country reports on terrorism 2013. *Annex of Statistical Information*, April 2014.

TBIJ. 2013. Emerging from the shadows: U.S. covert drone strikes in 2012. Monthly Updates on the Covert War, January 3, 2013.

UN. 2005. In larger freedom: Towards development, security and human rights for all. Report of the Secretary-General. Fifty-ninth session. UN General Assembly, March 21, 2005.

UNODC. 2014. The global study on homicide 2013, April 2014.

UNSC. 2011. Resolution 1378 (2001). Adopted by the Security Council at its 4415th meeting, on November 14, 2001.

U.S. State Department. 2014. Countering violent extremism. Bureau of counterterrorism: Programs and initiatives. Accessed on November 19, 2014.

Wall Street Journal. 2014. Afghan troop casualties are rising, October 22, 2014.

Washington Post. 2014. Denmark tries a soft-handed approach to returned Islamist fighters, October 19, 2014.

Welsh, B. 2007. Evidence-based crime prevention: Scientific basis, trends, results and implications for Canada. Final Report prepared for National Crime Prevention Centre, Public Safety Canada, June 2007.

World Bank. 2013. Brazil fights crime while bringing development to the Favelas. *Feature Story*, March 22, 2013.

World Bank. 2014. Afghanistan. *Data*. Accessed on December 2, 2014.

CONCLUSION

Massive data collection seems to reflect a too-often held view on terrorism since 9/11: that the threat posed by terrorism can and should be fully eradicated, or at least that we should be doing everything in our power to reduce the risk of terrorism even further, to an absolute minimum. However, we tend to overlook three basic facts about terrorism: (1) terrorism is a marginal problem, causing relatively little human and financial impact compared to other important challenges that the world faces; (2) there have always been and there always will be some level of terrorism in our societies, but government policies can have a positive or negative impact on the level of the threat; (3) through their actions, terrorists aim to instill fear in order to create government overreaction.

This book has attempted to reassess the policy response to terrorism since 9/11 and to provide a nuanced, yet meaningful contribution to current policy and academic debates. It has argued that Western governments have often overestimated and oversimplified the terrorist threat and overreacted to it since 9/11. Knee-jerk and hardheaded counterterrorism policies have proved harmful. Reform is therefore needed, toward more evidence-based, comprehensive, and proportionate policy responses.

What follows from these arguments is the following 10 recommendations, which could serve as strategic guidance for policy makers reviewing counterterrorism policies: (1) be mindful of the term *terrorism* itself, a divisive, all-encompassing, vague, and simplistic label; (2) understand that terrorism is a multifaceted problem that is often oversimplified and overblown; (3) recognize that overestimating the threat posed by terrorism and overreacting to it have a range of negative consequences that often outweigh their benefits, including creating opportunity costs, a disproportionate sense of fear, further alienation and discontent, and violating human rights; (4) allow more scrutiny, criticism, and oversight from other institutions and branches of government, parliament, the judiciary, and civil society, including with regard to intelligence activities and the use of drones; (5) address the emotional and psychological components of both terrorism and counterterrorism; (6) appreciate that government and media narratives may play into the hands of terrorists, by magnifying their importance or reinforcing their messages; (7) tackle the political, institutional, and socioeconomic factors behind terrorism and violent extremism, instead of only confronting their symptoms; (8) appreciate the limits of the state in responding to terrorism, and engage media and civil society actors in preventing and countering violent extremism; (9) adopt more balanced foreign policy postures that do not center on terrorism as their primary lens of analysis and response; and (10) review metrics assessing policy effectiveness to include a more comprehensive analysis including of the direct and indirect impacts of policy.

LIST OF ACRONYMS

ANC	African National Congress
ANSF	Afghan National Security Forces
AP	Associated Press
AQAP	Al Qaeda in the Arabian Peninsula
AQI	Al Qaeda in Iraq
AQIM	Al Qaeda in the Islamic Maghreb
ASH	Action on Smoking and Health
AVE	Against Violent Extremism
BAT	British American Tobacco
BBC	British Broadcast Corporation
CBO	Congressional Budget Office
CDC	Centers for Disease Control and Prevention
CEVIPOF	Sciences Po Center for Political Research
CGCC	Center on Global Counterterrorism Cooperation
CIA	Central Intelligence Agency
CIC	Center on International Cooperation
CIDB	Canadian Incident Database
CNN	Cable News Network
CNRS	National Center for Scientific Research
COPD	Chronic Obstructive Pulmonary Disease
CPOST	Chicago Project on Security and Terrorism
CRS	Congressional Research Service
CSIS	Center for Strategic and International Studies
CT	Counterterrorism
CTC	Counter-Terrorism Committee
DC	District of Columbia
DCRI	Central Directorate of Homeland Intelligence (France)
DEA	Drug Enforcement Administration
DHS	Department of Homeland Security
DIA	Defense Intelligence Agency
DIRNSA	Director of the National Security Agency
DNI	Director of National Intelligence
DOD	Department of Defense
EDL	English Defence League
ELN	National Liberation Army (Colombia)

EMCDDA	European Monitoring Centre for Drugs and Drug Addiction
ETA	*Euskadi Ta Askatasuna* or Basque Fatherland and Liberty
EU	European Union
EUCOM	United States European Command
FARC	Revolutionary Armed Forces of Colombia
FBI	Federal Bureau of Investigation
FCAS	Future Combat Air System
FCO	Foreign & Commonwealth Office
FLN	National Liberation Front (Algeria)
FOIA	Freedom of Information Act
FTO	Foreign Terrorist Organization
GAO	General Accounting Office
GCDP	Global Commission on Drug Policy
GCHQ	Government Communications Headquarters
GCTF	Global Counterterrorism Forum
GDP	Growth Development Product
GTD	Global Terrorism Database
GTE	Global Telecoms Exploitation
HIV	Human Immunodeficiency Virus
HMG	Her Majesty's Government
IAS	Institute of Alcohol Studies
ICCT	International Centre for Counter-Terrorism (ICCT–The Hague)
ICG	International Crisis Group
ICSR	The International Centre for the Study of Radicalisation and Political Violence
IDPC	International Drug Policy Consortium
IGC	Institute for Global Communications
IISS	International Institute for Strategic Studies
INCB	International Narcotics Control Board
INEGI	National Institute of Statistics and Geography
INS	Immigration and Naturalization Service
IPCC	Intergovernmental Panel on Climate Change
IRA	Irish Republican Army
ISD	Institute for Strategic Dialogue
ISIL	Islamic State of Iraq and the Levant
ISIS	Islamic State in Iraq and Syria
ISP	Internet Service Provider
ITU	International Telecommunication Union
LDC	Least Developed Countries

LSE	London School of Economics and Political Science
LTTE	Liberation Tigers of Tamil Eelam
MIPT	National Memorial Institute for the Prevention of Terrorism
MNLA	National Movement for the Liberation of Azawad (Mali)
MP	Member of Parliament
MPC	Migration Policy Centre
MTI	Mastering the Internet
MUJAO	Movement for Oneness and Jihad in West Africa
NATO	North Atlantic Treaty Organization
NATO PA	NATO Parliamentary Assembly
NBER	National Bureau of Economic Research
NCTC	National Counterterrorism Center
NSA	National Security Agency
NSC	National Security Council
NSTC	National Science and Technology Council
NSU	National Socialist Underground
NY	New York
OAS	Organization of American States
OSCE	Organization for Security and Co-operation in Europe
OSI	Open Society Institute
PCLOB	Privacy and Civil Liberties Oversight Board
PKK	Kurdistan Workers' Party
PPN	European Policy Planners' Network on Countering Radicalisation and Polarisation
QC	Queen's Counsel
RAF	Red Army Faction
RAID	Research Assistance Intervention Dissuasion (France)
RAN	Radicalisation Awareness Network
RDWTI	RAND Database of Worldwide Terrorism Incidents
RPA	Remotely Piloted Aircraft
RUSI	Royal United Services Institute
SACEUR	Supreme Allied Commander Europe
SAD	Suicide Attack Database
SDSR	Strategic Defence and Security Review
SIS	Secret Intelligence Service
SLC	Sri Lanka Campaign for Peace and Justice
START	National Consortium for the Study of Terrorism and Responses to Terrorism
TBIJ	The Bureau of Investigative Journalism
TED	Technology Entertainment Design

TE-SAT	EU Terrorism Situation and Trend Report
TIDE	Terrorist Identities Datamart Environment
TSAS	Canadian Network for Research on Terrorism, Security and Society
TSDB	Terrorist Screening Database
UAV	Unmanned Aerial Vehicle
UCAS	Unmanned Combat Aerial System
UCAV	Unmanned Combat Aerial Vehicle
UDA	Ulster Defence Association
UK	United Kingdom
UKIP	UK Independence Party
UKTI	UK Trade & Investment
UMP	Union for a Popular Movement (France)
UN	United Nations
UNGASS	United Nations General Assembly Special Session
UNHCR	United Nations High Commissioner for Refugees
UNODC	United Nations Office on Drugs and Crime
UNRWA	United Nations Relief and Works Agency
UNSC	United Nations Security Council
UPI	United Press International
U.S.	United States
USD	U.S. Dollar
USIP	U.S. Institute of Peace
WACD	West Africa Commission on Drugs
WHO	World Health Organization
WMD	Weapons of Mass Destruction

INDEX

O

P